Seeds of Virtue, Seeds of Change

A Collection of Zen Teachings

Edited by Jikyo Cheryl Wolfer
Foreword by Eido Frances Carney

Teachings by

Shosan Victoria Austin ◊ Jan Chozen Bays ◊ Enji Boissevain ◊ Domyo Burk
Eido Frances Carney ◊ Myoen Jisen Coghlan ◊ Eijun Linda Ruth Cutts
Meian Elbert ◊ Setsuan Gaelyn Godwin ◊ Myo-O Marilyn Habermas-Scher
Joan Halifax ◊ Hoko Karnegis ◊ Daijaku Kinst ◊ Etsudo Patty Krahl
Myoshin Kate McCandless ◊ Misha Shungen Merrill ◊ Teijo Munnich
Wendy Egyoku Nakao ◊ Pat Enkyo O'Hara ◊ Joen Snyder O'Neal
Josho Pat Phelan ◊ Jion Susan Postal ◊ Byakuren Judith Ragir ◊ Shinshu Roberts
Myoan Grace Schireson ◊ Myokaku Jane Schneider ◊ Meiren Val Szymanski

Temple Ground Press
3248 39th Way NE
Olympia, WA 98506

Cover and interior design and photography by Fletcher Ward.
Set in Minion Pro 8/19.

ISBN 978-0985565138 – Paperback edition
ISBN 978-0985565145 – Kindle edition

Library of Congress Control Number: 2014945483

Temple Ground Press, Olympia, WA

Dedicated with 108 bows of immeasurable gratitude to

all the Buddhas and Ancestors

who have transmitted, are transmitting, and will transmit the teachings

and to my teacher

Katsuyu Eido Frances Carney

who, with inexhaustible energy and courage, never ceases

to manifest the Dharma.

Table of Contents

Foreword

The current global crises demand a spiritual response equal to or great-er than the environmental, political, social, and economic problems we have collectively created. For those on a spiritual path, our work is clearly determined and this book of Zen teachings is one response to our world's needs. The book carries sufficient reason for its being since the words of the Dharma can endlessly be configured to help us gain insight into ourselves, direct our search for peace, develop awareness of our resistance to change, and bring about the inspiration and strength to positively assist the world we inhabit.

If humans are to survive as a planetary species and rescue other spe-cies that are threatened, we must collectively and individually listen to the voices directed toward sanity and right action. There has never been a time of greater need to speak publicly and face our responsibility to change the suffering world. Changing ourselves is an urgent prerequisite and these essays on body, speech, and mind, help support us with the tools to face the conflicts of our times and understand the contributory factors that influence and direct our future.

The writers in this collection are pioneers in helping to establish the heart of reason that rises out of Soto Zen meditation in America. All of these teachers are leaders and or founders of temples spread across the states and open to the many seekers who come to address their deep un-settledness in our current turmoil. How can we spiritually face the bur-geoning and complex problems—cultures, environments, climate change, economies, nuclear warfare, health, natural resources, employment, poli-tics, corporate greed, terrorism, local wars, ideology, education, technol-ogy—overwhelming problems too numerous to properly list? What are we to do? How can we cope? Is there an expression of solace? How can we help the world? Can we find a spiritual home from which to sort out and begin to address the problems in a meaningful way?

No one has a single magic answer to the tremendous challenges of our times. If anything, we are made uneasy and perhaps immobilized by the magnitude of the problems. Joanna Macy says, "The world itself has a role to play in our awakening. Its very brokenness and need call to us, summoning us to walk out of the prison of self-concern." Thus the teachers speaking in this collection came to Soto Zen because they believed their spiritual practice could make a difference in themselves and a difference for the world. They speak directly to us from the platform of their own awakening experiences because the world needs them to do so. When they took up Zen meditation they remained faithful through persistence and devotion—two virtues that favor continuation in a spiritual practice. Zen practice is not mysterious, and it is available to anyone to do who sincerely wishes to be at home spiritually and bring healthy inspiration and creativity to a needy world. Many people are hungry for direction and purpose. Listen closely to these teachings: "Stick with it, learn to trust your own body, the character of your speech, and the integrity of your mind, and respond with sincerity to the world around you" is the primary message and underpinning of these essays.

In the 1960's and 70's when the first generation of Soto Zen masters began teaching in America—Shunryu Suzuki, Kobun Chino Otogawa, Houn Jiyu Kennett, Dainin Katagiri, Taizan Maezumi, and Tozen Akiyama—we had no way of knowing that Soto Zen would find residence on every continent. Their groundwork in the Dharma paved the way for great teachers to appear in succeeding generations, illuminating the words of the Buddha and Eihei Dogen, our Founders, to worldwide cultures through numerous languages and expressions. This phenomenal development comes at a time when the world most needs the ethical values found in their teachings on body, speech, and mind. The teachers in this collection and its editor are direct descendants and transmitted disciples of those original masters, and their voices form a natural chorus of authentic presence firmly planted in the Dharma.

Through this book perhaps some may be touched by a particular essay and feel called to connect with and begin practice with a teacher. In so doing, we open to the world around us and join the increasing numbers of individuals worldwide who recognize the need to meditate together, for meditation is the recognition that the human race is completely connected in body, speech, and mind and what we do, and say, and think together may, in the long run, save us.

—Eido Frances Carney

Preface

Zen is a practice noted for the eccentricity and individuality of its masters. Each Zen master's Dharma—teaching talks, model of behavior, and method of interaction with students—is unique, which may be why Zen monks traditionally became "wandering clouds," traveling from temple to temple to experience the Dharma with different Zen masters. By reading this book, you, too, may become a wandering cloud. Each chapter contains a teaching or teachings that, like a seed, contains the potential to blossom into surprising fruit. All the myriad flavors of Zen practice are present—from the informal personal taste of a small, isolated Zen community to the formal banquet of Zen practice in large academic and urban centers. The sincerity and strength of each teacher's Dharma is manifest in her offering.

The names of some essayists are familiar to the reader of Buddhist literature, but several authors collected here have practiced for many years in small temples and cities with little recognition. Guiding a large urban organization presents significant challenges; but, speaking from my own experience in both types of settings, nurturing a small Sangha is a labor of pure love, often disheartening, sometimes incredibly rewarding, and always a test of one's own commitment to and faith in the Buddha Way. It is my great pleasure to introduce some of these Zen pioneers and their unique perspectives on Zen practice to a wider audience.

When I realized this collection would consist of twenty-seven essays, a rather large number for one book, I began reading through them to determine if a theme could be developed that would allow the book to be divided into sections and possibly suggest a title for the collection. Ultimately, the notion of sections was defeated by the multiplicity of subjects chosen by the authors. Although the reader will notice several common themes, I should stress that the arbitrary lists that follow by no means encompass the full scope of each author's essay, and many essays could belong to other categories as well. Hence my dilemma . . .

One notable theme is compassion. As I write this preface, my Sangha at Joyous Refuge is studying the practice of compassion as articulated by the oral tradition of the Buddhist Indian sage Atisha and preserved in the

Tibetan Buddhist tradition as the Seven Points of Mind Training. Norman Fischer in his commentary on this practice, *Training in Compassion: Zen Teachings on the Practice of Lojong,* laments "a serious weakness in Zen: its deficiency in explicit teachings on compassion." To be fair, Fischer is correct in his observation that Zen does not provide a specific training method for the development of compassion such as the one set forth in the Tibetan Lojong teachings. However, neither is Zen silent on the practice of compassion as the teachings in this volume demonstrate. In this weary world, no practice is more important.

Wendy Egyoku Nakao tells the story of her Sangha's compassionate response to the shattering discovery of a child molester in their midst; Eijun Linda Ruth Cutts teaches us the Listening-Response required to develop a compassionate heart; recalling the development of compassion during her chaplaincy internship, Myo-O Marilyn Habermas-Scher speaks of "this thin layer of protective plexiglass that surrounded my heart" melting away as the barriers between self and other collapse; and Hoko Karnegis explores the compassionate nature of *baika* songs used in Japanese memorial services.

Embodied practice is another timely theme if one considers the plethora of body practices advertised to Western culture. Zen tradition requires specific gestures and practices for many common activities, and these body practices are the foundation of mindfulness. Josho Pat Phelan explains how embodiment of Zen forms frees the mind, and Setsuan Gaelyn Godwin humorously encounters three levels of mindfulness while working in the garden.

Many teachers also encourage students to augment their meditation practice with a body practice, such as yoga or Tai Chi, that develops flexibility for long periods of sitting. Myoen Jisen Coghlan and Teijo Munnich provide lessons from dance and the Alexander Technique that benefit sitting posture. And, in what I believe to be the first instance of a published article on this subject, Shosan Victoria Austin distills her lengthy experience with Iyengar yoga into an illustrated exposition of meditation postures appropriate to the biological stages of a woman's life. Since this aspect of meditation practice is rarely addressed, I encouraged Shosan to publish a book-length version of her article in future, and if you benefit from her article, you can encourage her too.

No Zen collection would be complete without liberal attention to the writings of Eihei Dogen, the Japanese founder of Soto Zen. Dogen's writings, including his massive spiritual text *Shobogenzo,* provide an inexhaustible source of Dharma talks. Jan Chozen Bays uses Dogen's

"Genjo Koan" to clarify the meaning of enlightenment; Byakuren Judith Ragir investigates the state of busyness using Case 21 from *The Book of Serenity* and Dogen's "Uji"; Pat Enkyo O'Hara examines a passage from "Uji" to explore the overwhelming nature of modern life and Buddhism's compassionate response; Shinshu Roberts unpacks a portion of Dogen's "Guidelines for Practicing the Way," spiced with illustrations from the movie *Enlightenment Guaranteed,* while Daijaku Kinst uses a different section of the same text to analyze Bodhicitta—the intention to awaken. Misha Shungen Merrill illustrates her talk on stewardship with a well-known story of one of Dogen's encounters with an old monastic cook (tenzo) in China, and Joan Halifax includes another familiar tenzo story in her masterful contemplation of the continuous nature of practice.

Cultivation of Bodhisattva qualities and behavior is another prevalent theme. The four Bodhisattva Vows, a foundational practice of Mahayana Buddhism, are chanted every day in zendos and meditation halls around the world. Etsudo Patty Krall discovers Bodhisattvas trimming mistletoe around a California lake, quoted on a Starbucks' cup, and active on a hiking journey in Glacier National Park; Joen Snyder O'Neal recalls the Bodhisattvas whose words spoken at just the right moment seeded changes in her life; Meiren Val Szymanski explains the steps of cultivating equanimity, an important Bodhisattva quality; and Jion Susan Postal demonstrates how gratitude and repentance support the Bodhisattva Vows.

Finally, there is the broad theme of daily Zen practice on and off of the meditation cushion. Eido Frances Carney talks about hermit-priest Ryokan's example and the practice of right speech in a "gotcha" culture; Teijo Munnich explores the branchings of the Eightfold Path; Enji Boissevain ponders the many faces and effects of zazen; Meian Elbert analyses the diverse aspects of fear and its counterpart, fearlessness; Myokaku Jane Schneider provides a path to spacious mind with a guided meditation on the heart/mind; Domyo Burk poetically scrutinizes the driving force of longing for enlightenment; Myoan Grace Schireson examines the nature of awareness in long meditation retreats; and Myoshin Kate McCandless considers the anxiety of perfectionism.

Special attention must be drawn to Jion Susan Postal's "The Birth of Vow." As far as I know, this is the last project that Susan completed before her death on February 7, 2014. We began email correspondence in November of 2013 because, due to her deteriorating health, she wasn't certain she would be able to submit an essay. As Susan coped with headaches and double vision, she wrote, "I can no longer prepare a real Dharma Talk, but find myself sort of 'winging it' with encouraging words, and treasuring dokusan even though each student becomes a radiant being filled with her/his transparent double . . . ."

I encouraged Susan to send me what she had already written and admired her courage as she continued to practice while growing steadily weaker. She managed to review the final draft of her article, even as her vision failed, and responded by sending me the gift of her Sangha's newly-printed cookbook. I last heard from her in late December immediately after she was diagnosed with pervasive, metastatic cancer and stated her intention to enter palliative care. In her final email, she closed by saying, "Into the mystery. No wish to fight, just rest now. Sending gratitude to all of you for our good Dharma friendships over many years. Bows and love, Susan."

I followed the bulletins about Susan's condition on the website her Sangha created. I was deeply moved by the many expressions of love and gratitude posted there. It was obvious that Susan truly embodied her Vow of loving compassion and gratitude. I was inspired by a photo posted on the website of Susan in full robes with both arms upraised and a beatific smile on her face. In that photo, she epitomizes the joyous practice I aspire to. I feel fortunate to have encountered her during her final moments in this lifetime. May her Vow continue to inspire all beings.

I'm certain that everyone who publishes a book is convinced that this book—*This Book*—is special, and I am no different. From the beginning, as I began first to read, then to edit these essays, I marveled at the diversity of voice and viewpoint gathered here. I confess that more than one essay moved me to tears. I received new insights while working with these pieces, often wondering if I had been truly practicing Zen all these years. I am pleased to offer this opportunity for new insight to all.

I wish to express my gratitude to the Zen masters represented in this volume for their patience and care with the writing, editing, and publication process; to my teacher, Eido Frances Carney, for the opportunity to edit this book; to my Dharma brother Fletcher Ward for his thoughtful attention to design; to the Sangha of Olympia Zen Center for their many years of effort in support of the Dharma; to the many seekers on the North Olympic Peninsula who continue to practice and realize the Way; and to the global community of followers of the Buddha Way. May all beings benefit.

—Jikyo Cheryl Wolfer

Editor's Notes

Most of these essays are adapted from Dharma talks presented in the zendo. Such talks often contain references to Buddhist texts and Zen ancestors without citation. Since the intent of this collection is to present each teacher's voice as naturally as possible, citations are used only when inserted by the author or when questions about the source of a translation may arise. Some translations of commonly used Buddhist texts are unsourced because translations of these common texts sometimes vary from lineage to lineage and their origins may be obscured. A list of works cited is included at the end of each essay for the reader's reference.

During Dharma talks, Zen teachers often recite stories about or sayings of their teachers that may or may not have written or recorded verification. These treasured anecdotes are no less valuable for remaining unverified.

Many Chinese, Japanese, and Sanskrit words are included in the Zen lexicon and are also familiar to frequent readers of Buddhist and Zen literature. These words are italicized in the text only as necessary to provide emphasis or meaning. The essayist's capitalization of words such as Dharma, Buddha, and Sangha has been maintained and therefore is not consistent throughout the text. Diacritical marks for most foreign words are also excluded. And finally, some of our authors are of British or Canadian origin and their British spelling usage is retained.

Wendy Egyoku Nakao, Roshi, *is the Abbot and Head Teacher of the Zen Center of Los Angeles/Buddha Essence Temple. Her root teacher was Ven. Taizan Maezumi, Roshi and her Dharma Transmission/Inka and current teacher is Roshi Bernie Glassman of the White Plum Lineage. She is a founding member of the Zen Peacemaker Order and co-editor of* Appreciate Your Life: The Essence of Zen Practice *by Taizan Maezumi.*

The Authentic Tea Bowl Before Birth

Wendy Egyoku Nakao

Moon-Heart, a Zen Student, was serving tea to her special guest, Abbess Eko of a nearby temple. Mushin, a Dharma sister of the Abbess, happened to stop by and was invited to join them. Mushin was a "wild woman," and carried a bone instead of the usual ceremonial stick.

Moon-Heart handed the tea to Abbess Eko in an ancient tea bowl that the Abbess herself had given to her as a gift. In the midst of appreciating the exquisite bowl, Mushin suddenly shattered the tea bowl with her bone. "Now," said the Wild Woman, "Look at the Authentic Tea Bowl that exists before birth!"

Moon-Heart blanched, gasped, and nearly fainted. Abbess Eko said calmly, "I gave you this tea bowl, but now, I would like you to give it back to me. Before you do, gather the pieces, glue them, and fill the cracks with gold. Then have a box made for it. On the cover of the box, write the name of the bowl, which I now give as 'The Authentic Tea Bowl Before Birth.' I will reverently pass this bowl on to my Dharma descendants."

Now I ask you: What is the Authentic Tea Bowl Before Birth?

This is an adaptation of a story from the Japanese tea ceremony tradition. As a koan—a Zen story of awakening—it is an invitation, a prompt, to tap into the life force. The koan plunges us into the fullness of our amazing human lives: the authentic bowl before birth, the shattering, the emerging, the passing on. There is no tiptoeing around awakening and how an awakened life is lived. The Abbess and her Wild Woman Dharma sister are skillful and unfettered Zen women, calling us to claim our very lives through the immediacy of not-knowing.

In entering the sphere of a koan, we heighten our potential to be affirmed by the life force and become alive. We inhabit the people in the koan, meeting each intimately. Each is a piece of oneself that one is meeting for the first time or is meeting anew—the Student, the Abbess, the Wild Woman Dharma sister, and even the Bowl, the Bone, the Gold.

Each is a powerful and transformative agent for awakening, a catalyst for living the Buddha Way.

∨

Moon-Heart, a Zen Student, was serving tea to her special guest, Abbess Eko of a nearby temple.

A substantial amount of preparation is done for a tea ceremony. Moon-Heart as host would have carefully considered what was most appropriate for her guest, selected a Zen saying to express the spirit of the ceremony, arranged a flower that lasts only a day, and considered which utensils to use and which tea and sweets to serve. She would have reflected deeply on the ceremony as a container, ensuring that it would hold an intimate meeting of heart-mind between her and the Abbess. Perhaps Moon-Heart was proud of receiving this special tea bowl, perhaps she felt undeserving of such a precious gift, or perhaps she was so stuck that she needed skillful shattering of something that limited her.

Right now, who are you at this moment?

Tea ceremonies are highly ritualized containers. Ritual at its best is beautiful and truthful; it is grounded in the immediacy of the moment that exists beyond conventional notions of space and time. Many people are uncomfortable with rituals and some refuse to participate; they might obsess so much about their participation in the ritual that they become tight knots of self absorption and become paralyzed. Or they might succumb to mindlessly repeating ritual behavior without awareness and attention. To step into a ritual space itself is a tacit acknowledgement of one's capacity for transformation into a great unknowing truth. It can be very uncomfortable to the self that is mired in likes and dislikes, or in unskillful narratives that inhibit authentic expression of who one really is.

Many Zen students are familiar with various forms of rituals. For example, sesshin, consecutive days of intensive zazen, is a ritualized endeavor. The forms of sesshin—the way one moves about the zendo, the manner of chanting, the style of formal eating, the silence and stillness, the postures of sitting and walking—are created and maintained by all the sesshin participants together. While each participant has her or his own unique, personal experience, this ritualized form enables one to also experience the One Body of sesshin—everyone moving and acting together in unison, in mutual interrelationships. The sense of One Body is not limited to people, but extends to the food, the incense, the buildings, the grounds. The tight knot of self absorption loosens, mindless repetition falls away: everything, all together, is a living, breathing, immediacy of the intimate sharing of the web of the life force.

∨

Mushin, a Dharma sister of the Abbess, happened to stop by and was invited to join them. Mushin was a "wild woman," and carried a bone instead of the usual ceremonial stick.

The Abbess is a busy woman with many day-to-day temple and teaching responsibilities. She nevertheless makes time for this tea ceremony. It's unusual for an Uninvited Guest to appear during a tea ceremony, but not surprising that a Wild Woman of Dharma is the one who shows up. The unexpected wild Dharma woman is welcomed and invited to join the ceremony. Through Zen practice we learn to invite in everything that appears in our life, including those people or events we would prefer not to invite.

Wild Woman Mushin is not deranged, but wild in the sense of being natural and unfettered by conditions, awake and unencumbered. A ceremonial stick is given when someone receives Dharma transmission, but Wild Woman carries a bone, reminding us to awaken to life's transitory nature and the limitations of human knowledge. Her presence may have unnerved the Student—or, for that matter, you and me—because the Wild Woman is not attending to the needs of the small self. She is the archetypal bone woman who sings the original song of the life force. She is wild because she is so uncompromisingly alive; she plays freely in the boundless field of not-knowing.

∨

Moon-Heart handed the tea to Abbess Eko in an ancient tea bowl that the Abbess herself had given to her as a gift.

Most Zen teachers are careful not to favor their students with gifts, so we might wonder why this gift of an ancient tea bowl was given—as the Abbess's appreciation for her student, a token of gratitude, or something else? There was once an Abbot who gave a departing student a gift of a hot coal from the brazier as the student was leaving the monastery. "Here," said the Abbot picking up the hot coal with a pair of tongs, "I have a gift for you." Not knowing how to respond, the student retreated to meditate on this startling action. This was repeated several times, the Abbot offering a hot coal from the brazier and the student retreating, until one day the student realized how to receive the gift of the hot coal. If accepting a gift of hot coal seems impossible to you, it might seem easier to receive an antique tea bowl—that is, until it shatters.

To inhabit this Zen Student is to touch that part of yourself that has reached the limits of what you know, although you may not be aware of it. Perhaps the Student lived in her thoughts, in the gap between her ideas about life and what is. We outgrow the people we have been, think we are, or should be, but we keep trying very hard to continue fitting into these old images. We may fix and hold firm to what we have outgrown even in the face of the great truth of impermanence, or in the face of repetitive ways of being that result in suffering that is familiar, like old worn out clothes we insist on wearing. At times we seem to lack the imagination of life beyond these self-imposed limitations. We are constantly thrown back upon ourselves, buffeted about by circumstances and missing the spark of awakening inherent in each moment.

Antique tea bowls are highly prized in Japan. These are not little tea cups, but bowls around three to four inches in diameter that are the epitome of Japanese pottery. Some of the most highly prized bowls are those made by unknown potters. Not only is the potter's name unknown, but significantly, the bowl bears no trace of the potter's ego. Such bowls have emerged from not-knowing, radiating the fusion of life force of potter and clay. The antique tea bowl given by the Abbess was precious in this way.

In the midst of appreciating the exquisite bowl, Mushin suddenly shattered the tea bowl with her bone. "Now," said the Wild Woman, "Look at the Authentic Tea Bowl that exists before birth!"

Wild Woman Dharma sister is a powerful force. What arises for you when you inhabit her? The life shatterer? The life giver? The one who transcends hesitation before the glaring eyes of the unknown? We know the one who has pulled the rug out from under us; we know the times when our own actions have torn the fabric of other's lives—having an affair, not honoring a debt, becoming addicted to drugs. We may offer our reasons and justifications; we try to understand why we have done what we did. We come to realize that our reasons pale when we receive the suffering we have caused ourselves-and-others. Sometimes it is obvious that suffering results from actions ridden with self-serving agendas, or a blatant lack of awareness of cause and consequences; at other times we see that, even acting from honest intentions of good will, suffering ensues. Wild Woman Dharma sister wields her bone—this visceral reminder of death—and cuts through, "Look! What is this?"

The Zen Student is mortified. She is gasping, nearly fainting, speechless, in shock. She has been plunged into direct contact with that space before anything arises—before any words, opinions, or thoughts emerge. For a time, there are no words, no thoughts. Just open space. Stillness. Breath. Not-knowing. Non-arising. Only now, only presence, only this moment, only this Authentic Tea Bowl Before Birth. This!

Recalling such a life experience, what was shattered? This "I, me, mine"—a solid sense of yourself—that holds your life narrative together, what happens to it? Wild Woman Dharma sister cuts through the conditioning, the habit, the comfort zone of the ego; she exposes the great face of not-knowing—the Authentic Tea Bowl Before Birth. She knows that to be fully alive, one must die to the false sense of self that one has created and protects so carefully. She knows that the old narratives are dead; that they block us from possibility and from a fluid dance with the life force. She knows that the Authentic Tea Bowl Before Birth is not an ignorant or a fearful place, but a place of liberation and ease.

What is this bowl that you are: the bowl of Life? Buddha Nature? The Great Matter of Birth and Death? Can you affirm without hesitation that this very life that you are living now is itself the life of a Buddha? It seems obvious that life is precious, and yet this very fact itself often becomes obscured in the activities of daily life, or goes unseen in the face of unrelenting impermanence, or is lost behind the veil of self-absorption—our likes and dislikes, approval and disapproval, our standards of right and wrong.

In Zen we say that the giver, receiver, and gift are empty of a self: nothing is fixed—the empty bowl is without edges, it can receive anything, can give anything, and can become anything. The empty bowl speaks to this fundamental receptivity of a human life. Yet we often live from a sense of lack, out of touch with the inherent abundance—the empty fullness—of the life force itself. Receptivity is implied when a gift is given, but sometimes this is not necessarily so for us. Rather than being empty bowls, some of us find it difficult to give; others are unable to receive, even as they call themselves givers. As givers and receivers, we often find ourselves full of expectations of outcome, however subtle these may be. In this koan, awakening and the possibility of transformation is inherent in receiving what arises in one's life. The Abbess receives a student's offering and aspiration, the Student receives a lesson in not-knowing, the Wild Woman Dharma sister receives our inherent vulnerability.

This koan calls forth the archetype of Avalokitesvara Bodhisattva, the Being of Great Compassion. In Japanese Zen, this bodhisattva has two names: Kanjizai and Kanzeon. Kanjizai is "one who sees the nature of reality" and is called forth in the first line of the *Maha Prajna Paramita Heart Sutra:* "Kan ji zai bo sa gyo jin han-nya ha ra mi ta ji sho ken go on kai ku do is-sai ku yaku." In English, "Avalokitesvara Bodhisattva (Kanjizai) doing deep prajna paramita clearly saw emptiness of all the five conditions thus relieving suffering." Kanjizai sees deeply into the nature of reality, experiencing not-knowing, the reality of the tea bowl before birth. She sees the formless essence before any forms arise, sees the forms themselves, and realizes the transformational power of not-knowing. Her own suffering has been alleviated. What then?

Kanzeon, "The one who hears the cries of suffering of the world," works in the world to relieve suffering in all its forms. There is a great myth that when Kanzeon came face to face with the manifold suffering of this world, it was too much. No longer able to hold herself together, she imploded. She could no longer rearrange the pieces of herself as she had known them; she could no longer think her way to a new way of being in the face of such shattering, she could no longer find the old familiar pieces of herself. She could no longer act from preconceived ideas and agendas.

How does one emerge from the shattering? The myth teaches us that in this shattering there is an emergence, a coming back to life, not as a rearranged old self, but as our authentic self—as an empty vessel through which wisdom and love can flow. In the myth, Avalokitesvara emerges from the shattering with a multitude of hands and eyes. The old container of herself is much too small now. She has merged as Buddha; Buddha has merged as her. Who is Avalokitesvara? Who has merged with Buddha? Buddha has merged with whom?

Abbess Eko said calmly, "I gave you this tea bowl, but now, I would like you to give it back to me. Before you do, gather the pieces...

The Abbess remains calm and present; she recognizes the emergence of a Buddha. In this koan, there is the gift of two women holding a third in her own birthing. It is truly a great gift when someone bears witness to our suffering, when someone is vividly present and does not turn away. The Abbess goes one step further. She says, "I gave you this bowl, now I would like you to give it back to me." How extraordinary! Of what use is a broken bowl? Of what value are the cracked and scarred pieces of a shattered life that is no longer what it was? What now, now that the life force has come forth to claim us and now that all the things we have habitually done to make life work no longer apply?

Abbess Eko says, "Before you give this shattered bowl back to me, gather the pieces." The Abbess is so incredibly kind. She teaches us to bear witness to suffering and to the nature of life itself. "Oh, look at all these pieces. Let's gather them up; let's see each one; let's see all the pieces we have never seen before and which now have come into view." We discover a multitude of pieces; we see that one piece is not more valuable than any other. We ourselves have expanded beyond what we previously thought we were; now we recognize an infinite array of pieces that had been obscured by our self-preoccupations and ideas. The Abbess recognizes the Student's awakening to this fundamental inclusion of Life itself. Look!

When we bear witness, we meet face to face whatever aspects of life are revealed, regardless of how we may feel about them. There is a warning here for us to see without judgment, without the veils of likes and dislikes, to recognize the wholeness of each piece. Implicit in this story is a warning not to reassemble the pieces in the way we have known them to fit, because they do not fit that way anymore. There is a warning that it is not enough to awaken; the hard work of transformation awaits us, as well, and will be missed if we opt to reshape our lives into an idea of "what-is" instead of living in not-knowing.

Avalokitesvara emerged with many hands and eyes. There is a great lesson here. Who is Avalokitesvara? You are; I am. But, wait. What are the many hands and eyes? It is each of us all together. It is wonderful for each of us, as individuals, to awaken and transform, but it is not enough. Avalokitesvara is our many hands and eyes functioning together as One Body. We, as a community, as a Sangha, awaken and transform together. Each of us has a unique perspective of the One Body of which we are an inextricable part. How do we use these hands and eyes, individually and all together, to ensure that everyone has enough, deep wisdom is realized, and compassion flows unhindered in serving each other, the earth and all of its creatures, and all humanity?

Can a Sangha awaken together? Several years ago in the community in which I practice, we learned that a man who had served many years in prison for molesting children was practicing in our community. The situation was volatile; one could hear tea bowls shattering throughout the community, there was so much upset and upheaval. The Sangha was called together to see, to look, to not know, and to bear witness together. There we were—the abbess, the prison chaplains, the child molester, the Sangha—each person with her or his own narratives, sense of self, sense of right and wrong, and just and unjust, with varying degrees of clarity and confusion.

Our Sangha is practiced in creating containers. We created a bowl—a container in which to look deeply at what had arisen. We did our best to suspend judgment and listen deeply. We listened to ourselves, to the abbess, to the prison chaplains, the child molester, and to each other. Women and men in the Sangha came forward one after the other and recalled their own experiences of being molested as children. We had not expected this commonality of experience, but once it appeared, we invited it in. We were raw; we shattered together. We included together. When the gathering was over, we were neither the persons nor the Sangha that we had thought we were; the old narratives were gone. We were held together by the shared intentions of looking deeply, the faith that not-knowing would reveal the Sangha's wisdom, and that our brokenness would reveal our love.

Kanzeon/Kanjizai emerges from the shattering with many hands and eyes. The Sangha formed a Many Hands and Eyes Circle: each person in the circle was a hand and eye for the community. This situation called forth not the awakening of just one individual; each-of-us-all-together was called forth to emerge as One Body, using our individual hands and eyes to serve the whole, to respect all the pieces, to expand in order to include. There were so many pieces, including the child molester, each member of the Sangha, those who had been previously molested, the prison chaplains, the community resources, the organization itself, the shadows of community life, and so on. With each person as a hand and eye of the Sangha One Body, we emerged as a Sangha awakening together. Together we gathered the pieces and, by using the glue of our collective wisdom and love, became intimate with the inherent generosity of not-knowing. We were surprised at the loving actions that arose. A path of inclusion emerged: after a while, the Sangha was ready to welcome the former prisoner back and he was asked if he wanted to return. He replied, "I'll admit that I am scared, but I will because you all worked so hard to include me." He has since died, but not before we awakened together to great life lessons. In the years following, our Sangha created a life-affirming path of inclusion for those who have been incarcerated.

In shattering—whether it is an individual or a community—there is a great possibility for truth telling in all of its myriad dimensions. Don't squander it! To see this opportunity is to see into the beating heart of this koan.

When this "I, me, mine" implodes, it is a grave error to rearrange one's life, individually and communally, to fit into an old image of what life "should be." In such a moment, you, individually, and all of us together, are never the same limited person or community ever again. We learn to see from not-knowing; not the not-knowing of ignorance, but the not-knowing that is intimately attuned to the life force. In this koan, it manifests in the gasp of the Student, in the wide-open space of one's being before the Wild Woman commands us to look.

... and fill the cracks with gold.

It is a Japanese custom that cracked or broken pottery is glued back together and the cracks filled with gold leaf. What is this gold of one's life? Do we hide our cracks and scars and try to render them invisible? This koan challenges us: these are the very attributes that express our uniqueness as a Dharma vessel. When our self-centered agenda is forgotten and grasping stops, Buddha's light shines through. This is poignantly expressed in the words of Leonard Cohen's song: *Ring the bells that still can ring. Forget your perfect offering. There is a crack in everything. That's how the light gets in.* When the bowl is shattered, when things fall apart, look!

We are called forth to live in full accord with what has been revealed, with life as it is. The liberating openness of not-knowing is precisely the wholeness of life all together. This wholeness calls us to bear witness: What is this piece? What is that piece? Meeting this piece, meeting that piece, we practice the great wisdom of inclusion. Each of us, individually and communally, continually gathers the pieces and affirms the wholeness of life. Each of us, individually and communally, continually grows new hands and eyes, grows in wisdom, grows in love. Each of us, individually and communally, is the gold in the cracks. All of our thoughts, words, and actions, may they be loving actions serving the wholeness of life.

Not all shattering is traumatic, of course. Each of us, both individually and communally, can continue to shatter our own ideas, beliefs, and points of view by continually returning to not-knowing, by pulling the rug out from under ourselves, by living awake.

⌣

Abbess Eko said, " . . . Then have a box made for it. On the cover of the box, write the name of the bowl, which I now give as 'The Authentic Tea Bowl Before Birth.'"

Whose name is this? It is your name, it is my name, it is the name of the Sangha. It is everyone's name all together.

Abbess Eko said, "I will reverently pass this bowl on to my Dharma descendants."

What is passed on? The gift of awakening. The possibility of transformation. We are all Dharma descendants of each other. The Zen Student, the Abbess, the Wild Woman Dharma sister, and Each of Us All Together, support the awakening of each other. This is the great gift of Sangha, the gift of us affirming the intimacy of our interconnection by holding each other in the moment of our own birthing and in the arduous journey of transformation that follows.

Let us awaken to not-knowing and use all the pieces of life to serve each other, humanity, the earth and all its creatures. The Abbess and Wild Woman Dharma sister call out: Look! Life is transient; death is inevitable; love, essential.

Now, I ask you: "Using the Authentic Tea Bowl Before Birth, how do you serve the tea of your Life?"

Works cited:

Anderson, Reb. "Authentic Tea Bowl Before Birth" adapted from *Being Upright: Zen Meditation and the Bodhisattva Precepts.* Berkeley: Rodmell Press, 2000.

Josho Pat Phelan *is the abbess and teacher of the Chapel Hill Zen Center in North Carolina, where she has been leading practice since 1991. Josho trained at the San Francisco Zen Center, founded by Shunryu Suzuki Roshi, where she practiced in residence from 1971-1991, including three years at Tassajara Zen Mountain Center. She was ordained as a priest in 1977 by Zentatsu Richard Baker, received Dharma Transmission from Sojun Mel Weitsman in 1995, and traveled to Japan to participate in Zuise ceremonies at Eihei-ji and Soji-ji temples in 2008. She also has a chapter published in the book* Receiving the Marrow, Teachings on Dogen by Soto Zen Women Priests, *and short articles in* Mindfulness, *a journal published by Springer.*

The Sound of the Inanimate Expounding the Dharma

Josho Pat Phelan

In Zen when we practice together in the zendo or meditation hall, we place a lot of attention on the forms or the detail with which we do things. One function of these details or forms is that they help reduce the need to communicate verbally. I think the forms are felt both as a curse and as a blessing, at one time or another, by most of us. They seem like a curse when we feel them as empty forms or as rules—when we feel an expectation that they be done right. They become a blessing, or at least something positive, when we are able to enter them wholeheartedly; and when we do, the forms become an entrance to the formless. By wholeheartedly entering the forms, we forget about ourselves and how we are doing, which allows us to become free both from the forms and from our self-consciousness.

After many years of practicing with these forms, I have found that many of them are arbitrary or agreed upon ways of doing things. For example, the San Francisco Zen Center, where I trained, has a wide doorway to the zendo and we entered and left the zendo on the left side of the doorway, stepping in and out of the room with the left foot. The only reason I know of that we did this was because that was the way it was done in Japan. I don't know how or why this developed in Japan, but as far as I know, it was not done because the left side had some quality of being inherently right or because it had a sacred meaning, rather it was simply agreed upon. I do know, however, that it always made me pay attention. For a long time there was a board placed at the threshold that stood up about two inches that had to be stepped over, and when I didn't pay attention, I would bump my toe. When we decide to do something in a particular way, it helps us pay attention; it helps rescue us from our train of thought; and in this case, it helps us bring our awareness all the way down to our feet.

Using the forms: entering and leaving the zendo on the left side, turning clockwise when we sit on our cushion, bowing as the person taking the place next to us bows to his or her cushion, helps us notice our preferences—our prominent or subtle likes and dislikes. The forms give us a background against which to contrast our tendencies and conditioned activity. When we do such meaningless activity as bowing to cushions, or holding the chant card with two hands instead of one, or stopping and taking off our shoes before entering a room and then stopping and putting them back on when we leave, the activity itself helps us extend ourselves beyond our rational, logical minds.

We bow to our cushions or to the altar or to each other not because we, here, are Buddhists or the Buddha figure on the altar is sacred, or because this meditation room is special; we bow because everything is special. What all this bowing and stepping forward with a particular foot does is pull us out of the realm of our mental constructs, out of our incessant mental activity, into the realm of what is actually right before us.

Zen Master Dogen, who brought Soto Zen from China to Japan, wrote many teachings and one is "Hotsu Mujo Shin" or "Arousing the Supreme Thought." The supreme thought is the thought of enlightenment. Francis Cook includes this text in his book of translations, *How to Raise an Ox.* In this text, Dogen quoted Bodhidharma who said: *The One Mind and all minds are wood and stone.* Dogen commented on this saying: *What Bodhidharma calls "mind" is the absolute mind, the mind of the whole world, and so the One Mind is the mind of oneself and others.* Here absolute mind means non-dual mind. Dogen continues:

> *The minds of all beings in the world, the minds of Buddhas and ancestors everywhere . . . are wood and stone. There is no mind apart from these. These stone and wood, or things in general, are not themselves bound by the realms of being and nonbeing, and emptiness and form . . . . One arouses the thought of enlightenment, practices, and attains with the mind which is wood and stone because mind is wood and mind is stone.* (Cook, 1999)

I have been chewing on this for years. Does this mean that wood and stone are actually mind? Does it mean that wood and stone are my mind—that this lectern is my mind, that it is your mind? The phrase *One Mind* is *isshin* in Japanese, and it is used to mean whole mind, undivided mind, concentrated mind, and single mind. Undivided mind includes everything it experiences as itself, without dividing or separating into self and other, without engaging the naming, categorizing, judging or limiting aspects of consciousness. The expression *doing things single-mindedly* is used in Zen to describe how to extend the mind of practice into our ordinary activity. This single-mindedness or undivided mind reminds me of Master Tozan Ryokai or Dongshan Liangjie who lived in the ninth century and was one of the two founders of Soto Zen in China.

According to *The Record of Tung-shan* translated by William Powell, when Tozan was about seven years old, he was studying with the village priest, and they were reading the *Heart Sutra*. When they came to the passage, *no eyes, no ears, no nose, no tongue, no body, no mind,* Tozan interrupted and said, "Wait a minute. What about this? I have eyes, and ears, and a nose." Both the question and the way it was asked caused the village priest to feel that he was not adequate to teach Tozan, and he referred Tozan to a monastery with a more mature teacher where he began his formal Buddhist training, still a young child. According to the guidelines for Buddhist Ordination, one has to be twenty or twenty-one to receive full ordination. When Tozan was twenty-one, he was ordained and left the monastery and the teacher with whom he had been studying and began a pilgrimage to visit other teachers.

Tozan visited Master Isan Reiyu or Kueishan Lingyou. Tozan said to Isan, "I've heard that the National Teacher maintains the doctrine that inanimate objects expound the Dharma. I don't understand this. Could you please clarify it for me?" And Isan said, "Please tell me more, tell me the story in which this statement was made." So Tozan told Isan the story:

> A monk asked the National Teacher Nan'yo Echu, "What is the mind of the ancient Buddhas?" The National Teacher replied, "A wall and broken tiles." The monk asked, "But aren't they inanimate objects?" The National Teacher said, "Yes, they are." The monk asked, "Can inanimate objects expound the Dharma?" The National Teacher said, "Inanimate objects are continuously and vigorously expounding the Dharma." The monk said, "Well, I've never heard it. Why can't I hear it?" The National Teacher said, "Even though you cannot hear it, do not hinder that which hears it." After more dialogue, the monk asked, "Which sutra says that non-sentient beings expound the Dharma?" The National Teacher replied, "The Avatamsaka Sutra says, 'The earth expounds the Dharma, living beings expound it, throughout the three times, everything expounds the Dharma.'" (Powell, 1986)

Dogen commented: *The mind of the ancient Buddhas should not be understood as something irrelevant to your experience, as some mind which exists from the beginningless past, for it is the mind which eats . . . or tastes . . . food in your ordinary, everyday life, it is the mind which is grass, the mind which is water.*

When Tozan finished the story, Isan then said to Tozan, "That teaching also exists here. However, one seldom encounters someone capable of understanding it." Tozan responded, "I still don't understand it clearly. Would you please comment?" Isan raised his whisk or *hossu*, saying, "Do you understand?" Tozan replied, "No, I don't, please explain." And Isan said, "It can never be explained to you by means of the mouth of one born of mother and father." Isan then referred Tozan to another teacher, to Master Ungan Donjo or Yunyan Tansheng. The whisk is a wooden handle with the flowing hair from a horse's tail attached to it. Originally, it was used to brush flies away, but over time it came to signify heart-to-heart, mind-to-mind transmission of Zen from master to disciple. In Dogen Zenji's "Fukanzazengi," this story is being referred to when he writes, *to effect realization with the aid of a hossu.*

Tozan traveled to Ungan's mountain and asked Master Ungan, "When the inanimate preaches the Dharma, who can hear it?" Ungan replied, "The inanimate can hear it." Tozan asked, "Can you hear it?" Ungan said, "If I could hear it, then you would not be able to hear me teach the Dharma." Tozan persisted, "Why can't I hear it?" Ungan raised his *hossu* and said, "Can you hear it?" Tozan said, "No, I can't." Ungan said, "You cannot even hear it when I expound the Dharma. How do you expect to hear when a non-sentient being expounds the Dharma?" Tozan then asked which sutra teaches that non-sentient beings expound the Dharma. And Ungan replied, "The *Amitaba Sutra* says, 'Water birds, tree groves, all without exception recite the Buddha's name, recite the Dharma.'"

This was a turning point for Tozan; he got it. He realized that the inanimate, that everything, expounds the Dharma and composed a verse: *How amazing. How amazing! Hard to comprehend that insentient beings expound the Dharma. It simply cannot be heard with the ear. But when sound is heard with the eye, then it is truly understood.* This is the enlightenment story of Tozan Ryokai, founder of Soto Zen. Nearly four hundred years later, Master Dogen carried this teaching of practicing with the inanimate from China to Japan.

In *Enlightenment Unfolds*, Kazuaki Tanahashi translated a related text, "Mujo Seppo," where Master Dogen wrote: *. . . hearing dharma is not limited to the ear organ and ear consciousness. You hear dharma with complete mind, complete body, and the complete way from before your parents were born . . . . You can hear the dharma with your body first and* *mind last.* A little later he said, *insentient beings speaking the dharma cannot be heard because it is not a sound which is the object of the ear.* Here Master Dogen is referring to experiencing things immediately and directly with whole being, with undivided mind. So the dharma and the being are also undivided. He continued: *Insentient beings speaking the dharma is the awesome manifestation of the single way beyond sound and form* (Tanahashi, 1999).

Zen monastic practice had a strong influence on Tea Ceremony, *Chado*—the Way of Tea, and Tea Ceremony effected the monastic forms in Japanese monasteries. In an early issue of San Francisco Zen Center's journal *Wind Bell*, an article on Tea Ceremony stated that:

> These arts [tea ceremony and Noh chanting] embody the Buddhist insight that all things—even such ordinary things as a bowl, cloth, spoon, or space in a room—are alive, with the same aliveness that we are. (Wind Bell, 1973)

How can we practice with the inanimate; how can we recognize things as mind? We offer incense and bow. A bell rings, we stand up and fluff our cushions. The way we enter a space. The way we pick things up and place them down. The way we meet things. I find it useful to listen to the sounds that are made when I do things. The sound I hear when I eat with the *oryoki* or monastic eating bowls, the sound I hear when I close a door or put down a tea cup or walk across the room. *The minds of all beings . . . are wood and stone.* In this realm, all things are equally real, equally important. All things are alive. So, when we wash dishes, we are washing the minds of the ancient Buddhas.

Soto Zen stresses the non-duality between the everyday world of birth and death, or *samsara*, and ultimate truth, or *nirvana*. Because of this, doing very ordinary things single-mindedly, with our whole body and mind—our whole being—can be a direct experience of the ultimate. Zen also emphasizes that Ordinary Mind is the Way, meaning consciousness, wholeheartedly engaged in ordinary activity without grasping or aversion, can be an experience of engaging the ultimate.

For Dogen, the *things* in our world also include space. Dogen considered space to be alive and inherently enlightened, the same way he considered mountains, rivers, grasses and trees, a wall and broken tiles to be alive, to be the mind of the ancient Buddhas. In his text, "Bendowa," Master Dogen wrote: *When . . . you sit properly in samadhi, . . . all space without exception is enlightenment* (Waddell/Abe, 2002). In the article, "Dogen's

Cosmology of Space and the Practice of Self-Fulfillment," Taigen Leighton commented on this saying that ... *space is not merely a dead, objective container in which there are forms. [For Dogen] Space is presence ... space has power. Space itself awakens when one person awakens.*

Japanese Tea Ceremony could be described as one long conglomeration of details, one after another, or as a world complete in itself. In Tea Ceremony there is a very precise way of doing everything: of walking, of sitting down, as well as the way you sit, the way you stand up, and the way you place each foot when you walk and turn around in the Tea Room. Each utensil has a specific way that it is picked up and held. All of this is in addition to the actual procedure for making the tea. When I studied Tea, I decided that I did not want to memorize each step; I didn't want to track it with my thinking mind. So I tried to encourage my body to learn the ceremony. I wanted to be able to rely on something other than my thinking to know what to do next.

I had a similar feeling when I was learning to ring the bells for zazen and service and when eating the formal zendo meal. When I eat with my *oryoki* I try to set aside my thinking mind and let my body respond to what comes next, so that I am free to engage in the activity of just sitting and eating. And when my attention becomes distracted, when I start thinking, it is often sound that brings me back to the present, the sound of rough movement or the sound of a rough, distracted mind.

When we eat with our *oryoki*, we sit in zazen posture with a straight back and hold our bowl rather high and close to our mouth so we don't need to lean over or curve our back while we are eating. In effect, we bring our food up to our mouth rather than bringing our mouth down to the food. We hold our bowl resting in our palm, as if it were a part of our hand or an extension of ourselves, rather than treating it as if it were an external object that we manipulate for our use. As we move our bowls—picking them up and placing them back down, we try to use two hands. Bringing both hands to an activity helps bring our full attention to what we are doing. If you have a tea bowl or a cup without a handle, you can experiment by drinking a cup of tea at home while holding the tea cup with two hands. Using both hands, in any activity, helps collect and focus the attention; it unifies our body and mind. In this way we can use drinking a cup of tea as a concentration or unification practice.

In Tea Ceremony the emphasis is not on making tea perfectly without mistakes. When I took tea class, we had class once a week in which you made tea for your partner and then watched while your partner made and served you tea. In the course of a year, we either made tea or watched someone else make tea close to a hundred times. This was done for the most part in silence. Several times a year, all the students would come together for a formal ceremony where four or five students prepared and served tea to the rest of the students. Everyone in the room knew tea well and the hosts had practiced many, many times, but I never went to a Tea Ceremony expecting that it would be done completely right. There are too many chances to have a gap, or to do something out of sequence, or to pick something up in the wrong way.

Although we would spend a lot of time and effort learning the forms, the point of Tea Ceremony, the emphasis, is not on recreating the forms perfectly. The emphasis is on taking care of your state of mind in the midst of the forms, with the support of the forms, and whatever happens moment after moment, you stay with your state of mind. Whatever situation arises, whatever happens, you address that and take care of it as your state of mind without worrying about making mistakes. Your state of mind is your priority, not the activity you are trying to accomplish. Each instant becomes a unique, non-repeatable opportunity to experience your state of mind. In this context when you serve tea to someone, you are not serving tea as much as you are serving your state of mind. Actually, what more do we have to offer?

In *Zen Mind, Beginner's Mind*, Suzuki Roshi said: *When you do something, if you fix your mind on the activity with some confidence, the quality of your state of mind is the activity itself* (Suzuki, 1970). When the bell rings, we stand up and fluff our cushions; the activity of fluffing our cushions is a direct expression of our state of mind. When we put on our shoes, we are wearing Buddha, and when we walk away, we are walking on the mind of the ancient Buddhas.

In Zen practice the goal isn't to sit zazen in full lotus position with a straight back, never moving, or even to have an enlightenment experience. The emphasis, the point is . . . What? . . . Why are we really here?

In a sense, our practice is to get the self out of the way so we can meet ourselves, meet everything, at a more fundamental level.

Although you do not hear it, do not hinder that which hears it.

Works Cited

Cook, Francis Dojun. "Hotsu Mujo Shin." *How to Raise an Ox: Zen Practice as Taught in Master Dogen's Shobogenzo*. Boston: Wisdom Publications, 1999.

Dogen, Eihei. "Mujo Seppo." *Enlightenment Unfolds: The Essential Teachings of Zen Master Dogen*. Ed. Kazuaki Tanahashi. Boston: Shambhala, 1999.

---. "Bendowa." *The Heart of Dogen's Shobogenzo*. Trans. Norman Waddell and Masao Abe. Albany, NY: State University of New York Press, 2002.

Leighton, Taigen Daniel. "Dogen's Cosmology of Space and the Practice of Self-Fulfillment." Excerpted from "Pacific World" journal, 2004. www.ancientdragon.org/dharma/articles/dogens_cosmology_of_space.

Liang-Chieh. *The Record of Tung-Shan*. Trans. William Powell. Honolulu: University of Hawaii Press, 1986.

Suzuki, Shunryu. *Zen Mind, Beginner's Mind*. New York/Tokyo: Weatherhill, 1970.

"Tea Ceremony." *Wind Bell*, XII (1973): 24.

Myoen Jisen Coghlan *is a practitioner and teacher in the Soto Zen lineage of Jikai Dainin Katagiri. Since receiving Dharma Transmission in 2012 from Rev. Kyoki Roberts of Zen Center of Pittsburgh, she practices and teaches at City Dharma in Pittsburgh, Pennsylvania. Jisen is trained in music, dance, and physical therapy and is a certified Alexander Technique teacher. She is member of the Soto Zen Buddhist Association and practices with Dosho Port of Great Tides Zen, Portland, Maine in the Vine of Obstacles Zen training, an online project.*

Without these teachers and mentors, the journey would have been impossible: Rev. Daien Bennage, Abbess, Mt. Equity Zendo; Rev. Shohaku Okumura, Founder and Guiding Teacher, Sanshin Zen Community; Ani Tsultrim Palmo, Gampo Abbey; Rev. Master Shiko Rom, and the monastic community of Shasta Abbey.

Dancing with the Ancestors

Myoen Jisen Coghlan

This writing is dedicated to Ani Tsultrim Palmo, my first Buddhist teacher,
and offered with deep reverence to all the Ancestors for transmitting
this wondrous practice of "just sitting."

"You must do two things when you leave here. Sit with Zen Buddhists. They know how to sit. And offer the Alexander Technique when someone asks," said Abbess Ani Tsultrim Palmo. We stood together in the entryway of Gampo Abbey, a Tibetan Buddhist Monastery high on the cliffs overlooking the St. Lawrence Gulf. It was a cold, sunny summer day in June 1995 on Cape Breton. I had just completed a Lojong retreat. At that moment, a lifelong journey began, and I knew I would take her words to heart.

Without Ani Palmo's keen insight, my life would have taken a very different course. Regretfully, I never returned to Gampo Abbey to thank her and tell her that I ordained in the Soto Zen Buddhist tradition. I can't remember if she knew I had been a dancer. However, I am sure if she had known, she would have told me to dance through my life.

We can sit down *spacious and content without confusion from inner thoughts of grasping . . .* as Hongzhi Zhengjue described it in *Cultivating the Empty Field* (Leighton, 2000). Here we pay attention to the body, breathing, being breathed, leaving thoughts as they are and adopt a gentle upright posture that expresses an open awareness to everything that arises, including thoughts meandering and curiosity intertwining with the breath. Relaxing into this spaciousness is the journey of realization. How we prepare the body sets the stage. This upright posture begins by swaying left and right with attention to the whole torso.

The torso is defined as the spine, pelvis and hip joints; arms and legs are actually the appendicular skeleton (appendages). This insight may be surprising as many of us think of the pelvis and hip joints as part of our legs. When we see the pelvis and hip joints as part of our torso, we can experience them lengthening upwards together with the spine. This simple discovery permits the legs to release and relax into the earth.

After moving the torso forward over the legs, allow the head to release in relationship to the torso. Notice the relationship between the spine and head by imperceptibly nodding "yes." The base of the head has feet too. These occipital feet glide on the first cervical vertebra, and the "nodding" occurs exactly at that joint. Breathing in, breathing out, allows the head to lead the movement and return to upright, gentle sitting.

Now bring your attention to the base of the pelvis, the sits-bones. Feel the pelvis and hip joints as part of the torso. The arms and legs release outward and are easily supported by a lengthening spine. The hands nest on top of each other, completing a perfect seal with the thumbs lightly touching. The tongue, originating from the lower jaw, fills the palate; it is soft, flexible and wide. There's no need to swallow repeatedly as the tongue's resting point behind the front teeth slows the flow of saliva. The lips touch lightly and the teeth close, resting together. The jaw releases at the joint across from the external ear openings—the exact point where the head balances on top of the spine. The eyes are open half width and rest in their bony sockets with a downward view. The gaze looks both outward and inward.

When the head balances on top of the spine, there is no need to pull the chin inward. Simply lower the eyes without allowing the head to fall down and back. As you inhale and exhale one full, complete breath through the mouth, the whole body expands in all dimensions. This is Hongzhi's posture of an *upright independent spirit*.

Breathing naturally through the nose, the belly softens. Become intimate with the breath, and let the mind settle and rest here at the core. Sense an energetic line connecting the eyes, the nose, and the body's center at the belly. As gravity flows down through the bones, an innate, natural response lengthens and widens the torso. When the mind is settled, permit a question to join intimately with the breath. Invite that which is hidden to come into plain view. We sit down and directly become Buddha with this body and mind. There is nothing to change to directly realize the Way; sitting is the gate for practice-realization.

By sitting you can dance through your life! Marion Scott, my modern dance choreography teacher, was someone who had a full life of dancing. She choreographed and danced until her death. She was a master of skillful means and found a way to bring forth our creativity from the inside out. The lessons she taught us went far beyond dancing. She taught us to fall down and pick ourselves up; to care for injuries with compassion; to express emotions and feelings through movement; to move like trees, birds, and fish; to relax within the complexity of the choreography; and finally, yes, to dance full out.

Also from her I learned the principle of "let come what may." Turning to meet everything and discover balance, I began moving from stiffness and tension to grace and poise. And through the Alexander Technique, I learned the process of moving from unsatisfactory, habitual patterns and allowing these very specific directions, "let the neck be free so that the head can release forward and up, so that the back can lengthen and widen," as a means to rediscover a natural use of the body. I explored moving through old crippling patterns of tightness and narrowing into ease and lightness. Learning these techniques of dance and the Alexander Technique took over ten years; embodying them is an ongoing, ever unfolding process of continual refinement.

Even after years of sitting, I continue to discover endless layers of tension intertwined with layers of ease that disclose hidden patterns. We often sit with tension, slumping into familiar acquired patterns. Preconceived attitudes and feelings spring forth as habits. These habits prevail almost involuntarily and are revealed through physical distortions and emotional outpourings. Holding onto strong emotions, opinions, and beliefs results in hidden tension in the body. Long-held tension causes physical impairments and reflects and contributes to habitual ways of interacting with others and with our environment.

Hongzhi states that we can *overcome habitual behavior and realize the self that isn't possessed by emotions.* As we let go of habitual patterns in our bodies and minds, we discover a sense of lightness and ease. There is no way to make this discovery other than by intimately knowing our habitual patterns. This is the place of connecting with our vulnerability. We see the transient nature of everything and directly experience this in our bodies. When sitting right down in the middle of our lives, what transpires can be quite surprising. Perhaps we are inspired to look deeply into this happening place.

Underneath all strong emotions, there is a treasure—tenderheartedness. This soft-heart could be likened to a wound. As a physical therapist, I performed intricate wound care. Many wounds were chronic, never healing, always tender, raw, and painful to the touch. In fact, some wounds never heal and the pain never goes away. Through peaceful, upright sitting, we can immerse ourselves in emotion and touch the tenderness without being overwhelmed; there is no way out but through the discomfort.

Finding a way through uneasiness means becoming very intimate with it. Befriend it, welcome it, and invite it to join you. The journey becomes one of courage and confidence. Here courage is defined as being open to whatever is arising without turning away; confidence and resilience evolve through our willingness to abide with all strong emotions. We see the causes of suffering and happiness; however, it's not a kind of la-di-da happiness. It's a sobering happiness that deepens over time in relationship to the willingness to stay within it all. This is a place where there is no wiggle room. Everything is in the mix. Nothing is concealed within the phenomenal world, nor is it about surpassing ordinary experience. Each of us can be here as we are. We can realize, penetrate the true nature of everything and completely express it in one total dynamic action. When we intimately meet everything, the whole world opens. There is nothing else.

How does the ordinary physical activity of sitting transform into a spiritual process? We settle into the zafu, beautifully upright, willing to be present, with an attitude of open awareness. The field of attention is spacious and includes a vast, broad, all-inclusive interior, so what seems very conventional is actually quite unfathomable. Confusion, despair, and fear can transform into clarity, joy, and compassion. "Just sitting" isn't "just;" it is challenging and difficult to stay in the thick of it all, especially when we want to escape. Within our experience, we get caught between right and wrong, this and that. We pick and choose, clinging to an opinion or an idea. We perceive ourselves as separate from everything. We all grasp something, each of us in our own way. Relying on things outside of ourselves for comfort and support, we hold onto our beliefs and opinions and miss the point that right here is where everything is happening.

Sitting year after year, we see a path right under our feet. In fact, it is our own feet. When we recognize the true teaching, we become responsible for practicing without exception. Finally, when we give up pursuing outside things, give up figuring things out, then the gate opens. What is most precious is this moment now, right here, and in that moment we can rest. Without running or looking for comfort, we can face what is arising and "just sit" right here without any choreography.

Returning home, we sit down and meet ourselves just as we are. We encounter our bodies as expansive and broad, or constricted and narrow, and the mind as it is, roaming or settled. That's it. There are no improvement programs. This is our birthright, sitting upright, breathing, thoughts coming and going with a willingness to be present. Upright, vivid sitting is resting with nothing added; it includes all thoughts, feelings, and emotions. Everything is fully alive and we penetrate everywhere. This is how we expand beyond conceptual understanding and open the door to becoming as Hongzhi describes, *clean, pure, and lucid.*

With endless possibilities, we relax into the moment, turning our lives inward in order to leap forward. Here, where absolutely nothing is excluded, we open our hearts, our bodies, our minds. It can't be seen from the outside. It is hidden in the wide open, and when we know the secret, and it is confirmed by the gatekeeper, we dance cheek to cheek with the Ancestors.

There's no need to search outside of ourselves; no need to change this body and mind to directly realize the Way. Sitting upright, being straightforward, means opening to realization. Settling down right here, the heart opens naturally. This is Dogen's practice-realization, the gate of joy and ease, and Hongzhi's *practice of true reality.* Practice is not a means to an end and realization isn't separate from our activities. Practice and realization are intimate dancing partners and can be fully actualized in daily life. In the spirit of our great ancestors, have courage, patience, resilience, and stick to the principles of peaceful upright sitting.

Here, in this precious moment, we are dancing with all of the Ancestors.

Works Cited

Zhengjue, Hongzhi. *Cultivating the Empty Field: The Silent Illumination of Zen Master Hongzhi.* Trans. and ed. Taigen Dan Leighton with Yi Wu. Boston: Tuttle Publishing, 2000.

Eijun Linda Ruth Cutts *is currently the Central Abbess of San Francisco Zen Center. She came to practice at San Francisco Zen Center in 1971 and was given Dharma Transmission in 1996 by Tenshin Reb Anderson in the Soto Zen Lineage of Shunryu Suzuki Roshi. She has lived at Green Gulch Farm since 1993 and teaches there, at Tassajara Zen Mountain Center and elsewhere.*

Compassion Practice: Call and Response

Eijun Linda Ruth Cutts

A talk given at Green Gulch Farm on August 17th, 2013

Recently someone said to me, "Oh, Zen doesn't talk about compassion very much." I didn't agree. Actually, all of the Zen stories, all the teachings, and all the meditation instructions flow from the vow of compassion and the wish to work for the welfare of sentient beings. There isn't any ulterior motive or something besides that.

In a sutra describing characteristics of a Buddha it says: *A Buddha is steadfast, due to great bliss and joy in the taste of the Dharma, . . . continuing to practice in order to bring about the welfare of all sentient beings.* Sometimes people think practice is for some other reason—perhaps to be in some fantabulous altered state. Actually the sole grounded reason for Buddhas or Awakened Ones to appear in the world is for the welfare of all sentient beings. This is the vow of compassion.

Now one might feel that some people are compassionate and other people are not compassionate, and you either are or you aren't. Compassion is not like that. What is so marvelous is that we all are born with the capacity for compassion; however, each person may not have the conditions in which to develop and nurture the "compassion instinct." Recently there has been lots of research about compassion, the findings of which do not come as a surprise to those who have been practicing zazen and meditation. There are studies about the biological and evolutionary importance of compassion, how it is essential for our good health, and how we are genetically predetermined to be kind and compassionate in order for our very species to survive.

Compassion can be defined as an emotion or feeling that arises when we see suffering, and, at the same time, as a true wish to relieve that suffering. If we are stable, calm, and have access to our inner resources when we see suffering, then compassion arises. If we ourselves are distraught, out of balance, and distracted, in the face of suffering we will want to distance ourselves and we will be unable to help.

A person with an aspiration to practice compassion can change the way the psycho-physical self responds to difficult situations. Compassion can be developed, can be trained, and can be deepened.

Of course, our practice, without saying anything about neuroscience or research, shows us that this is possible. Taking up practices of meditation, of mindfulness, of non-harming, of precept study, and of living an ethical life, as well as the practices of Generosity, of Ethics, of Patience, Joyful Effort, and Loving Kindness, develops us to be compassionate ones in the world.

In Buddhist iconography, there are personified images of infinite compassion called bodhisattvas, beings who have taken a vow in the same way as the Buddha, to live for the benefit and the welfare of all beings. The images of bodhisattvas, in statues, paintings, and *thangkas*, help awaken in us our own capacity for infinite compassion. It is not that compassion resides in a figure or painting. When we see compassion personified in a statue, we see our own heart-mind. When we take up practice and the vow of compassion, we make a turn in our lives. It may be a complete turnaround. We go from activities that are basically self-serving, where our own self-concern is of utmost importance, and turn to living for the benefit of others, which includes our benefit too. This is how bodhisattvas are born.

Shunryu Suzuki Roshi's title of his classic book, *Zen Mind, Beginner's Mind*, is well known. What isn't as often quoted from Suzuki Roshi is: *The beginner's mind is the mind of compassion. When our mind is compassionate, it is boundless* (Suzuki, 1970). Zen Mind is beginner's mind and a beginner's mind is a boundless compassionate mind.

One of the bodhisattvas of infinite compassion is Avalokiteshvara, or in Chinese, Kuan Yin, whose name means The One Who Hears the Cries of the World. One of the forms of this bodhisattva is a figure with a thousand arms and hands, and on every hand there is an eye—a wisdom eye. This bodhisattva of infinite compassion has myriad ways to help. There's no limit to the ways that compassionate activity manifests.

Compassion means an appropriate response. We often think of compassion as the same as being nice or sweet. The appropriate response or the appropriate action is not necessarily *nice*. It may be a shout or a "NO!" It could be anything. These thousand hands with the eyes of wisdom also have skill in means. If you see one of these figures with a thousand arms, there are different implements in each hand, all sorts of things: lassoes, mala beads, willow twigs, wish-fulfilling gems, and vases of compassion. I actually saw a statue in China that was carrying a cell phone! It was a modern statue in a new temple, and along with these lassoes and beads, willow branches and vases, and all sorts of symbolic things, was a cell phone. I think sometimes a call at the right time is exactly what's needed, is the appropriate response. Compassionate action uses whatever means necessary to relieve suffering. It may be sweet, but it could also be yelling at somebody, or refusing to do what someone says.

There are many, many figures of the bodhisattva of infinite compassion. Some figures have the thousand arms, some have eleven heads, some sit by the water in the bodily posture of "royal ease," with one knee bent and one leg hanging down ready to move, ready to come when her name is called. The eleven-headed form has eleven different faces. The front face is peaceful and a very beautiful face, and then if you go around to the back, there's a face that's really fierce, really frightening. Compassion can have this kind of face sometimes, when we need it. When we need some kind of strong medicine, then compassion may come in that form, and that will help us to wake up, to relieve our suffering.

The *Lotus Sutra* speaks of the thirty-three forms of Kuan Yin, The One Who Hears the Cries of the World. Whatever you need, compassion comes in that form. If you need compassion to come in the form of someone yelling at you, it'll come in that form. If you need it to come in the form of a good friend, it'll come in that form. If you need it as your pet, it takes that form. Zen mind, beginner's mind, compassionate mind. Be ready because it will take any form. Be ready.

I'm in a year long Contemplative Caregiver Course that San Francisco Zen Center is offering. It's not specifically hospice training, but a program that trains in caring for the elderly, sick, children, or anyone. It offers a way of connecting with people in a caregiving situation, a new way that is probably the oldest way. It's "compassionate care" when you are not pitying someone or setting yourself above, and you're not below and looking up; you're eye-to-eye with people. We may have habits of mind of how we are with family members, or friends who are having a hard time, or are dealing with loss, or grieving or in bereavement. We may find that it's hard to be with people who are in this much difficulty; we may not want to stay around them. So this training is helping the participants to become very aware of what's going on inside themselves, and helping them to have a deep acceptance and compassion for their own difficulty in staying with beings who are suffering.

It is possible to become more and more aware of how we deflect staying open and compassionate. We deflect in many ways: by trying to fix what's going on, by presenting solutions, by problem-solving. We want to say, "Listen to me, I did it this way," "I read an article about this . . . ," "Try it like this," "Don't do this." Advice, lots of advice. Or we're not able to be with our own painful feelings that arise when someone is suffering, and so we close down and step back, isolating the person a little bit; they're not fun to be around anymore. We are learning to be very aware of these tendencies, to watch what happens, to just stay with. We are learning to just be with, be present, without doing anything, without fixing, without trying to change the person, or to change the circumstances—that probably can't be changed anyway.

Being with in this way is a difficult practice that we can develop. Developing this Zen mind, beginner's mind, compassionate mind, and being able to stay with our own feelings, our own strong sensations of pain and difficulty, will allow us to fulfill our vows of living a compassionate life, of living for the benefit of others. We have to start with ourselves; we can't skip over and somehow look outward. To take care of someone else we start close to home. Developing true compassion for ourselves is the heart of a genuine compassion for others.

So this kind of eye-to-eye or evenness, rather than taking a position of above or below, or not wanting to be around at all, is essential for an appropriate response, but we don't know what it's going to look like. There's no formula, no set way, and if we get used to a set way that worked one time, we will become discouraged, because it won't work the next time. This is why beginner's mind is so important. If you hold onto what worked the last time and think, "I'll try that one again," you may get discouraged and confused, "How come that didn't work?" We keep coming back to beginner's mind over and over, "I don't know, but I'm going to stay present. I'm going to stay open. I'm going to listen." This is one of the main practices of Kuan Yin or the Bodhisattva of Infinite Compassion: listening, hearing.

True listening and appropriate response are not two separate things. There's the call, calling out for help, and there's the Listening-Response. Call and response come up together when we are practicing compassion.

There's a Zen story that illustrates this kind of call and response. It's a story that I love and the more I turn it and tell it and reflect on it over and over, the more the story has meaning and gives back. This is the same with all stories whether they are myths or fairy tales or Zen stories or family stories. As we continue to turn them, we can learn more and more or wake up to the story and its inner teaching structure.

As I said, often people don't associate Zen stories with compassion. They are stories of waking up, of someone realizing their true self and awakening to the reality of self, the reality of existence. Because so often the story includes somebody slamming the door on someone and breaking their leg, or twisting somebody's nose really hard, one might think, "That's not very compassionate; I hope I don't meet that fellow!" However, if you reflect on the teaching story and ask, "Where is compassion here?" it may surprise you.

This story is a story of compassion, a story of call and response and often when I get to the end of the story I feel like crying. This happens to me when I tell certain Zen stories.

This is a story about Ananda and Kashyapa who were both disciples of Shakyamuni Buddha. Ananda was the Buddha's cousin. The word Ananda means *joy* and supposedly Ananda brought joy to beings. He was a very fine-looking young man, and probably a fine-looking baby, and just to gaze upon him brought joy. If you see statues of Ananda, he is very sweet-faced and he often has plump cheeks that you want to give a little pinch. You always know it's Ananda if he's a really cute fellow.

Ananda was not only the Buddha's cousin and disciple, but he was also his attendant for about twenty-five years. Serving as the attendant of the Buddha meant seeing to the Buddha's personal and physical needs— mending, washing clothes, accompanying him—as well as attending all of the Buddha's talks. Ananda had a particularly incredible memory, and he learned all of the Buddha's talks by heart and could recite them word for word. Can you imagine reciting after this talk whatever it was that I said, word for word? Ananda was able to do this. He heard everything the Buddha taught and it was said to be *like pouring a glass of water into another glass without spilling a drop.* Every single thing was passed on. After the Buddha died, Ananda was asked to recite the Buddha's teachings at a council, and he recited everything. It was said that this was as if the Buddha had come alive again. All the sutras begin with, *Thus have I heard . . .* , which is Ananda's voice speaking and telling exactly what the Buddha said.

The Buddha transmitted the Dharma to Kashyapa, who became his successor in a very wonderful story. The Buddha was teaching at Vulture Peak and twirled a flower and winked. Kasyapa was in the assembly and he smiled. That was the transmission between them. The Buddha said, *I entrust the True Dharma eye and the fine mind of Nirvana; I completely entrust it to Kashyapa.* Then the Buddha asked Ananda to please communicate the teaching. He entrusted Kasyapa, and he also entrusted Ananda, with the assignment of passing on the teaching. After the

Buddha died Ananda practiced with Kasyapa for twenty more years and served Kasyapa. Ananda, however, had not realized his true self during the Buddha's lifetime; even though he intellectually knew every single thing the Buddha had said and could recite it, he still hadn't woken up to his true self.

So this brings us to the story of compassion called *The Banner Pole.*

> *Ananda said to Kasyapa, "What did the Buddha transmit to you besides the golden-sleeved robe?"*
> *Kasyapa said, "ANANDA!"*
> *Ananda said, "YES!"*
> *Kasyapa said, "Take down that Banner Pole at the gate."*
> *And Ananda was greatly enlightened.* (Cleary, 1990)

This is the story.

You might say, "What? What is this? I give up. What does this story have to do with anything? Banner poles . . . shouting?"

Here is Ananda who has not realized his true nature. He knows the Buddha's teaching intellectually, academically; he understands it and can teach it. He says to Kasyapa, "What else?" He's been with Kasyapa for quite awhile. He is saying, "I know the Buddha gave him the robe and transmitted to him the teaching. Did he give him something else besides the robe with the golden sleeves?" (They were said to be made of golden felt.) Ananda is saying to Kashyapa, "Did the Buddha hand on to you something beside this? What else did he give you? Come on, tell me! Isn't there something else? Let me in on it, please!"

And Kasyapa said, *Ananda! Yes!* Ananda! Yes! Ananda–Yes!

The two of them together, Kasyapa and Ananda, were just one call and response. He called Ananda's name and Ananda immediately responded without thinking. He didn't think, "Gee, how come he's calling me? I wonder, hmm . . . ." Just, "Ananda–Yes."

This is deep, deep compassion. Kasyapa just cut through what Ananda was fishing for. *Ananda! Yes!* It's enough. There's nothing you're lacking Ananda; you are abundantly filled with Dharma. And Ananda's *Yes!* expressed that completely. There's nothing lacking. There is a call and you respond.

Then: *Take down the banner pole.* In India when there was going to be a debate between two teachers about the Dharma they would put up banner poles, or flag poles, and then I think they would take down the pole of the teacher who lost the debate. Erecting the banner pole meant,

"I'm about to teach or speak the Dharma!" The banner pole is something that you put out, it is set forth to say, "This is who I am." Kashyapa said, "Take it down. You don't need it. It's enough. You are enough." And Ananda completely realized his true nature and stayed with Kashyapa, teaching and practicing after that.

It isn't enough to just realize your true nature. This is an important point. There needs to be the actualizing of the truth of that realization. This means responding in any way that is appropriate to the cries of the world. Over and over we hear that once our true nature is realized, we can really work for the benefit of all beings, and the vow that we've taken and aspired to all these years can truly manifest in any situation with compassion. Ananda and Kasyapa are non-dual. Your self and others are non-dual. You can really be compassionate because helping self and helping other is not different.

When we cling to our old accomplishments, our own sense of who we are, when we are clinging to that which is already over, we are clinging to the past. How about this moment? How about, what is the call now? Rather than dragging in our attachment to who we are, *Take down the banner pole!* You don't need it. You don't have to put up a sign that says, "Look, this is who I am. See, remember me? I'm that one who . . . said that really good thing one time." It's over.

Ananda! Yes! All of us have this capacity to live in that way, to be this present and this responding. What gets in the way of that; what are the obstacles? All sorts of things can be obstacles to "Ananda–Yes!"

Ananda's name is *joy*. One of the supports of joyous effort is rest. The four supports of joyous effort are aspiration, stability, engaging in our practice with full enthusiasm like a sport, and rest. Taking repose and rest are essential for joy. The obstacles to compassion might be that we are over extended; we are overwrought, and we are constantly busy and doing things, so we can't even hear.

Call and response is the name of infinite compassion. We're being called and requested all throughout the day in big and small ways, internally and externally.

May you be encouraged and feel enthusiastic and feel joyous effort in taking up this practice of compassionate response, appropriate response, and look into it, test it, ask about it, reflect on it. The more one does so, the more one develops and deepens the vow to live for the welfare of the earth and all beings.

Works Cited

Keizan, Zen Master. *Transmission of Light: Zen in the Art of Enlightenment.* Trans. Thomas Cleary. San Francisco: North Point Press, 1990.

Suzuki, Shunryu. *Zen Mind, Beginner's Mind.* New York/Tokyo: Weatherhill, 1970.

Jan Chozen Bays, Roshi, *has studied and practiced Zen Buddhism since 1973, receiving Dharma Transmission in the White Plum lineage from Taizan Maezumi, Roshi, in 1983. Also a pediatrician, mother, and wife, Chozen Roshi has been the teacher for the Zen Community of Oregon in Portland, Oregon since 1985. In 2002, she helped to found Great Vow Monastery outside Claskanie, Oregon and serves there as co-abbot with her husband, Hogen Bays. She helped found Heart of Wisdom Zen Temple in Portland, Oregon in 2011.*

Chozen Roshi has published many articles about Zen in Tricycle *and* Buddhadharma *magazines. Her books include* Jizo Bodhisattva, Guardian of Children, Women and other Voyagers; How to Train a Wild Elephant: And Other Adventures in Mindfulness; *and* Mindful Eating: A Guide to Rediscovering a Healthy and Joyful Relationship with Food.

When the Truth Fills
Our Body and Mind

Jan Chozen Bays

People are very curious about enlightenment. Zen teachers don't talk about it much, however, as talking about it conceptualizes enlightenment and encourages people to strive for certain experiences. As a result there seems to be a lot of confusion as to what enlightenment is. Zen masters exhort students to "die on the cushion" or "die before you die and you will never have to die again," but these instructions don't give us a picture of what enlightenment might be like or how to proceed forward.

A lovely treatise on the path to enlightenment was written by the thirteenth century Zen Master Eihei Dogen. It is called "Genjo Koan, or the Way of Everyday Life" (Maezumi, 1978, throughout). Dogen Zenji wrote:

> *When the truth does not fill our body and mind, we think that we have enough. When the truth fills our body and mind, we realize that something is missing.*

This is why we begin spiritual practice. We know that something is missing. It isn't a different place to live or a new car, job, or partner. We try those out, but they only seem to satisfy for a time, and then the creeping sense that something fundamental is out of kilter arises again.

What is it that's missing?

Dogen Zenji gives us a hint.

> *For example when we view the four directions from a boat on the ocean where no land is in sight, we see only a circle and nothing else. No other aspects are apparent.*

Most of the time we look at life from the perspective of a little boat, a boat called "I, me, and mine." Everything we see, hear and touch, smell, taste and even think is crammed into this little boat. We perceive everything in reference to this small boat. The weather? How will it affect me and my little boat? The stars wheeling in the heavens, national events, all other boats? We see them as existing only to benefit or harm this little boat. Everywhere we go in the world, we take this boat with us. It's here with us in the meditation hall. As soon as we sit down it's my place, my cushion, my bowls—and over there? That's your boat. Don't come too close to my boat, my circle of imagined control.

What is missing cannot be found in the world of material objects. What is missing cannot be provided by other people, no matter how dearly they love us. Transient objects, including people, can never satisfy us completely, because they will change and disappear. Deep down, we know this, and it makes us uneasy. We start to search in earnest for what is missing, something that is unchanging and deeply satisfying.

The Sufi poet mystic Hafiz writes about it (Ladinsky, 1999). *First the fish needs to say, "Something ain't right about this camel ride—and I'm feeling so damned thirsty!"* This thirst is fundamental, and fundamentally good!

Now Dogen Zenji gives us another hint. He tells us to look outside the boat, outside the circle called self.

> However this ocean is neither round nor square and its realities are infinite in variety.

We know this intuitively, that we must be more than a short-lived, soon-forgotten person. We know intuitively that some larger aspect of ourselves is missing.

It stirs in us occasionally: when we hear beautiful music, when we lie next to a sleeping child or lover, when a deer stops and looks at us with liquid eyes, when, for a moment, everything is perfect. It stirs in us like a whale turning over deep in the ocean.

As we sit, up here on the surface, we feel a rocking of our boat, a quickening of our pulse. For a moment our mind extends down into the depths, into the vastness of the ocean and its innumerable creatures, microscopic and immense, tame and savage. We see that we are insignificant specks on this indifferent ocean of vast power. We might glimpse, just for an instant, that we are also the ocean, that it flows in our veins, that it will reclaim us when we die. But it is too frightening to be the tiny speck, too alarming to be the immensity of the ocean, too impossible to be the speck and the ocean at once, so we pull back and begin thinking about what color to paint our boat when we get back to shore.

> However this ocean is neither round nor square and its realities are infinite in variety.... It just seems circular as far as the eye can reach at the time.

At the time tells us that our inner eye will be able to see further. It is the promise of enlightenment to come. This is an amazing promise— that who we truly are is not just *round or square*, not just five feet, two inches or seven feet tall, sixty-eight or twenty-one years old, not just American or Canadian, a woman or a man, not just talented at music or poor at math. No matter how it is configured, that is still the little boat. What we truly are is *infinite in variety*. That is the promise of a path of discovery that goes on forever. In long retreats, as our mind quiets, the path opens before us and we get a glimpse of another aspect of who we really are. We are enticed to continue on.

Many people have insights during or as a result of sesshin. Enlightenment is not an insight. An insight is an *aha* moment when you realize, "Oh, I should go to college," or "This is not the person I should marry," or "Oh, that's the reason they behaved so strangely!" or "Here's what I should say in this talk." Those insights are very helpful and more likely to occur when our mind is open and settled, but that is not enlightenment. People wax eloquent about their insights, but how often do those insights lead to real and lasting change in their lives?

Enlightenment is like being turned inside out—completely inside out—so you can never go back. You become the ocean and forget the boat. The boat becomes unimportant. Not for a moment, but as a permanent change. When you forget yourself, your energy is freed from the bondage of the small self's constant anxieties and strategies, and it turns outward to help others who are suffering because they are convinced that they are in tiny boats, defective boats, sinking boats. Your particular boat becomes a tool at the service of the ocean and the other boats sailing through it.

Enlightenment is not a goal, not an ending. It IS, ALL THAT IS.

> When a fish swims in the ocean there is no end to the water,
> no matter how far it swims.... Know then that water is life.
> Know that air is life. Life is the bird and life is the fish.

We are enlightenment swimming in enlightenment. Our experience of it is a process, a continual opening to the home we have always known but somehow forgot. Enlightenment has no end and no beginning. We can swim in it forever and never come to an end, like a fish swimming round the world, never leaving the ocean.

Gaining enlightenment is like the moon reflecting in the water. The moon does not get wet nor is the water disturbed.

Dogen Zenji tells us that enlightenment is a natural event, like the light of the moon reflecting in a drop of water. As practice deepens we come to an edge, an edge of fear. Encountering our unconditioned, un-bounded nature is like encountering the ocean for the first time. Its size and power are overwhelming. But we don't need to be afraid of it. Just as the drop becomes completely filled with the moon's light, so the light of enlightened awareness fills us. It is remarkable and at the same time completely simple and natural.

Although its light is extensive and great, the moon is reflected even in a puddle an inch across.

This is amazing! Although we might think of ourselves as a little murky puddle, actually we reflect ... we contain ... we *are* the light of enlightenment, the light of the entire Universe, of all Universes. Because our inner eye is clouded we cannot see that light, and we get confused, grope around blindly and suffer.

Hafiz wrote: *It rained during the night and two puddles formed in the dark and began chatting. One said, "It is so nice to be at last upon this earth and to meet you as well. But what will happen when the brilliant sun comes and turns us back into spirit again?"*

Why are we afraid of disappearing into the ocean of the Unbounded? Because we have to let go of everything we've put together to form a self. It takes faith to step out of the small boat, even though this boat is imper-fect and so small it is suffocating us. It's all the protection we have. We are afraid to let it go and swim around, naked and vulnerable. We are afraid to evaporate and merge with the sky. To do this takes faith, and courage.

This is why we might prefer to take it slowly. When people begin practice they often think that they'd like sudden enlightenment—a bolt of lightning that knocks them over, transforming their life in an instant, granting them instant perfection. As they begin to realize how thor-ough the transformation needs to be, however, they may come to prefer Master Issan's version of the enlightenment process: *Walking in a fog unaware that your clothes are getting wet.*

Actually both gradual and sudden aspects of enlightenment are nec-essary. The slow, steady practice that creates minor adjustments—more mindfulness, less reactivity, more loving kindness, a mind that learns to enjoy being quiet—these are like the small slips in the earth that pave the way for a big earthquake. Gradual enlightenment is like removing one rotting board at a time from a defective boat, and replacing it with a sound board. The sound board, however, is made of emptiness. One day we realize that the entire boat is nothing but emptiness sailing unhindered through emptiness.

> *When all dharmas are Buddha Dharma there are enlightenment and delusion, practice, life and death . . . . When the ten thousand dharmas are without self, there is no delusion, no enlightenment . . . no life and no death.*

Dogen Zenji points out that from one side, the side of multiplicity, of individual selves, there are differences between enlightened and unenlightened, between life and death. But from the side of only One, of no single self, there is no difference. Sometimes we feel torn between these two opposites. From the self side, I am unhappy. I have to practice hard in order to get enlightened so I can be happy before I die. From the without-self side, I'm intrinsically enlightened. Every activity of my life is my Original Nature manifesting. Grasping for enlightenment is extra, adding a boat on top of a boat.

Both sides are true. As you have all discovered, sometimes in long retreats we have to work hard, but sometimes that hard work gets in the way. Then we have to relax and do nothing. Just sit and be aware, not picking and choosing. Everything perfect as it is. But then someone near you chants off key or keeps clearing their throat, and everything falls out of perfection. You have some work to do again. In an informal talk Dogen Zenji once quipped: *A deluded person and an enlightened person at the same time use one boat but . . . each is not obstructed* (Leighton/Okumura, 1995).

In the *Genjo Koan*, Dogen Zenji doesn't leave us trying to hold the tension of two apparent opposites, being at once enlightened and not enlightened. He points to the next stage of enlightenment.

> *The Buddha Way transcends being and non-being, therefore there are life and death, delusion and enlightenment . . .*

But they are not the same life and death or delusion and enlightenment as before. These opposites are transcended. Where? In our unique life, when we experience them as the same, as identical non-identical twins, as manifesting in harmony. No life, no death, infinite lives, infinite deaths, in the moment-by-moment functioning of our very life.

Once again Dogen Zenji tells us how this happens, step by step.

To study the self. Necessary.

To forget the self. Necessary.

Seeing forms with the whole body, hearing sounds with the whole body, one becomes them intimately. Submerged in zazen, mind and body one whole, seeing sounds, hearing forms, no inside, no outside, no one to watch it all. Necessary.

To be enlightened by the ten thousand dharmas is to free one's body and mind and the body and mind of others. Another promise—when this happens, we will be free and others will simultaneously be freed. From what? From the dense net of delusion we cast over the entire world when we putter about in a little boat fueled by desire, fishing for stuff we think we want.

Through enlightenment, the boat, the boater, the fish, the net all disappear. There is just the ocean, and, just being ocean, it does not know itself AS ocean. It just is. Not even perfect as it is, because perfect means comparing, and if there is only One, there is no comparison. Then, everything appears again, but we know forever that everything is optional. Everything is useful, even wonderful, while we are alive, but letting them go is not a problem, because we've already done it.

People wonder, "What is an enlightened person like?" Here are some possibilities.

They tend not to take things personally, because they know that there is fundamentally no person. They also do not see others as objects.

They tend toward equanimity, because nothing can give offense.

They are flexible, not attached to roles, and able to move about easily in many worlds, comfortable in robes, a tux or overalls.

They are compassionate without getting mired in the suffering of others.

They benefit others. As they pass through life you see, in their wake, a lessening of suffering and an increase in freedom.

They have a sense of humor, taking the predicament of inhabiting a self lightly. Hafiz said, *God and I have become like two giant fat people, living in a tiny boat. We keep bumping into each other and laughing.*

They are happy, because quiet happiness is fundamental to the awakened heart/mind, underlying everything, even sorrow. This is not a top-of-the-roller-coaster-with-fireworks-in-the-background kind of happiness. It is the simple happiness of being thirsty and drinking cool water, of awakening healthy after days of illness, of arriving home after a long journey.

The depth of the drop is the height of the moon. As for the duration of the reflection, you should examine the water's vastness or smallness and you should discern the brightness or dimness of the heavenly moon.

Although we are the entire light of enlightenment, Dogen Zenji admonishes us to honestly evaluate the brightness of the moon in our life—to see clearly what we have to work on and then do that work.

Some may realize it and some may not.

Practice is not a necessary condition for us to *be* enlightenment. It is a necessary condition if we want to *experience* that enlightenment, for ourselves, in our own being. May this be possible for us all, in this very life.

Works Cited

Dogen, Eihei. *Dogen's Extensive Record: A Translation of the Eihei Koroku.* Trans. Taigen Dan Leighton and Shohaku Okumura. Boston: Wisdom Publishing, 1995.

---. *The Way of Everyday Life.* Trans. Hakuyu Taizan Maezumi. Los Angeles: Center Publications, 1978.

Hafiz. *The Gift: Poems by Hafiz, the Great Sufi Master.* Trans. Daniel Ladinsky. New York: Penguin Compass, 1999.

Jion Susan Postal, *teacher and founder of the Empty Hand Zen Center in New Rochelle, NY, entered Buddhist practice in 1970 with a teacher of Dzogchen in the Tibetan Buddhist tradition. She began Zen studies with Bernie Glassman Roshi at the Zen Community of New York in 1980 and continued in 1987 under the guidance of Maurine Myo-on Stuart, teacher of the Meeting House Zen Group in Rye, NY, from whom she received tokudo in 1988. In 2000, Susan began studies with Darlene Cohen, Zen Teacher of Russian River Zendo in Guerneville, CA. In 2008, Susan received Dharma Transmission in the Soto Zen lineage of Suzuki Roshi from Darlene. Susan died on February 7, 2014 while this book was in publication.*

Susan pursued graduate studies in social anthropology and geriatric counseling and worked for many years in homes for the aged. She was also active in interfaith dialogue in both church and university settings and was a member of the American Zen Teachers Association.

The Birth of Vow

Jion Susan Postal

Vow gives us courage; repentance totally crushes our arrogance.
This is the posture of a vivid, alive religious life.

Kosho Uchiyama in *Opening the Hand of Thought* (Wright, 2004)

Hasn't Uchiyama Roshi put his finger on precisely our own fundamental question—how is it possible to live an alive religious life? While not disagreeing with Uchiyama, I would like to expand and rephrase a bit.

During a talk on Vow a few years ago, I found myself making the rather outrageous statement that Vow isn't something we do, but rather something that happens to us. Vow is born in us. The aliveness, actually living a life of Vow, is not the same as making a decision or a promise, a commitment, or a New Year's resolution. In my experience, the birth of Vow is a turning, almost like being physically turned around, or turned inside out. It seems to me that Vow is given life, is born, from both repentance and gratitude; Vow has two "parents" so to speak.

Repentance

Dairyu Michael Wenger points us in the direction of repentance in his book *49 Fingers, A Collection Of Modern American Koans*. He cites the following case: *Katagiri Roshi was once asked, "Why did you add the Verse of Purification to your morning service? Is it traditional?"* (This verse is not part of the usual Soto Zen service as found at San Francisco Zen Center, for example.) *"Is that because we Americans need it more?" Katagiri responded, "No, it is because we humans need it."*

The Verse of Purification says:

> *All my ancient twisted karma,*
> *From beginningless greed, hate and delusion,*
> *Born through body, speech and mind,*
> *now I fully avow.*

Katagiri was not the only teacher to emphasize the Verse of Purification. I recently discovered that Torei Zenji, Dharma Heir of the great Rinzai Zen Master Hakuin Zenji, gave his students a list of three things to do to clean their karma: bow fully, sit zazen, and recite the Verse of Purification. Shantideva said: *One law serves to summarize the whole of the Mahayana. The protection of all beings is accomplished through examination of one's own mistakes.*

In our zendo, every weekday and Sunday morning, we follow our nine bows with this verse of repentance. Thus we accept our own responsibility, acknowledging how we may have caused harm and also cleaning it, purifying it, not carrying it farther. We set it all down, fold it up, and move on with emptier hands. Since the time of the historical Shakyamuni Buddha, repentance, or confession, has been seen as the preparation for taking the Bodhisattva vows.

Shohaku Okumura, in his inspiring book *Living by Vow*, comments that awakening to our own imperfection is repentance. He also reminds us that, in Buddhism, repentance is not just an apology for a mistake we have made. Apologizing may be relevant and helpful, but it is only a partial step. As Buddhist practitioners, full repentance requires clear awareness of our limitations and imperfections. Then the release and purification of our karmic actions can actually happen. That release means that we don't go around for the rest of our lives filled with guilt and self-criticism. Our endless stumbles are often the finest teachers.

In my experience, bowing and chanting are close and helpful partners for repentance. Both chanting and bowing offer a direct doorway into practice that is physical—a body practice that allows us to become sound, to become gesture. Dropping to the floor is a whole body expression of letting go of the self, of "me-mine." Reb Anderson in *Warm Smiles from Cold Mountains* notes that bowing is not to bow down to something. He says *to bow is to crack duality.* Maybe it is this cracking, this experience of no-separation, which makes room for Vow to be born, to begin to grow. In morning service, when wholeheartedly giving voice to a *sutra*, a *dharani*, a reading, we release the struggle to understand its "meaning" and simply let the sounds we are uttering teach us directly. Again, no room left for "me," just an outflow of sound from our vocal chords and an inflow through our ears.

I am reminded of a scene at the beginning of the *Vimilakirti Sutra*, a setting similar to the *Lotus Sutra*, where a multitude of Buddhas, Bodhisattvas, monks, nuns, and lay disciples are gathered around the Buddha. On the horizon a large group of young men appears, all sons of Brahmans, all with strong aspiration for the Way. Each is carrying a beautifully decorated parasol. Each parasol is uniquely covered with jewels, ribbons, and rainbow colors. As they approach the Buddha, each young man folds up his umbrella, lays it on the ground, and drops to the ground in a deep prostration. When all the umbrellas are folded and put down, the Buddha transforms them into one giant magnificent umbrella that covers all space and time. What a powerful illustration of complete surrendering, complete setting down, folding up, and letting go of the self.

So what are you carrying today? How is your parasol decorated? Are you ready to fold it up and lay it down?

Gratitude

Eihei Dogen in our Soto Zen line and Torei Zenji in the Rinzai Zen line, both wrote eloquently about Vow and gratitude.

In his treatise *The Undying Lamp of Zen*, Torei wrote:

> *What is received from the teacher, inspiring gratitude for the teaching, is something you should not turn your back on, even at the expense of your life. When you include gratitude for the achievements of successive generations of Zen masters, each one equal, no amount of effort is adequate to requite it.*
> (Cleary, 2010)

Master Dogen's Vow, ("Eihei Koso Hotsuganmon"), is found embedded within chapter nine of the *Shobogenzo:* "Voices of the River-Valleys and Form of the Mountains." At some later time, it appeared as a separate verse in the version we treasure. To read *Buddhas and Ancestors of old were as we. In the future, we shall be Buddhas and Ancestors*, never fails to bring me shivers of disbelief, of doubt. Dogen then assures us that *as they extend their compassion freely to us, we are able to realize Buddhahood and let go of the realization.* This release of realization—something we seek and make great effort to "get"—may sound strange, but in this release lies the key. Empty hands cannot hold any notion of realization.

Gratitude for the endless compassion of the Buddhas and Ancestors is so beautifully expressed in Dogen's Vow. We are invited to honestly see our failure to practice, our lack of faith. We are assured that by repenting in this way, we will receive deep and unending help. Upwelling of boundless gratitude begins to flow. We are thoroughly soaked. It feels like all the dried out, discouraged, doubtful places have now been moistened. Now we are open to being surprised, to being astonished by the birth of something new.

Our own two karma verses, Purification and Gratitude, serve as bookends in our daily service at Empty Hand. In the opening Verse of Purification, we acknowledge our ancient twisted karma. Then in Verse of Gratitude that closes our service, we give thanks for all the beneficent karma, all the blessings of this life.

The Verse of Gratitude says:

> *For all beneficent karma ever manifested through me, I am grateful.*
> *May this gratitude be expressed through my body, speech and mind*
> *With infinite kindness to the past,*
> *Infinite service to the present,*
> *Infinite responsibility for the future.*

The "three infinities" embedded in the middle are actually vows themselves or maybe prayers. Wherever we find the word "may," what follows is a vow or a prayer. This prayer is not directed to any being or deity outside of us, but to the *Endless Dimension Universal Life*, as Soen Roshi called it.

Gratitude seems an essential element for the birth of these vows in us. It is the wellspring that allows an outflow to begin. This is a huge turning, where we find ourselves not practicing to get something for "me," but rather with a pouring out, a lateral flow out in all directions. Even when we are filled to overflowing with gratitude, not only is there some space, some growing room, for vows to be born, but perhaps the embryonic vows are also deeply and directly nourished by our gratitude.

Birth of Vow

This birth of a life of Vow is, in fact, the birth of Bodhisattva functioning. A Bodhisattva is an awakened being who vows not to enter Nirvana until all beings are saved. As Vow is born, a shift happens; we are no longer sitting just for "me," but actually with all beings. The Bodhisattva is not doing this for others. There are no others. There is, in fact, no duality, only not-two. There is an outward flow in our zazen that just happens. We may be subtly aware of this movement, but we cannot make it happen.

In my own small tastes of this turning, it has been like being turned inside out, like a glove, like a sock. The "me," the person in charge that ordinarily exists on the surface, running the show, with unique habits and conditioning, is still here; but now it is on the inside being useful, serving. What was on the "inside," a kind of soft open awareness, becomes that which meets the world, which interacts with people and circumstances as is appropriate. This is a quality of warmth, of open acceptance, which serves to relieve suffering even in the middle of great difficulty.

Some of us have discovered that is possible to experience "being practiced." Our zazen begins to practice us. "You" are not doing it. In the same way, I would suggest that the life of Vow can be born in us, can become alive in us, can practice us through the ongoing, deep, introspective release of true repentance and the profound, joyful outflow of boundless gratitude.

Works Cited

Anderson, Reb. *Warm Smiles from Cold Mountains: Dharma Talks on Zen Meditation*. Berkeley: Rodmell Press, 2005.

Enji, Torei. *The Undying Lamp of Zen: The Testament of Zen Master Torei*. Trans. Thomas Cleary. Boston: Shambhala, 2010.

Okumura, Shohaku. *Living by Vow: A Practical Introduction to Eight Essential Zen Chants and Texts*. Ed. Dave Ellison. Boston: Wisdom Publications, 2012.

Uchiyama, Kosho. *Opening the Hand of Thought: Foundations of Zen Buddhism*. Trans. and ed. Daitsu Tom Wright, Jisho Warner, and Shohaku Okumura. Boston: Wisdom Publications, 2004.

Wenger, Dairyu Michael. *49 Fingers: A Collection of Modern American Koans*. San Francisco: Dragons Leap Press, 2011.

Rev. Meian Elbert *is the Abbess of Shasta Abbey in Northern California. She was ordained by Rev. Master Jiyu Kennett in 1977 and received Dharma Transmission from her in 1979.*

The Gift of Fearlessness

Meian Elbert

In order to talk about fearlessness, first I have to talk about fear. Everyone is subject to fear, no matter who we are; none of us is exempt. Just by virtue of being human animals we are wired for fear so that we may survive. At present in this world, the level of fear seems to have escalated far beyond normal limits. Here in the West, in addition to all our usual fears, we also have fear of terrorist attacks, fear of ourselves or our families being killed, fear of irreparable damage to the environment, fear of severe economic deprivation, and so on. In many countries people have lived with these fears for a long time, and for many people, not just in other countries, these fears have become their reality. However, on a day-to-day basis, most of our fears are much more mundane. And it is by working with these daily fears that we learn to deal with the bigger ones. Fear is fear, from mild anxiety to stark physical terror.

What are we afraid of? The most obvious fear is of harm to the body, which in itself is a basic, useful fear that keeps us from falling off cliffs and getting mugged in dark streets. We fear getting hurt or sick; we fear physical pain, we fear death. Up to a point this fear is useful, but only up to a point. We can spend enormous amounts of time, money, and effort in trying to maintain our physical health, avoid pain, and prolong our life. In fact, we will inevitably get sick, undergo pain, and eventually die. We need to deal with our fear of these things so that they do not enslave us.

Then there are all the other fears: to name just a few, we have fear of insecurity, fear of the unknown, fear of losing the people we love, or of harm coming to them, fear of abandonment, fear of making mistakes, fear of being judged and blamed by others, fear of looking foolish and being embarrassed, fear of not being in control, and the Nameless Dread, not knowing what we are afraid of but feeling fear anyway. Any one of these can be a source of great suffering and can paralyze us. A person may be afraid to go outside, and be literally imprisoned by their fear, or they may not have the courage to make some change in their life that they need to make, whether it be ending a harmful relationship, or making a change of career to doing something their heart longs to do. Whether the fear seems real or unreal, it's real to the person concerned.

Often we are ashamed of our fears. We don't want to admit that we are afraid of another person, or of social functions. If we are afraid of heights, or of closed spaces, or of spiders, we may feel foolish, but we still have the fear. A soldier going into battle doesn't want to admit he is afraid, but of course he is. No matter how courageous he may be, there is fear there. Courage is not the absence of fear; it is not letting it prevent us from doing what we need to do.

Fear makes us selfish. When we are afraid, we become enclosed in a little frightened shell, and it is hard to think of others. When we are afraid for our loved ones, we bring them into our little shell with us—a slightly bigger shell but it's still a little shell. When we are afraid for our town, or our country, or even our world, our shell is bigger but it's still a shell. We are still in the world of the opposites, and our fear can make us angry: "me" vs. "them," "us" vs. "them," "the good guys" vs. "the bad guys."

So, how do we deal with fear? It's interesting that, although the Buddha talks about all sorts of states of mind, he doesn't talk much about fear. I was wondering aloud about this and someone suggested it may be because fear is not an intentional thing like anger and desire, it's just fear. It's not one of the hindrances to meditation; in fact Theravadin monks often meditate in places that inspire fear to help them overcome it, whereas they don't go to places that inspire lust or anger. One thing the Buddha did say was that, before his enlightenment, he decided that if fear and dread came to him, he would remain in whatever posture he was in (walking, standing, sitting or lying down) until he had subdued that fear and terror. If he was walking, he would continue walking until he had subdued his fear; if he was standing, he would continue standing, and so on, and that is what he did *(Bhayabherava Sutta)*.

This is exactly what we need to do. When we are afraid, we need to recognize that we are afraid and face it head on, whether we are in a dark forest or in a business meeting that isn't going well. Fear is a slippery beast, and it's easy to distract ourselves by pretending it isn't there, or by justifying our unease in some other way. If we can see that we are afraid, then we are less likely to act on it blindly and perhaps hurt someone. We try not to judge our fear, but just to notice: there is fear here. I am afraid of this person, or this situation. Sometimes we are afraid of someone with no apparent reason, whether it seems rational or not, and sometimes they are also afraid of us. If we can talk about it together, it often dissipates or is greatly reduced; we may be astonished to find that someone is afraid of us.

When we are angry, usually we are afraid. If we are attacked, physically or verbally, we might respond with anger, but really, we are afraid. Even when it feels like righteous anger, or anger on behalf of someone else, there is still fear there; we are afraid that bad things will happen, that people we don't trust will have power over others that they will misuse and thereby harm them, or harm us or those we love. We may not realize that there is fear underneath our anger, but if we can recognize it, we can work with it a lot more effectively.

Desire is also related to fear. When we really want something, there is the fear that we won't get it, or that if we do get it, we will lose it. If there is a person we are longing for, the fear grows in proportion to our desire. In our intimate relationships, we can be tormented by jealousy, fear of inadequacy or being abandoned, or fear of things just not working out. When rich people try to amass more and more money, I think it is because they are afraid; they are trying to create safety for themselves and the people they love. Thinking of it in this way, we can perhaps be a little more forgiving when we hear of scandals involving millions of dollars that do harm to a great many people, and such a person will suffer the karmic consequences of their actions. But if they had been able to face their fear and deal with it in another way, an enormous amount of suffering might have been avoided.

In fact, it seems that most of human (and animal) suffering is caused by fear. Wars often start because people are afraid. If one country wants what another country has, they are afraid of not getting it, and each becomes afraid of the other. Disharmony in a family is often because people are afraid of each other or for each other. One family member may see another doing harm to themselves or to other people, or they are worried about money, or worried about their children. On the personal level, anxiety, depression, inadequacy, despair, and many other forms of suffering are mainly based on fear.

We need to recognize when we are afraid, recognize the sensation in our body. Sometimes it is quite subtle, just a little uneasiness; sometimes it is sudden and unexpected. Then we may ask: why am I afraid? What exactly am I afraid of? What do I think I am afraid of, and what is really going on? If I am afraid of someone's anger, what will actually happen to me if they get angry? Are they likely to hurt me or humiliate me? Do they have some power over me? What do I actually fear here? Am I afraid for my safety, or afraid of losing face, or am I afraid that the person will get their way with something I don't agree with or think is harmful?

Not being in control can be very frightening to some people; if I am in control maybe things will go the way I think they should. If someone else is in control, then they will have power over me, and I might feel belittled, or unsafe, or I might be required to do something I think is wrong. Sometimes if we investigate like this, we can help ourselves bring our fear into perspective, and we are better able to deal with it. Sometimes it's best just to sit with the fear. Sometimes we can reason it away, as when we're alone at night and our imagination is getting the better of us, and sometimes not. Investigation is a handy tool but it's limited.

Most of all, we need to sit still in the midst of fear. We need to recognize fear arising, to see what it is we are afraid of, if we can, and to sit still right in the midst of it. If we rush around trying to fix everything and make it all safe, there is a limit to what we can do; we can't make it all safe. Life is not safe. We are vulnerable beings with a brief, fragile body on an increasingly fragile planet. We are all prone to old age, sickness, and death. No matter what lengths we may go to in order to preserve our health, we may still get sick. If we are lucky, we will live to grow old and eventually die. This may sound depressing, but it is completely true, and if we can look at it straight on and accept it, it helps us enormously. People who spend a lot of time with those who are dying tend to have a much brighter and more accepting view of death than those who avoid it. We fear the unknown, and death is the great unknown.

Fear of physical pain and suffering is often greater than our fear of death, and the fear of pain is often worse than the pain itself. If we can sit still right in the midst of pain as it arises and accept it completely, while doing what we reasonably can to alleviate it, our experience of it is completely changed. The pain may still be there but we are not driven by it or dragged around desperately trying to get rid of it. It is our fear of the pain that is the worst part. If we can simply take it moment by moment, it is not so bad. This can be very hard to do, but we can keep working on it. I have heard people who have had a lot of pain in their lives say that pain is a great teacher; it teaches us patience and acceptance, because in the end that is the only way to handle it. Illness can be a great teacher too, if we let it teach us. It can get our attention. Instead of simply running along, taking things for granted, we are brought up short and we might ask: what am I doing? How am I living my life? What is really important in life? Again, if we can sit still with it, really accept it and even embrace it, pain and illness can help us and our suffering is greatly reduced. We still treat it; we still try to relieve our pain and sickness, but we are not denying it or kicking against it. Our acceptance and stillness are an enormous help.

Of course, it is the mind that is the key in all of this. Our imagination can make our fears much greater if we let it, and our mind can run rampant. Anyone who has camped in the woods knows that a squirrel outside our tent can sound just like a bear to us. On the other hand, we may tend to distract ourselves from the things we are afraid of, or pretend they don't exist, such as refusing to deal with our money problems, or putting off going to the doctor when we have some worrying symptom of illness.

We don't want to suppress our fear, but we don't need to feed it either. This is important. If we can sit still and feel the fear *in our body* (which is where we feel it) and not feed it with the mind, it begins to lose its grip and eventually it dissolves. When we notice fear arise, what does it feel like in the body? Is there tightness in the chest, or hollowness in the stomach, or are we trembling or sweating? Or all of the above? If we can sit still and simply feel the fear, look at it but not let the mind run off imagining the worst, it will dissipate. This is what the Buddha meant by continuing to walk, stand, sit or lie down until he subdued the fear; to look it right in the eye and not let it move him. We investigate when we need to, and then we sit still with it. When we sit still right in the midst of it, it dissolves; it is empty.

A very common and pervasive form of fear is worry. Fear can be of something immediate, a "clear and present danger"; worry is nearly always about something that might happen in the future. At this moment, usually we are not in immediate danger. If we are, then we do our best with the situation, fear or no fear. Worry and, usually, fear are about things that might happen. In fact, the things that do happen are almost always different from the way we imagine them. Our worst fears are usually not realized, and when they are, it's generally quite different from the way we imagined. We may be afraid of illness, then we get sick and we just deal with it; it's all right. We may be afraid of losing all our money, and if we do, we just do our best and manage somehow. The fear and worry are nearly always worse than the reality. Often the worst things that happen to us are things we hadn't thought of at all, and still we deal with them; we just do our best with whatever comes to us. This is because we eventually accept them. Worry is a form of non-acceptance, of resistance to what might come to us. It's just the mind.

Nameless Dread can be a very useful tool in working with fear. I think we may all be prone to this inexplicable unease that suddenly comes upon us, quite unexpectedly, often in the middle of the night for some of us. If we are attentive we can be still and observe it arise, abide, and pass away. Our investigation may not help us here; the nature of Nameless Dread is that we don't know what it is exactly that we are dreading. We can ask, "What am I afraid of?" and we may or may not get an answer. We simply have to sit still in the midst of it and let it come and go. This is a very helpful practice in dealing with all kinds of fear. It helps us to see that fear is really empty; it has no real substance. Even when there is something or someone immediately present to be afraid of, fear still comes and goes. When the situation abates, the fear abates too. If we suffer from chronic fear of some person or situation, it still comes and goes; it is not solid and static.

In dealing with fear there has to be compassion, not self-judgment. It does not help if we disparage or castigate ourselves. Even if we know that our fear is groundless or exaggerated, we have to accept it with compassion and sit still. We can also remember that other beings feel fear, and they may be afraid of us. If we know that fear arises for everyone, we can feel compassion for others and not just dwell on our own self-centered fear. This helps us to be less afraid, knowing that other people are pretty much the same as we are; we are not especially vulnerable or flawed or insecure.

A great antidote to fear is generosity. Generosity with material goods helps us to be less fearful of losing them or of not having enough for ourselves. It helps us to reach through that little selfish shell that can enclose us in fear; it helps that shell to soften and melt. When we give something, we are refusing to be imprisoned by fear. Similarly, when we stop and give our time and attention to someone else, it helps us to break the habit of rushing anxiously from here to there with no time for anyone or anything but our own agenda.

One of the great gifts is the gift of fearlessness. Fearlessness is not the absence of fear, and it's not doing things like bungie-jumping to prove our courage. Fearlessness is doing what needs to be done, and not letting our fear prevent us, even when it is difficult. It may be taking on something that scares us, rising to a challenge, or it may be standing up for what we feel is right in the face of opposition. It may be continuing with something in the face of obstacles. It is a form of giving. We see great examples of fearlessness in people like Mother Teresa, Venerable

Maha Ghosananda, Nelson Mandela, and so on. These people inspire others and help them to go beyond their fear too, thereby bestowing fearlessness on them. Our own practice of fearlessness may not seem so grand; however, simply sitting down to meditate takes courage and is very hard for many people, but we do it anyway.

We can also give fearlessness by not causing other beings to fear us, by practicing kindness and trustworthiness, and by keeping to the Precepts, so that people know we won't manipulate them or use them or treat them poorly. In fact, another of the best antidotes to fear is the practice of *metta*, loving-kindness. This works both ways: when we practice it, beings don't fear us, and its practice also helps with our own fear. Again it is a form of giving; it helps us to break through that shell of selfish fear, offering loving-kindness to other beings and thinking of them rather than just ourselves. This is very simple but very effective.

There is one more fear I have not mentioned. It's what I call the fear of drowning in the delusive world without knowing the Truth, seeing Buddha Nature. This fear can help to motivate us in getting on with our practice, but in the end it isn't very helpful. It tends to get in the way and cause us to get worried and look for results. It is much better to apply the other antidote: faith. The practice of faith helps us with all the many fears we may have, and it is the one thing that really sustains us in the end: faith in Buddha Nature, whether we think we see it or not, faith in the practice of the Dharma, imperfect as our practice may appear, and faith in those who try to practice the Dharma, even when they make mistakes. Faith goes deeper than the mistakes and imperfections of human beings, deeper than our own perceptions and opinions, deeper than all that seems reasonable. It takes courage to practice faith, to entrust ourselves to That which is greater than we are, That which sustains us and supports us, whether we know it or not; the Unborn, Undying, Buddha Nature, whatever we like to call it, from which we come and to which we will return. This is why we do not need to be afraid of death, or anything else for that matter; we come from the Source of Compassion, and we return to that Source. There is nothing outside of it. We don't have to worry; we just have to do our best. We do our very best with this life that we have, this very moment that we have, to live with faith, with kindness and generosity, with courage, and with joy.

Works Cited

"Bhayabherava Sutta, Fear and Dread," Sutta no. 4. *The Middle Length Discourses of the Buddha: A New Translation of the Majjhima Nikaya*. Trans. Bikkhu Nanamoli and Bhikkhu Bodhi. Boston: Wisdom Publications, 1995.

Shosan Victoria Austin *is a Dharma Teacher with the San Francisco Zen Center. She studies with Sojun Mel Weitsman and received Dharma Transmission from him in the Shunryu Suzuki lineage in 1999. Shosan has taught Iyengar yoga for thirty years and continues regular study in the U.S. with Manouso Manos and in India with the Iyengars.*

Artist Christine Bailey *created the drawings that illustrate the text. Christine is also an educator and Zen practitioner who currently resides in San Francisco, CA. She received her Master of Fine Arts in Interdisciplinary Studies from the Maryland Institute College of Art, has exhibited her work in numerous galleries and museums, and has received grants and awards for her work in drawing, photography and new media.*

The Seated Meditation Pose for a Woman's Life

Shosan Victoria Austin

This offering is dedicated to the Buddha's first practice, which was yoga, with nine bows to Yogacarya B.K.S. Iyengar, who teaches stability, comfort, and great awakening through the Dharma gate of the infinite specific characteristics of human life.

Meditation And Being Human

Before becoming free from delusion, men and women are equally not free from delusion. At the time of becoming free from delusion and realizing the truth, there is no difference between men and women. (*Shobo Genzo:* Fascicle 9, Tanahashi, 2010)

The main point of meditation is the same for all humans: to rest in the ultimate, and to experience the connection between ultimate and conditioned existence, in the present moment. To do this, we sit in an upright, aligned way, one with the universe by nature of being composed of its elements, naturally receiving it in and offering it out through the process of normal breathing. When we sit down on the cushion, it is just like the Buddha approaching his seat. When we arise, it is just like anyone who arises. The simplicity of sitting allows us to study ourselves and the human condition with as little extra in the way as possible. When body and mind align, composure and depth gradually develop. The nature of human birth and death becomes apparent, as does its deeper meaning. The meditator's structure and personality naturally mature bit by bit, to receive, hold, and express this teaching.

Meditation And Being Female

If you practice sitting Zen, [you will know that] Zen is not about sitting or lying down.
—*Nanyue, Zen Master Dahui* (*Shobo Genzo:* Fascicle 28, Tanahashi, 2010)

Though the main point of meditation is the same for all humans, the majority voice in the transmission of the teachings is male. As a female Buddhist teacher, I believe that it is important to explore the impact of this historical fact in the bodies and minds of women practitioners. In particular, following the lead of one of the foremost female yoga teachers in the world, Bri. Geeta Iyengar, I feel that it is necessary to set forth specific postural teachings that reflect the changing circumstances in the body of a female meditator through the various stages of life. I cannot praise Geetaji's teachings highly enough. Through her devoted practice and persistent teaching, I have been able to discover a sense of stability and comfort each morning as I sit on my cushion.

It is proper to note here that Geetaji's teachings are for the pure practice of Iyengar yoga, in which seated meditation is done in an upright posture with the palms in *anjali-mudra* (joined at the level of the lower sternum, with thumbs touching the sternum and fingers touching), and with the eyes closed.

In contrast, seated meditation in the Soto Zen tradition is done with the palms in *dhyana-mudra*

(one palm on the other, palms up and overlapping by two joints of the middle finger, hands in an oval, thumb tips lightly touching), and with the eyes open enough to admit light. Though the meditation posture is slightly different, Geetaji's approach, based on B.K.S. Iyengar's teaching, is supportive, informative, and inspirational for any female meditator in any tradition. Though in a few pages we can only scratch the surface of the vast array of conditions a woman meditator might face, I hope that these teachings from the yogic tradition followed by the Buddha, help a wide group of female Buddhists of the present day to find steadiness and comfort in sitting.

In general, choose a pose that respects the Buddha's teaching of the Middle Way—neither too difficult to maintain, nor so relaxing that you fall asleep. Sit equally on the two buttock bones, and extend the sides of the chest equally upward. This will support the spine to be upright and tall, with the tailbone and the top of the spine, and all the spinal curves in between, balanced in re-

lation to each other. Then balance the actions of legs, arms, and trunk.

These general instructions are adequate for many men, and for some non-menstruating women in the prime of life. However, the ease or difficulty of the following instructions will vary during the course of a woman's life, and may be out of reach altogether in the sitting posture during certain phases of a woman's life:

- Avoid sinking the front of the pelvis; don't let the uterus drop. In cross-legged poses, while the inner groins need to release downwards, they should not sink, or create compression.

- Balance flexibility with inner strength and support, but not hardness. The knowledge of how to do this must be slowly and patiently built; it does not come quickly, even if a woman has a sincere desire to sit upright. Because the hormone relaxin is secreted during menstruation and pregnancy, and because female hormone levels change greatly and sometimes fairly rapidly at various points in a woman's life, there can be a huge learning curve on any given day of a woman's life. If we assume that our posture today can be the same as yesterday, we stress and tax ourselves, creating physical, mental, and emotional stress. The female body needs structure, which creates a realistic sense of courage. When we patiently build ourselves up, emphasizing a practice of nourishment rather than a quick fix, these issues resolve from within, and the balance of flexibility, strength, and support is built as a natural maturation of self-study in changing conditions.

- Keep the mind focused, but wide: at crucial points in a woman's life, the mind becomes diffuse or loses its known quality due to the all-encompassing nature of the physiological changes. Fighting the diffuseness only creates agitation. Nor should we confuse diffuseness with *sunyata* (the positive experience of emptiness); this delusion leads to dullness. As followers of the Middle Way, our job is to build a wholesome physical, physiological and mental structure that gives a sense of continuity and stability through any change. The experience of *sunyata* becomes naturally accessible and wholesome when it is appropriately held.

- Keep face, ears, eyes, nose, tongue, groins released: this depends on our willingness to subtract unnecessary effort, once postural stability is learned.

In different stages of a woman's life—puberty, pregnancy, menopause—to find a state of alert repose, she will need to arrange her meditation posture in a manner that is responsive to her physical and physiological condition. Though the basic concept of upright, alert repose in the meditation posture is the same throughout life, the specifics vary:

seated or reclining, leg position, sitting height, and the need for and type of support. For insight to be possible, a woman's meditation posture must be stable and nourishing. According to the Buddha's teachings of nourishment, not only the physical body must be nourished, but also the woman's senses, intention, and consciousness. Due to the physical and physiological changes, how a woman meditator nourishes herself in these four important ways, varies throughout the course of her life.

Puberty

For young girls and teens, meditation practice needs to be short and simple—five to ten minutes maximum. Puberty, the transition from a physiologically neutral to overtly female body, is marked by drastic social, physical, and emotional changes. First the arms and legs, then the torso, grow at an unprecedented rate. There are structural changes— from the leanness and quickness of youth to a young woman's curves, interests, and pace. Menstruation begins, but the menstrual rhythm is not yet established. The young woman now has the potential to go inward—and often interest in doing so—but what she finds, when she does, is newly complex, often to the point where time spent with the self can become a morass rather than a refuge. The process of becoming overtly gendered, whatever direction it takes, can be embarrassing and painful, exhilarating, or anything in between.

Key words for an adolescent's meditation posture are: interest, responsiveness, safety, and simplicity.

A teenage woman needs the simplest variations of poses, particularly at the time of menstruation. She can sit or lie down for periods short enough not to trigger strain or restlessness, in any posture that establishes a connection with the earth and with her normal breath. Appropriately propping the pose can help with cramps, bloating, over-flexibility, any heavy feelings, fatigue, and emotional changes. Since the menstrual cycle is not yet regular, her needs and inner emotional climate may change unpredictably. That is why simple poses that can be maintained in a variety

Using a blanket for psychological safety

of conditions work well at this time. If breasts and hips are embarrassing, provide safety by using a blanket, shawl, or sweater.

Adult Menstrual Rhythm

Once the menstrual cycle has established its rhythm, the woman enters physiological adulthood, the time of greatest physical ability for meditation posture, and most predictable monthly rhythm to establish a practice of self-study. Barring medical conditions, this stage of a female meditator's life includes practice from her mid-twenties to her forties. This is a time to examine the large rhythms of life, and there are unique meditation teachings for women at this time. The menstrual cycle alerts us to impermanence and the primacy of birth and death. The very sense of self rhythmically changes over the course of a physiological month.

For the first few days each month, estrogen increases to prepare a woman for conception until mid-month ovum release. If conception does not occur, progesterone rises to maintain a rich uterine lining for another few days. In the last one to two weeks, both estrogen and progesterone drop, inner abdominal fibers open, and the uterine lining sheds with blood.

This physiological monthly rhythm produces fluctuations in a woman's body, emotions, and intellect that can be inhabited and known through meditation. For instance, in the third physiological week each month, weight may rise, breasts may ache, skin may break out, and irritation level may rise. A woman may be in a womblike mental state, annoyed, or teary each month. In the last few days, the flow changes, and perceptual ability and emotional life changes with the hormonal rhythm. There is a period of gradual recuperation.

If a woman is not looking inward, she may take these changes for granted and believe in them as part of her self-image. If she practices meditation, she can realize and become one with the ebb and flow of the sense of self. Being one with the menstrual cycle gives a wide, accepting and accurate sense of receptivity to what is.

Key words for adult meditation practice: nourish, stable, right effort, and real.

To support an adult woman's meditation practice, any of the traditional postures may be chosen depending on the time of month. Depending on the internal state of lightness or heaviness, one may support the buttocks higher or lower. The choice of props should create a soft abdomen with naturally grounded breathing. If she needs to

resolve stresses and strains, she may prop for effortlessness, and maintain awareness of exhalation. For this time of life, comfort is built by lifting and opening the chest, softening the face, creating a sense of depth in the chest, and taking enough time to meet what is within. During menstruation, supported reclining or seated poses can provide a sense of softness and refuge.

As the flow stops, and internal environment returns to a steady state, the supports can be gradually removed to retrain abdominal postural support. Internal lifting actions, lateral actions, and an emphasis on inhalation work for this time of month. A firmer cushion and hard props will help to reestablish an active relationship with the ground. Though practicing firmness

A variety of props may be used to meet the special physical, physiological and emotional needs of menstruation

of internal support, most female meditators must apply their attention to extend and expand the lower back, and to keep the female organs soft and natural. Without attention, female structure tends to collapse over time. If there is back or abdominal pain, physical props are useful to support those areas, and to maintain a natural sense of balance, flexibility and relaxation. The goal is to find a state of alert repose.

Conception/ Desired Conception

The middle of the month, when an egg has been released to a fallopian tube and the uterine lining is at its thickest, is the time of greatest fertility. For conception to be successful, a woman's internal environment must be stable and comfortable enough to implant and nourish the fertilized egg. Age, stress, frequency and quality of sexual intimacy, and general level of health, are a few of the many factors that may affect the ability to conceive.

Key words for a meditator either conceiving or trying to conceive: stable, balanced, safe, and nourished.

At this time, personal discipline with weight, food, sleep, and exercise to maintain a healthy hormonal balance, is a prerequisite to right effort in meditation. The posture can be nourished from the base by choosing a meditation posture in the middle of the possible physical range, establishing evenness of the buttock bones on the cushion, and supporting the trunk or arms to maintain an even balance of lift and softness. For instance, rather than kneeling in *seiza* (knees together, feet apart, buttocks on a bench or cushion) as is sometimes taught, sitting in a simple cross-legged pose with buttocks higher than knees, and support between the ankles and shins, creates a much more hospitable internal environment for conception. In the posture, im-

Supporting the lower legs helps soften the abdomen while remaining upright and balanced

mediately before or after conception, a woman would do well to focus on balance—front and back, left and right, inner and outer, bottom and top, body and mind. A continuous practice is to extend the trunk up, and to create internal width and depth, without hardening or narrowing the lumbar region, abdomen or throat. The spinal muscles need to be strong or supported to maintain a sense of lift without holding or adversely affecting the breath.

Pregnancy

The benefits of establishing a stable, comfortable meditation posture extend to both mother and child, throughout both of their lifetimes. Because hormonal changes of pregnancy begin immediately upon conception and become physiologically noticeable only after a few weeks, and because the process consumes a great deal of creative energy, a woman's meditation posture for pregnancy greatly depends on her prior practice. Though developmental change in pregnancy is continuous, we conceptualize it in three-month periods called trimesters, which include recognizable sets of changes in each third of the nine normal months of gestation. During the three trimesters, a woman's meditation posture changes to stably, continuously hold her own inner life and that of her developing child.

In the first trimester, a female meditator needs to give up any harmful habits, and to proactively nourish the body of both herself and the baby through their continuous mutual process of growth and change. New experiences and allostasis develop quickly: by the end of the second month there may be morning sickness signaling a changed system of nourishment, and by the end of the third month the embryo has developed to be recognizably human in form and internal systems. In the first trimester, *key words* are nourishment and continuity through change. Though the external form of the posture may not change, internally the mother is learning how to respond to change.

In contrast, the second trimester is a time of external physical change. The body becomes heavier and physiologically more sensitive. There may be dizziness, frequent urination, discharge, or changes in circulation. The process of sitting down and getting up becomes an issue, as does the quality of the skin and space of the lower body. *Key words* for the second trimester are: support, circulation, and nourishment. Props can be used to maintain a sense of lightness and maintain the circulation in the lower body, for instance by sitting cross-legged on a high, wide cushion with support under the knees. In the seated meditation pose, a second-trimester mother can learn that not only is it possible to refrain from descending into physical, physiological or emotional fatigue, but rather to proactively grow her knowledge and ability for external and internal happiness, not just for one, but for two.

Key words for the third trimester are: preparation, patience, friendliness. By this point, the extra weight and the physical pliability built by a new hormonal balance may have side effects of fatigue, discomfort or pain. There may be lumbar or pelvic pain, discharge, or even mild contractions. Internal space in the body must be cultivated for digestion, assimilation, breathing, and excretion. To create space, the pregnant meditator needs extra props, not just under the seat, but sometimes under the forearms as well. If she separately supports each leg, their separate function, relaxation, and the space between will become known to her. She must avoid closing the space, holding the breath, or putting weight on the growing baby. At this time, a healthy posture is non-demanding, so the nerves can relax and the parasympathetic response become

active. The most productive practice will not come from compliance to a schedule, but rather from responding to internal need and happiness. A spacious, friendly, nourishing internal environment creates conditions for the pregnancy to culminate naturally. This is a good time for back support rather than abdominal action; the abdomen needs to soften and spread. Therefore, sitting in *Baddhakonasana* (back to the wall, buttocks on a cushion, soles of the feet together, knees wide) will be useful at this time, perhaps with a folded towel behind the mid-back, or with a wide folded blanket under the forearms. Supporting, lifting and opening the upper body in such a manner gives natural space, relaxation, and breath to the lower body. Supporting arms as well as legs gives a feeling of firmness and safety, to hold the emotional changes that can range from impatience and anticipation, to anxiety, to great contentment.

Labor And Delivery

Women with a very established meditation practice may choose to meditate during labor, particularly between contractions, during the hours or days of the latent phase before full dilation. Though only an experienced meditator will have the physical and mental preparation to return to concentration between contractions, attention to posture and breathing can help stabilize the woman's experience and make it possible for her to feel safe and receptive throughout one of the most transformative experiences of her life.

For those women faced with the prospect of a C-section, establishing a stable "seat" allows internal space to contemplate major surgery. In non-emergency situations, meditation is possible and helpful before and after a C-section; the exact posture depends on the specifics of the woman's condition, so should be discussed with a teacher experienced in therapeutic applications of yoga. In general, the most appropriate posture will be reclining with supports to maintain circulation and avoid further internal disturbance.

Post-Partum, Lactation

Meditators in the first few weeks after delivery need to establish a posture that promotes healing and the return to normal internal rhythms. The posture needs to safely hold the physiological transition to regular lactation, and the huge emotional transformation of becoming mother to a new life that is now

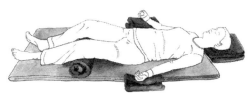

physically separate from her body.

In the first two months particularly, women new to contemplation will find the most healing posture to be a simple reclining pose with back or leg support. Once bleeding ceases and healing has progressed to the point of considering a seated posture, a simple choice such as *Virasana* (knees together, feet apart, with buttocks elevated and a blanket behind the knees) keeps the lower abdo-

men in a safe posture conducive to gradually re-establishing the abdominal support of a normal adult rhythm. Gradually the buttock support may be decreased and more complex postures can be introduced. At this time, wide-legged postures such as *Baddhakonasana* (soles of the feet together, knees wide apart) or *Upavisthakonasana* (straight legs wide apart) are not healthy for meditation practice. Particularly if there are still health issues, no posture should be held to the point of fatigue.

After about twelve weeks, most women can resume any seated posture that gives them a sense of composure and balance. A new mother can now return almost to her normal adult rhythm if she realizes that the period of lactation has its own physiological needs that must continue to be supported until the child is weaned. She can use a stable, comfortable meditation posture to resolve suffering before it gets entrenched. For instance, contemplation, observed breathing, and meditation in a well-supported posture helps her resolve internal tensions, irritation and agitation that might otherwise affect her milk or communicate themselves to her child.

Peri-Menopause And Menopause

With the exception of periods of childbearing or disease, most women can continue to use the postural rhythm that they have established to support their normal menstrual rhythm, until the menstrual cycle begins to slow between age forty or fifty. This is the period of peri-menopause, during which a woman will have to re-establish her seat in a posture suitable for soothing any extra bleeding, body aches, emotional changes, or pelvic pain. For many women, simpler postures such as those used after delivery will work. A woman in peri-menopause needs to create stability, lift, and openness in the upper body to hold the

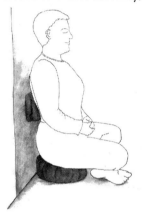

emotional changes, which are otherwise often experienced as negative. More suffering comes to the foreground and needs to be safely held. She needs to keep her head and face balanced, relaxed and silent, and spend more time with both inhalations and exhalations normal, unconditioned, rhythmic, and reassuring.

Many women will find it appropriate to take back support of a wall for the seated posture. Arm support may help both with aches and pains, and to establish a sense of safety, nourishment and continuity. Reclining meditation poses can be difficult to endure for many women at this time; lying down will be more productive with thoracic support. *Key words* for a woman's posture at this time: explore the new balance, safety, soothing, cooling.

After Menopause

After menopause, once the endocrine system has entered a state of greater balance, a female meditator will find herself once again physically facing the unknown. The balance continues to change, though much more slowly, through the time of old age. Because the change is very slow compared to the transformation of menopause, she may experience a relative state of calm. As gradually her natural state becomes more sensitive, drier, more frail, and more vulnerable to environmental change, the choice of an appropriately supported seated posture can allow her to experience the wide perspective, emotional maturity, and grandmotherly wisdom that characterize this time of life.

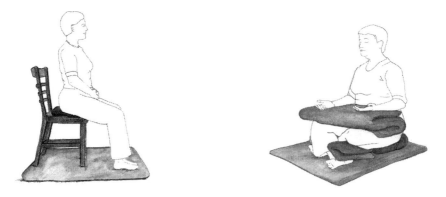

Like a young adult, a post-menopausal woman can choose from a wide variety of postures for seated meditation. She may want to support any vulnerable joints. To respect the changes that come with aging, a decrease in the effort or excitement level may be appropriate. The main point is to keep the posture happy and comfortable, and to lessen any harsh or controlling qualities in her practice.

Key words for a postmenopausal meditator: steadiness, comfort, ease, respect, natural range. If her posture safely and comfortably holds her, a woman in this stage of life is naturally contemplative.

The Seated Meditation Pose For A Woman's Life

> *[The Buddha] was not interested in some metaphysical existence, but in his own body and mind, here and now. And when he found himself, he found that everything that exists has Buddha nature. That was his enlightenment. Enlightenment is not some good feeling or some particular state of mind. The state of mind that exists when you sit in the right posture is, itself, enlightenment . . . . In this posture there is no need to talk about the right state of mind. You already have it. This is the conclusion of Buddhism.*
> —Shunryu Suzuki, Roshi (1970)

With apologies to Eihei Dogen Daiosho, here is a version of his "Fukanzazengi" (Trans. Sotoshu Shumucho, 2001) rewritten for a woman's body:

> *The Way is originally perfect and all-pervading. How could it be contingent on practice and realization? The true vehicle is self-sufficient. What need is there for special effort? Indeed, the*

74

whole body is free from dust. Who could believe in a means to brush it clean? It is never apart from this very place; what is the use of traveling around to practice? And yet, if there is a hairsbreadth deviation, it is like the gap between heaven and earth. If the least like or dislike arises, the mind is lost in confusion. Suppose you are confident in your understanding and rich in enlightenment, gaining the wisdom that knows at a glance, attaining the way and clarifying the mind, arousing an aspiration to reach for the heavens. You are playing in the entranceway, but you are still short of the vital path of emancipation.

Consider the Buddha: although he was wise at birth, the traces of his six years of upright sitting can yet be seen. As for Mahapajapati, though her lineage is lost, her persistence as a mother and awakened being continues. If the ancients were like this, how can we today dispense with wholehearted practice?

Therefore, put aside the intellectual practice of investigating words and chasing phrases, as well as the social practice of dissimulation, and learn to take the backward step that turns the light and shines it inward. Body and mind of themselves will drop away, and your original face will manifest. If you want to realize such, get to work on such right away.

For practicing Zen, a quiet room is suitable. Eat and drink moderately. Put aside all involvements and suspend all affairs. Do not think "good" or "bad." Do not judge true or false. Give up the operations of mind, intellect, and consciousness; stop measuring with thoughts, ideas, and views. Have no designs on becoming a buddha. How could that be limited to sitting or lying down?

At your sitting place, spread out a thick mat and put a cushion on it. Sit either in the full-lotus or half-lotus position; or kneel with knees together and feet apart; or sit with one shin in front of the other and ankles crossed; or with shins crossed. At certain stages of life, it is suitable to recline with the torso supported; or to rest on your side with one arm supporting your head. In the full-lotus position, place one foot high on the opposite thigh, then the second foot high on the first thigh. In the half-lotus, simply place one foot high on the opposite thigh. Switch legs every day if using an asymmetrical position. Tie your robes loosely and arrange them neatly. If sitting, place the hand on the side of the second leg first, palm up, with the little finger touching the abdomen between the pubic bone and the navel. Place the other hand on top, palm up, and lightly touch the tips of the thumbs. If reclining, adjust your hand position in a dignified manner. Align the body and sit upright, leaning neither left nor right, neither forward nor backward. If reclining, align the body so legs, hips, trunk and face are centered on the midline, and keep your forehead higher than your chin. Align your ears with your shoulders and your nose with your navel. Rest the tip of your tongue lightly on the front roof of your mouth, with teeth together, lips shut, and the skin of the face smooth. Keep your eyes open and breathe softly through your nose.

Once you have adjusted your posture, take a breath and exhale fully, make subtle adjustments, then settle into steady, immovable sitting. Think of not-thinking. Not thinking— what kind of thinking is that? Nonthinking. This is the essential art of zazen.

The zazen I speak of is not meditation practice. It is simply the dharma gate of joyful ease . . . .

Works Cited

Dogen, Eihei. "Fukanzazengi" from *Soto School Scriptures for Daily Services and Practice*. Consensus translation. Tokyo: Sotoshu Shumucho, 2001.

---. "Receiving the Marrow by Bowing," Fascicle 9 and "The Point of Zazen," Fascicle 28. *Treasury of the True Dharma Eye: Zen Master Dogen's Shobo Genzo*. Ed. Kazuaki Tanahashi. Boston: Shambhala, 2010.

Suzuki, Shunryu. "Posture," Chapter 1. *Zen Mind, Beginner's Mind*. New York/ Tokyo: Weatherhill, 1970.

Meiren Val Szymanski *is the Dharma Teacher at Bamboo in the Wind Zen Center in Sunnyvale, California, where she has taught since 2001. Val was ordained as a Soto Zen priest by Sojun Diane Martin in December, 2002. She received Dharma Transmission from Sojun in the Dainin Katagiri lineage in June, 2010. Val retired from thirty years in corporate technology as Director of Engineering in 2012. She lives with her husband in Cupertino, California.*

The Fudoshin *calligraphy that accompanies this article was created by Meiren Val Szymanski.*

Cultivating Equanimity

Meiren Val Szymanski

Fudoshin

Everyone wants to be happy. Happiness is the most sought after experience in human life. What does it take to be happy? Our first Ancestor, Shakyamuni Buddha, taught the Four Immeasurables as practices to guide us to liberation and happiness. The Four Immeasurables are loving-kindness, empathetic joy, compassion, and equanimity.

While each immeasurable is important, our focus today is equanimity. What is it? What are the steps in its cultivation? And since Mahayana Buddhism focuses on bringing all beings to awakening, which teachings about equanimity support awakening?

The English language defines equanimity as *the quality of being calm and even-tempered, implying mental balance as a characteristic state*. A synonym for equanimity is serenity, defined as *tranquility of nature that suggests imperviousness to agitation or turmoil* (American Heritage Dictionary). Each of these words describes aspects of equanimity that can be cultivated through Zen practice.

From our Japanese Zen ancestors comes the Japanese word for equanimity, *fudoshin,* which can be translated as *immovable mind-heart.* This succinct definition captures the essence of equanimity in Buddhist practice while also offering clues about how this quality might be cultivated. Here, in this moment, one practices equanimity wholeheartedly in this body, not wavering, from the center of one's own being. There is immovable tranquility.

The steps to achieving equanimity that are supported by Buddhist teachings are: zazen, investigation of suffering, setting forth an intention, mindfulness practice, and personal study and realization of impermanence and dependent co-arising from the Mahayana tradition.

Zazen

The practice of cultivating equanimity involves a form of detachment, a conscious letting go, a releasing or surrendering. What better way to begin than with zazen? Zazen sitting practice is essential, for it provides us with the opportunity to watch our personal hindrances arising.

Through the process of repeated observation of the content of these entrenched habits and personality traits, we are able to recognize their destructive natures operating in our life, and to let go of them over time. Then, when these mind habits appear when we are off the cushion, we have learned to intercept their reactive patterns and can choose different responses before speaking or taking action. Now who is in control? That's how we develop calm and mental balance.

With the regularity of daily zazen practice, we face everything that arises and falls away, no matter how painful or joyful. Because we see the content of daily life expressed in our minds, we process memories, intense feelings, strong beliefs about who we are, or plans for the future—and let them go. Over time, we experience spaciousness amid the barrage of thoughts, the endless stream of consciousness. This is the transformative power of zazen. Not thinking about *this* or *that* gives way to non-thinking. Suddenly, body and mind drop off. In this moment we experience ourselves as being one with the source of existence—a view of reality that we are not separate from everything that is. Through this practice, we lay the bricks and mortar for the foundation of equanimity.

Investigation of Suffering

Our time on the cushion becomes a natural time to investigate the content of our suffering. Often when new students seek Zen practice, they are motivated by a desire to become calm, to reduce the noise in the mind. In other words, they are looking for mental balance and evenness in temperament. They have already become excellent observers of their minds. In their quest for happiness, they recognize how they have been tugged by desire for some object, person, or position, only to be disappointed when their desire is achieved. When they experience dissolution of their desire, dissatisfaction follows.

Likewise, they may have been caught in negative and destructive thinking or in conceptual views different from their own beliefs, and may have experienced suffering and unhappiness as a result. Accordingly, they seek relief from repetitive thoughts and an end to destructive behavior patterns. A new desire is formed to escape from their suffering and to understand the causes of that suffering. Questions come up. How does suffering arise? What are the triggers for these outlandish reactions? Why are such reactions peppered with frustration and anger?

So what does Buddhist practice offer to relieve our suffering? What are the teachings of our ancestors? Our unhappy twenty-first century student follows in the path of Shakyamuni Buddha who also sought to understand the causes of suffering, aging, and death. After Buddha's enlightenment in Varanasi, India, his first teaching was The Four Noble Truths. In this teaching, he spoke about suffering, its cause, its cessation, and the path to healing.

Buddha's message is strong encouragement for each of us. By following Shakyamuni's example of deeply examining suffering and its causes, we can experience an end to our negative behavior. That's a hopeful teaching, not only for the beginner, but for all practitioners. The beginner is not the only one who experiences these forms of suffering. We all do.

Setting Forth an Intention

In our quest for self-knowledge, we become aware that we have mind habits. Mind habits are repetitive thought patterns that are expressed with little awareness on our part. The use of intention is a highly effective awareness tool that aids the practitioner in maintaining mental balance and observing mind habits in action.

Intention works with the mind at an unconscious level to bring to conscious awareness those thought patterns that are difficult to observe arising in the mind. For example, a mind habit such as criticizing others can upset us, even though we cannot see it clearly during everyday activity. This is because the thought process of criticism happens so quickly that we are often speaking or reacting before we can choose to act differently. The setting forth of an intention to observe a mind habit can focus energy in an area we want to transform.

Here is how the process works. Formulate an intention around a mind habit that is troublesome. To ensure the intention is expressed, write it on a post-it note and place it where you will see it as soon as you wake up. When you see this reminder, make a vow to observe the mind habit during your day. At some point during the day, you will notice the mind habit identified in the intention note at least once or perhaps more frequently. Each time you notice these thoughts, your powers of observation are heightened and you see more clearly into the causes and conditions that give rise to this habit.

While this technique may sound too simple to be true, try it for yourself. Experiment to discover if your experience is similar or not. In Buddhist practice, we are training the mind. Setting forth an intention sharpens observation and response. Both are necessary components for cultivating equanimity.

Mindfulness Practice

Mindfulness is bare awareness focused on an object in a non-judgmental way. Bare awareness means observation without application of any attributes or labels to a person, object, or idea.

With the practice of mindfulness, we can observe our emotional responses. For example, we can see frustration arise as we defend our ego if someone calls us "inconsiderate" or "insensitive." Mindfulness can also bring us back to the present moment if we take a deep breath and are able to let go of anxiety and frustration. With continuous investigation into our suffering, coupled with a daily intention to see into suffering, mindfulness practice can strengthen the mind in cultivating equanimity.

When we continually practice mindfulness around troublesome afflicted emotions, we notice over time that a purification, a cleansing of repetitive thoughts, takes place. Willingly observing what arises in the mind, no matter how unpleasant, and then letting go is the process that develops concentration and equanimity. This transformation of afflicted emotions creates a distinct and abiding shift in one's view of reality. A Zen Master once said that mindfulness that has been purified in this way becomes equanimity.

Study of Impermanence and Dependent Co-arising

Buddhist study and realization are interconnected. Impermanence and dependent co-arising are two Mahayana Buddhist teachings that have deep relevance for cultivating equanimity. We can study impermanence ourselves by observing the changes that happen to people, objects, feelings, beliefs, and ideas, as well as to our own senses. Still, we may not be able to recognize the magnitude of change that occurs in life. At every moment, change is occurring in us, around us, and in the entire universe.

Not recognizing the impact of change can create problems in our relationships and life situations and can be a major block to our own progress on the path to awakening. As humans, we have a tendency to hold on to what we know and to turn away from change. When the direction of a change is in our favor, then we like change. It is more difficult to accept the change we don't like. This resistance to change is a pivotal moment in cultivating equanimity. Can we embrace everything that is, not just what we like?

In his essay titled *Faith and Mind*, our third century ancestor, Kanchi Sosan, taught us to *just avoid picking and choosing*. That means we must drop our preferences, our likes and dislikes. It is no longer a matter of a dualistic view of our experience. As we become aware of our habits of picking and choosing, observe our thought processes around these choices, and hear ourselves utter words of preference, we take steps toward developing equanimity.

Commit to begin today. Prepare a vow that can be said every morning upon waking. Vow to see preferences expressed during the day. Become intimate with your preferences. Evaluate their importance. Is your preference frozen in time, fixed and hardened? Consider the suffering that accompanies attachment to preferences. Reflect on the impermanence of preferences.

While practicing this attention when approaching persons and things, we can be open and willing to suspend judgment; we can also be patient and tolerant to what is arising. In other words, we will be aware of the tension experienced in not choosing and we will be able to hold a neutral position in spaciousness, without judgment.

The teaching of dependent co-arising is closely related to the teaching of impermanence and change. The teaching of dependent co-arising states that no person or other phenomena exists separately from anything else. There is a causal relationship between everything, as expressed in the statement, "Because of *this, that* arises." All people, all things, all events arise in dependence on something else; nothing arises alone.

Another term used to express this teaching is interconnectedness. Our normal view of the world is from the perspective of the self—from *I, me,* or *mine.* With a shift to *other* instead of *self,* there is a radical change in relationships that extends beyond family and friends to include every encounter.

With the diversity of life we see on this planet, it can be challenging to accept, much less embrace, the interconnectedness of all reality. But it is so. Today, even quantum physics identifies natural processes such as entanglement, and biological research in genetics confirms the interconnectedness of all life.

In Buddhism, we believe in the ultimate nature of reality, in oneness. It is from oneness that the ten thousand things come forth as expressed in Buddha-dharma. Based on the reality of interconnectedness, self and other are never separate. We need to ask ourselves, if we are not separate, how can we treat others badly, acting rudely or arrogantly towards another? Fundamentally, we are everyone and everything.

If we are interconnected, and everyone and everything is changing moment by moment, is there a self that can be found? This question brings us full circle to the teachings of Shakyamuni Buddha: the cause of suffering stems from a fundamental ignorance about the nature of our own existence. We are not separate from other beings. And no permanent, unchanging self can be found. Yes, we have a body and a personality that both appear as phenomena, but ultimately we are all interconnected and impermanent. These truths of interconnectedness and impermanence must be realized—directly experienced—by each of us.

Conclusion

Cultivating equanimity through Buddhist practice involves a deep study of non-attachment, conscious letting go, purification, and transformation. Through practicing zazen, setting forth intentions, practicing mindfulness, studying Buddhist teachings, and applying these teachings to one's life, equanimity can be found.

Experiencing the interconnectedness of existence through these steps, a serious student of Buddhist thought can eventually experience equanimity in relation to all people and events as they arise in the moment. And this is true happiness.

Myo-O Marilyn Habermas-Scher *is an interfaith staff chaplain at the University of Minnesota Medical Center, Fairview, in Minneapolis, MN. She is the guiding teacher for Dharma Dance Sangha, which is affiliated with Hokyoji Zen Practice Community under the leadership of Rev. Dokai Ronald Georgesen. Myo-O received Dharma Transmission in the Dainin Katagiri Roshi lineage from Rev. Dokai in 2012. Katagiri Roshi was Myo-O's root teacher.*

Myo-O would like to acknowledge Patrice Koelsch and Jerri Hurlbutt for their generous editorial assistance.

Being the Bridge

Myo-O Marilyn Habermas-Scher

Adapted from a 2008 talk given at Clouds in Water Zen Center, St. Paul, MN

In 2006 I went off to study Clinical Pastoral Education (CPE) in order to train to be an interfaith chaplain, in the "Inside-Out, Upside-Down Monastery." This monastery was the University of Minnesota Medical Center, Fairview, in Minneapolis, Minnesota. In this monastery, instead of silence there were words, words, and more words. In this monastery there were reflection papers and verbatims to write, and I found myself talking with scores of people, every single day, for a year. It was shocking to me. This constant use of words, when I had been used to the language of silence, was one of the things I had to reconcile in order to be in this new environment with equanimity.

What took me to this work was that I felt called to see what could happen when the rubber hits the road—that is, how it is when our practice meets the whole world—and I wanted to be with everyone, from every walk of life and circumstance. I wanted to test my idea that at bottom we can meet each other where it counts, no matter what our religious, cultural, class, or educational story might be.

Throughout the sixteen months of my CPE training, I struggled to internally reconcile several aspects of difference that constituted my lens onto this chaplaincy work. This work of reconciliation was a very big koan:

    ⤫ Growing up in a Jewish family in the Midwestern United States, I was never at the center of the mainstream. During the year of my CPE training I placed myself directly in the heart of that Midwestern mainstream culture—that is, Christian culture.

    ⤫ Before my CPE training I spent years of my life being an artist—one who often comments on the culture and tries to call it to something larger and deeper, through beauty and creation. In this year of training I deliberately set myself down in the middle of this culture.

    ⤫ I rarely use Western medicine, yet I was working in one of the largest research hospitals in the state.

❧ I often find myself drawn to explore the edges of things. I am curious about how things connect, what is really going on that I can't yet see. I often see possibility before there is a structure to support it. It was an interesting struggle to live with this view right in the middle of a behemoth of a corporate and academic world.

❧ Being a Zen practitioner, which, according to Bodhidharma, teaches no dependence on words and letters, and whose practice is the profound dismantling of concepts, I often found it amazing to be in the culture of Clinical Pastoral Education, which demanded a constant flow of words, letters, and story in the shape of papers, conversations, and presentations.

Near the end of my CPE year-long residency, a strong metaphor arose for me out of my practice with this koan. I began to realize that I am the bridge that crosses the river of separation.

In my years as an artist, I had discovered that I am a bridging person. As a choreographer in my youth, I had made work with movement, voice, images, instruments, and text. I had asked, for example: How might the kernel of a dance be realized through multi-dimensional and multi-sensorial lenses? Now, in this once-Catholic hospital whose patients are ninety-five percent Christian, I functioned in a role that often brought me very close to intense and intimate situations of fear and loss. In this role, I experienced a sense of constant translation that required me to bridge the worlds I found myself in with the worlds I knew: those of contemplative silence, art making, and teaching, particularly how the voice has its life in the body and in space. One of the ways I did this was with silence. During my internship I worked with a young native American woman who had been told that her baby was being taken to foster care. She did not speak, and so I sat with her in silence for a long time, nearly an hour. Finally, she chose to give voice to her thoughts and feelings.

Upon embracing this role in my residency year as a chaplain, on August 1, 2007, at 6:00 p.m., the 35W highway bridge, just near the University of Minnesota Medical Center, actually fell into the Mississippi River, killing thirteen people and injuring many others. I can see this bridge from the window of my office. The state of Minnesota and the city of Minneapolis were in great shock.

One of our physicians, Dr. Pat Hart, talked to me about the bridge's falling as a metaphor. She thought it suggested to us that we needed to find new pathways. She thinks medicine is bound by a narrow view of outcomes and presumes it has the right to name and value such outcomes. As a chaplain working in this context, I had to find a way to reconcile my presence in this very challenging conundrum, in which I offered care that presumed my *patient* was the source of wisdom he or she needed to feel whole. I saw myself as being the wisdom *with* my patient, and together we opened to the movement of the heart.

The language of intimacy is used throughout the commentary on the literature of our tradition. The basis of insight and compassion stems from intimacy with every nuance of creation. It was this very intimacy that both grounded me and constantly showed me how to become the reconciliation I sought. This was Love, functioning. The insights that come from our practice are about the direct experience of Reality. They seem to me to mirror exactly the insights of all mystics in all traditions—however they come to those insights. That this is so has reinforced my trust of the practice and allowed me to be there, in that upside-down monastery, offering spiritual care. Seeing this also helped me to translate between cultures in my own heart.

The way I did this was to cross over the bridge. It is my way to be a bridge between inner and outer, to find and manifest new pathways, to move between boundaries, to point to what's possible. *Where the transformation is truly possible proved to be within my own heart, in the shredding of my own conditioned habits of heart/mind.*

One weekend spent at home during my internship, early in this investigation into chaplaincy, I found myself weeping. Looking carefully, I understood that a thin layer of protective plexiglass that surrounded my heart was melting away. I realized that I had tried to hop over this protection in order to minister to Christians, whom my Jewish conditioning had deemed unsafe. In order to truly manifest my heart's vow, this plexiglass could no longer stand. This insight was surprising; my conditioned mind claimed that this was counterintuitive and unfair, but wisdom mind understood more deeply what was required for Love to live.

That year of journeying set me to move between my *own* boundaries. It helped me to manifest new pathways within my *own* heart, to point *myself* toward what's possible when the old, narrow bridge falls into the river.

In honor of the inter-faith nature of my journey I offer this *niggun* (wordless song) from the Hassidic Jewish tradition, created by Reb Nachmann of Bratslav. In this song, Reb Nachmann is echoing this process of being and walking on a bridge. The song goes like this:

*The whole world is a very narrow bridge and the main thing
is have no fear at all.
[Kol ha'olam kulo, Gesher tzar me'od, Veha'ikar lo lifached
k'lal.]* (Traditional Jewish song)

Towards the end of my residency year I found myself able to carry
wood in one direction and water in the other. In other words, I saw the
gift that the mind training and silence was to my CPE world, and I was
able to bring it to that world with more grace. I also saw the gift in the
naming of dynamics and speaking to them directly that my CPE training had offered me. I longed to bring these to my Zen communities, who
have struggled with silence and right speech.

This carrying of wood and water can also be found in the stories of
Job, and in those of the Zen master Joshu.

Here is our friend Job, the one who suffered. He is us, isn't he? Isn't
that why we practice?

> *For seven days and seven nights Job's friends sat beside him
> on the ground, and none of them spoke a word to him, for
> they saw that his suffering was very great.* (Job 2:13)

This is what we did as chaplains-in-training: like Job's friends, we listened to stories and stories and stories. We not only listened, but we also
interacted with the stories. We also told stories to our teachers and col-
leagues. At first this was very confusing to me. How could I help people
by doing this? Instead of dismantling and cutting off the story line, we
were fishing with stories.

Arthur Frank, a sociologist who has studied the body and illness,
wrote: *The story, to be worth that name, is a ground on which subjectivities meet in mutual knowing. This fundamental need is to know and to
be known.* It seems to me that he is outlining Zen master Thich Nhat
Hanh's teaching on deep listening, from another angle. Thich Nhat
Hanh has offered Buddhist practitioners the beautiful practice of listening with a quiet and open heart, and this is now widely practiced all over
the world.

This sounds exactly like mindfulness and exactly like Zen: to be
known, intimately, in moment-to-moment arising and dissipating. To
listen without an agenda, as Job's good friends did for him; this is *don't
know mind.* Also, the subject/object paradigm, which spiritual practice
sees through, and which modern medicine usually does not see through,

breaks right here on the *ground on which subjectivities meet in mutual knowing*. This leads to healing, because there is only subject; inside and outside are fundamentally not separate.

When we can listen like Job's friends, and neither help nor hinder the teller of the story, beyond being with him or her, and see the story completely on the one subjective side that is the whole universe, healing occurs. This is compassion, or "suffering with."

Joshu, the famous Chinese Zen master from the eighth century C.E., was known for his bridge. The story goes like this:

> *A monk came to Joshu and said, "Joshu's Stone Bridge is very famous and I came to see it. I thought it would be big, but it is very tiny." And Joshu replied, "You are just looking at a small bridge, but you are not seeing the real bridge."*

There is a famous poem from Joshu that goes with this bridge:

> *Donkeys cross over.*
>
> *Horses cross over.*
>
> *Cross over! Cross over!*

This bridge is available to everyone, no matter if they are slow as a donkey or graceful as a horse.

Keido Fukushima Roshi, Chief Abbot of the Tofuku-ji Zen Temple, has commented on this story:

> *In Zen, that means Joshu, the master himself, becomes the bridge. In Zen, it's very important to "become" something. When you see bridge, become bridge.*
>
> *In the Joshu Stone Bridge story, donkey can cross over. This expression shows great compassion. Small donkey and large horse can cross over, and they are not the only ones that can cross over. So Joshu's expression shows great compassion.*
>
> (Fukushima Roshi Lecture, 2003)

Here is a story from my ministry about crossing over the bridge, the bridge of birth and death.

> *There was a patient on my unit who was very ill. He was Lutheran and extremely quiet. I'd ask him how he was feeling,*

and then sit in silence with him for quite a while before he answered with a couple of words. One day, his wife was sitting with him. They were preparing to discharge from the unit. I asked, "Are you ready to go home now?" After a long silence he said, "No." After some more silence I said, "You are not ready to go home." Suddenly the energy in the room turned inside out and all three of us felt something. There was no birth, no death, no suffering. Nothing was a problem. His wife was in tears and I noticed tears on my face as well.

Joshu says horses and donkeys—that is, every kind of being—can cross the bridge, fall into the river, cry out to God like the psalmist naming his suffering. Once, when working with a patient who didn't want to complain, I cited the laments in the Psalms, and I heard myself say, "If you don't tell G-d where you are at, how can He find you and help you?" In Zen practice, this cry is known directly in the embodied experience of the practitioner. This is Buddha, Dharma, and Sangha dancing the great function.

Fukushima Roshi says, *Zen amplifies experience*. In the intimate knowing of the exact experience of this moment, redemption awaits. It waits for everyone—Buddhist, Catholic, Lutheran, Jew, Hindu, Muslim. It has no notion of suffering or being separate.

In Judaism and Christianity the cry is addressed to a powerful external force. Whether the cry is an internal experience or is addressed to an external force, it does not matter. In terms of helping beings, which is our vow, we can use whatever is skillful at the moment—that is, upaya, or skillful means. At the Upside-Down Inside-Out Monastery this meant that I used whatever language spoke to my patient and to their family. I prayed to God, Jesus, Mary—whatever had power for them. I called on "all my relations" in the Ojibway language, and on the Creator and the power of the great Mississippi River. In gathering the hopes and the pain of my patients, as well as their aspirations that they may not have known they had voiced, and in giving these back to them again in the container of prayer, something holy, something non-dual often arose. If I called Jesus, he came; if I called Mary, she came; whatever and whomever I called upon came into the space of the open heart.

Hourly, perfectly ordinary people have poured wisdom from their hearts and tongues into my heart and mind. I find that this is a redemption experience. Who is helping whom? It is a gift to do this work. It was a gift to learn it, and it is a deep, challenging, opening, and demanding gift to practice it. In August 2007 I graduated from the Inside-Out Upside-Down Monastic program. Now I work as an inter-faith chaplain at this same hospital.

Most of the people I work with wish for comfort and consolation. Stephen Batchelor says that Christianity is about *existential consolation* and that Buddhism is about *existential confrontation*. As my Dharma sister, Byakuren Judith Ragir of Clouds in Water Zen Center in St. Paul, Minnesota, always says: *At the intersection of time and space the absolute and the relative meet in this one moment.* And in this one moment the fruit of confrontation and the peace of consolation are dynamically unfolding over and over.

I leave you with Ikkyu, Japanese Zen master and crazy wisdom poet. Ikkyu says:

> *Many paths lead from*
> *The foot of the mountain,*
> *But at the peak*
> *We all gaze at the*
> *Single bright moon.*

Works Cited

Ikkyu. *Wild Ways: Zen Poems of Ikkyu.* Ed. Rengetsu. Trans. John Stevens. Buffalo, NY: White Pine Press, 2007.

Keido Fukushima Roshi. *Zen and Bridges.* Lecture at Spencer Museum, Lawrence, KS. 6 March 2003.

Roshi Pat Enkyo O'Hara, Ph.D., *serves as the abbot of The Village Zendo, Dotokuji, in downtown Manhattan. As a contemporary American Zen teacher, she integrates zazen and koan practice with personal introspection, and social justice issues. She received priest ordination from Maezumi Roshi and Dharma Transmission and Inka from Bernie Glassman Roshi, all of the White Plum Asanga. A Founding Teacher of the Zen Peacemaker Order, she taught for many years at New York University's Tisch School of the Arts, centering on social issues and new media. Her publications include* Most Intimate: A Zen Approach to Life's Challenges.

Overwhelmed

Pat Enkyo O'Hara

Opening the morning paper—O my!

Every morning I read the newspaper, feeling a desire to connect with the world I live in. It is usually painful. I wince just looking at the headlines, realizing all the suffering they report: poverty, violence, and disasters both ecological and ordinary. Of course, the world of the newspaper is only one version of the world we live in, but is a powerful and often disturbing one. Sighing, I put the paper down and reflect on my own personal suffering and that of the people around me: loss, illness, old age, anger, and poverty. Many days I feel overwhelmed. Whether it is the structural violence of human institutions, or the innocence of an infected tick that bites a human being, there is no end to the suffering we can witness if we are willing to open our eyes.

In the *dokusan* (interview) room, I often hear dharma students speak of a sense of being completely overwhelmed by their own suffering, and by the suffering of the world around them. Being overwhelmed, we don't know what to do. We may freeze or resist, and feel defeated by life itself.

What does this "overwhelming" actually feel like? Maybe it seems like waves are crashing over our heads—we see images of Fukushima, of children starving, of overflowing prisons, and people wearing guns to the coffee shop; perhaps we are dealing with a sad or angry teenager, a toxic work environment, our own addictions, or simply a sleepless night. It can feel like we're drowning!

Naturally, Zen students wonder what the dharma teaches us about this feeling of being overwhelmed. For me, the word *overwhelming* always calls to mind a line from an early translation by Kaz Tanahashi of Dogen's "Uji" or "Time Being": *Overwhelming overwhelms overwhelming and sees overwhelming* (Tanahashi, 1985).

Dogen is saying that the antidote for feeling overwhelmed is to *allow* the overwhelming feeling to overwhelm the overwhelming, and to "see" or to be present to the vastness of our experience.

Dogen continues:

> *Overwhelming overwhelms overwhelming and sees overwhelming.*
>
> *Overwhelming is nothing but overwhelming. This is time.*
>
> *As overwhelming is caused by you, there is no overwhelming that is separate from you. Thus you go out and meet someone. Someone meets someone. You meet yourself. Going out meets going out. If these are not the actualization of time, they cannot be thus.* (Tanahashi, 1985)

It seems to me that Dogen is normalizing our experience of feeling overwhelmed: *Overwhelming is nothing but overwhelming. This is time.* We could say, "Life is nothing but life. This is our actual life, no matter what. To avoid it, to hide from it, to resist what is right here, is to separate from ourselves, from our time, from our reality, from '*just this*'." In our denial, in our resistance to the soup we are actually floating in, we are frozen, and lost. We are without agency; we are, indeed, *overwhelmed*.

Many years ago, I went with some friends to the Stanislaus River area in Northern California. There was a huge aqueduct, carrying water from the mountains—the speed of the flow was amazing, and so it became a natural place for tubing. I had never experienced "tubing" and, although I am a good swimmer, the sight of this narrow churning channel was a bit unnerving. Still, I went ahead and got a tube. The truck left, everyone else jumped into the water and rushed down the canal, but I was still standing on the bridge. Although staring at the water was pretty scary, I really had no choice. I jumped in and the freezing cold, heaving, swirling water rushed me forward. *Help! I want to stop this!* Suddenly I glimpsed a branch from a tree and grabbed it but while I stopped, the water did not! You can picture what happened next: my arms were outstretched, holding onto the branch, the water was beating my head and face—and the rushing current was shoving the inner tube down toward my feet—not a stable situation!

There was only one possible action: I had to . . . let go!

And the minute I let go, my body slipped back into the tube and I was carried along the canal, bouncing along like a ball on the water. What happened? It is as if my body realized that the only way to survive my situation was to let go and to flow along with the surging waters.

Letting go of control, I could *steer* within the flowing motion. And this is how I understand what Dogen implies with: *As overwhelming is caused by you, there is no overwhelming that is separate from you. Thus you go out and meet someone. Someone meets someone.*

In the case of the tubing experience the "someone" was the swiftly flowing water, and the "meeting" was my unavoidable acceptance of my situation. I then "met" the water, "met" the recognition that I was not separate from the stream, and I began to meet that reality.

How about us today? Are we able to meet our "overwhelm"—or do we stiffen, freeze, hide, or distract ourselves from the flow of our lives as they are right now? Our lives, after all, are our whole being: not only our individual struggles and joys, but also the struggle and joy of every being and everything—particularly in our time of life, but actually throughout all time.

What do I mean by "throughout all time?" Is it possible to recognize our vast self, our relationship to the whole of time and the whole of space? What would that be like? How would it be, to look at the stars, and recognize our own selves? Would we be so overwhelmed that we could not function? Or would we be inspired to live a life of generosity and compassion?

Maybe that is what Shakyamuni Buddha wondered on that pivotal night when he recognized the truth he had been seeking for so many years.

In the Zen story of Shakyamuni—in the version by Keizan in the Denkoroku—when Shakyamuni, having sat in meditation through an entire night, looked up at Venus, the Morning Star, he realized enlightenment, and said (Cook, 1996): *How wonderful, how marvelous! I, the great earth, and all sentient beings are simultaneously enlightened!*

Amazing! Not just "I" but "all sentient beings!" Then Keizan—who was a student and successor of Dogen's—asks: *Who is this "I" that says "I, the great earth, and all sentient beings are enlightened at the same time?"*

And he answers: *This so-called "I" is not Shakyamuni Buddha, and Shakyamuni Buddha also comes from this "I."*

What does this mean? It is not *only* Shakyamuni Buddha who is speaking, but Shakyamuni *arises out of* this boundless, limitless wholeness. It feels as if Keizan, through the Shakyamuni story, is reminding us of something that persists through space and time, something that is present right here. If Shakyamuni arises out of the boundless wholeness, so do we. This is not just an old story. It is happening now, if we could just see it that way.

Shakyamuni's statement evokes Whitman's *I am large, I contain multitudes.* It intimates Rumi's *hearts of boundless oceans without limit,* and all the mystics who remind us of our relationship with all that is.

In Thomas Cleary's *Transmission of Light,* when Keizan explains who this "I" is, he says:

> *Just as when you lift up a large net, all the holes are raised.*
> *In the same way when Shakyamuni Buddha was enlightened,*
> *so too were all beings on earth enlightened. And it was not*
> *only all beings on earth that were enlightened, but also all*
> *the Buddhas of past, present and future, at that time attained*
> *enlightenment.* (Cleary, 2002)

So there is nothing that is left out.

It's hard for us to conceive of a reality where there is nothing that is left out. We can't actually *perceive* such a reality, because perceiving is an act by a subject that sees an object. In order to not leave anything out, we have to dissolve into the one great reality . . . we have to *be* it; we have to let go of the subject that stands apart. It is just as when I perceive the churning waters and am paralyzed with fear; but when I am in the water, I flow with it, and can steer within it.

What I am interested in investigating these days, given the world as it is, is the power of this insight that Shakyamuni had—is how it helps us navigate the demands of our civic responsibility, our responsibility for the world and its well-being, and our own well-being. Beautiful literature is beautiful literature, but how does it move you to action?

I believe this insight into our interrelationship, our fundamental one-ness with all that is, opens our ability to serve with compassion. Let me try to explain how I understand this.

Consider that Shakyamuni, who had been strenuously seeking an answer to his questions for many years, stayed up all night long with the intention to wake up. "I'm not getting up until I'm enlightened," he said. Such determination! He was a seeker who would sit there until he got something that was outside of himself—something "over there"— "enlightenment!" He was seeking a key to understanding the suffering of all beings. And, we could say that he was feeling different, set-apart, from that which he was seeking. He was separate, he was not "the same as"—he was not intimate yet. But he was reaching out toward something.

Shakyamuni had been practicing meditation for six years, but what happened that night was different. At that moment of insight, when he felt a cool breeze on his face, he took a deep breath and he looked up from his precious unbroken concentration to see the Morning Star. He had a moment of complete intimacy. It was what you might feel in any situation when suddenly, for no particular reason, a tear comes into your eyes, a feeling in your throat, or a warmth in your chest. Seeing the Morning Star was like that, a sudden realization of the wholeness of everything.

The Morning Star is a wondrous image, of course, but you might be awakened by the sound of a mourning dove, or by a familiar car horn, or by watching the shadows fall on a wall of buildings in your city. Surely, some people might think that is ridiculous—they might say it is kind of corny! But you could say that what Shakyamuni experienced was kind of corny, too! Be careful of what you dismiss in yourself and others.

What he saw, what he felt, was a unity; a relationship with Venus. He didn't leave Venus out of what was awakened—*everything* was awakened: the vast, limitless nature of reality, the constantly shifting relational bundle of energy that is entwined with everything that has ever been and ever will be. And we too are in the midst of it; we're not separate from it. Only when we think about it does it seem like we might be separate from it. This is a powerful, wondrous insight; a profound mystical insight: to realize the interconnected, interdependent, interrelated nature of the self and all of reality.

Was Shakyamuni overwhelmed by his realization? How did he respond to this insight? What did he do with it? Did he retire alone? Did he just sit and enjoy it for himself? Did he spontaneously combust with the power of this?

In fact, he set out to teach for forty-five years and to mix it up with people who were in distress and discouraged, people who often didn't heed his teachings. He didn't say, "Oh, there's too much misery in the world, I can't deal with it." Remember, he had set out to find the cause of suffering; to answer the question, "When we look at humanity and we see that all of our life is attenuated by the reality of old age, sickness and death, why do we suffer?"

So when he sat through the night and the next morning saw the wonderful unconstructed nature of reality—that which has no edges—that which flows through space and time—was that the answer to his question?

Certainly it is the very perspective that enables us to accept our karma, and to accept that we are responsible for all karma. When we perceive our interconnectedness, we can finally say, "Yes, I too am injustice; not just those people over there. I too—because I am part of the whole—I too am responsible for the injustice throughout space and time. I am responsible for the wars, for the terror. I'm also responsible for the generosity and kindness and goodness."

This insight is what we sometimes call "emptiness"—though I've often thought it should be called "fullness." It is a way of seeing reality without all the categories, the walls that we have set up, that we've learned, that we've been conditioned to believe in. When we're able to see that those walls exist only as mental constructs, we can let them drop; and that's what gives us power to serve and to work without expecting a particular outcome.

Shakyamuni's insight was overwhelming but not paralyzing. He managed a large group of followers. He raised resources for retreat centers. He spoke to political figures, to stop the violence and wars during that time. You could say *he was not overwhelmed by his insight*. It did not impede his functioning in the world. *Overwhelming overwhelms overwhelming and sees overwhelming.* He was not flooded or conquered or covered over by the power of his insight. Instead, he *used* his insight into the boundless nature of reality to serve others. In our common understanding of the word, he was not "overwhelmed."

To be overwhelmed is to be flooded or inundated. And perhaps that's what Shakyamuni initially experienced when he looked at Venus, the Morning Star. It's what we see when we recognize the world from a non-dual perspective—when we allow that realization. It might be watching a sunset, or meditating on our cushions facing the wall, or an utterly unpredictable moment that opens up the non-dual, the limitless, boundless reality that's always there. Usually we just get a peek: a moment, then it's gone.

But for that moment there's this juicy, wonderful reality! I think that's what the first *overwhelming* means in *overwhelming overwhelms overwhelming*—it is the oceanic flooding of everything. So what does this first "overwhelming" overwhelm? It overwhelms our divisive, ordinary self.

We can say, and I hear often, that the suffering of the world is overwhelming, that we can do nothing. Or we might say that we are overwhelmed by the demands on us by our own life, and that we don't know what to do. In both cases there's a kind of a paralysis; we grab for the branch—or we fly into a kind of frenzy of distraction, which is another way in which we run away from our overwhelmed feeling.

Overwhelming overwhelms overwhelming. Overwhelming, that oceanic feeling, floods out overwhelming, it conquers that feeling of being overwhelmed. How does it conquer our busy-ness or our paralysis?

First we have to be willing to take in this grand view. You know, even when we're not conscious of experiencing the non-dual, we can participate in an understanding of this awesome aspect of all of life: the misery and suffering and the joy, the loving, compassionate qualities of the Way. We can allow it to pour over us, to overwhelm us, until all sense of overwhelming oneness subdues the overwhelming of the particular. The overwhelming quality of reality floods through us and subdues and confounds the overwhelming that we feel in our small lives.

Is this too abstract? Let me be specific.

We are in a time of newly awakened consciousness of the economic injustice in our country. Thank goodness there's some discourse about what only a few people have been willing to talk about in the last thirty years. We're at a time when we are perhaps newly aware of the incarceration of poor people and people of color—a massive incarceration. This is a time when innocent people are losing their homes, their savings, and their jobs because of large unregulated economic forces. We're in a time when only those who can afford it can get a decent education, or health care, or training for skilled labor. This is a time when health care and even food is not available to a vast number of people on this planet. This is a time when the earth is being exploited, polluted and it feels like no one is stopping it and saying no!

These are only a few specific examples of what can overwhelm us and what *we cannot afford to be overwhelmed by.* To think of the hunger in the world, the torture that goes on, the violence, the devastation of the planet—it is so overwhelming we could be paralyzed—or we could distract ourselves to death!

But if we can tap into that realization that Shakyamuni Buddha had on the 8th of December, 2500 years ago, if we can draw on the realization that we are part of this vast, limitless, boundless, eternal quality of reality, the realization that enlightenment is not something happening "over there," but that it *is us,* that we are part of it—then we receive the power, the strength, to serve, to make a difference, to offer compassion. *Because we realize that everything is contingent on everything else: everything is contingent on everything else!*

Two years ago many of us were excited, stimulated by the "Occupy" movement. Then there was disappointment, and a sense that it had failed. But I see that there has been a tidal change in the worldwide discourse about power and money as a result of the Occupy Movement. Yes, it began locally as Occupy Wall Street; and yet it is still spreading the idea that each of us can occupy, can *inhabit* our family, city, nation, and world. And inhabiting, occupying one space, we may recognize our global and universal interdependence.

It's like Dogen's line in "Uji": *As overwhelming is caused by you, there is no overwhelming that is separate from you. Thus you go out and meet someone. Someone meets someone.*

We meet each other and we begin to make a difference in the world, in the many different ways that each of us manifests. We're not going to solve all the problems in this vast, limitless, boundless reality. But we will create ripples of effect, which will make a difference.

It's not so much our particular view of the right strategy, but rather, the willingness to engage, the willingness to practice awareness and interdependence.

And this awareness, this "juice" of seeing the Morning Star, of recognizing our place in the whole world, in history, and in the future, is what keeps us keeping on, involved and alive.

My hope and prayer is that we will build a society that is not based on separate, selfish self-interest. I think it's possible. I do! I may not live to see it, but I think it's possible, and I'm willing to work for it. I'd like to see a society that was relational, compassionate, that offers service to everyone. That's what was powerful about the Buddha's insight 2500 years ago. He gave us a key. We don't need to be overwhelmed by all the suffering we encounter. We can amplify that vision with our own personal, local responsibility. What is it that needs to be done? Can we remain functional? What can you do tomorrow that would make a difference?

Let me conclude with a gatha to remember this teaching:

Looking up at the Morning Star
Old Shakya was blown away.
But he came back and worked his ass off.
Let's thank him by serving someone every day.

Works Cited

Cook, Francis Dojun. *The Record of Transmitting the Light: Zen Master Keizan's Denkoroku*. Boston: Wisdom Publications, 1996.

Dogen, Eihei. "Uji (Time Being)." *Moon in a Dew Drop: Writings of Zen Master Dogen*. Ed. Kazuaki Tanahashi. San Francisco: North Point Press, 1985.

Keizan, Zen Master. *Transmission of Light: Zen in the Art of Enlightenment*. Trans. Thomas Cleary. San Francisco: North Point Press, 1990.

Enji Boissevain *is a transmitted disciple of Soto Zen master Kobun Chino Otogawa, and completed Dharma Transmission with Vanja Palmers. She has been teaching in the San Francisco Bay Area for thirty-five years. She was one of the founders, with Kobun Roshi, of Jikoji, a Zen temple and retreat center in the Santa Cruz mountains, and now is teacher for Floating Zendo, which meets in San Jose, California. She has three sons and is a published poet.*

A Few Words About Practice

Enji Boissevain

In our Zen practice, we talk about mind so often that it's a surprise to sit down and find out that the really big deal is our body. It's the earth; it's the ground itself, deeply affected by gravity, feeling almost constant little pains of one kind or another. Usually we keep moving and don't notice them, but when we sit and allow ourselves not to move, we feel the effect of gravity, the effect of being a fragile body on this earth. As Westerners, when we begin, we might feel that whatever we meet, we're strong. We can do it. But in the zendo, we meet ourselves on the other side of that "can do" attitude. We take what Dogen called "a backward step" and begin to find a deep and tender place inside us.

It's important to address posture first of all. Each time you sit you find the place that creates the best breath for yourself. It won't be the same every time you sit; it won't be the same from one retreat to another. As our bodies slowly fall apart, we're always modifying, always changing, always asking, "What's needed now?" As we sit, the main thing is to breathe as freely as possible. Throwing our shoulders back and holding ourselves immobile doesn't work so well. We're flexible, soft, little beings and resilient. When we breathe, all of us is breathing. Our toenails are breathing. The roots of our hair are breathing. The whole kit and caboodle is participating in such a way that we can't even say it's "me," and yet, we're given away to it as we sit and breathe. Add to the breath a little Buddha-smile, and our zazen lives.

My teacher, Kobun Chino Otogawa, often said that our job in sitting is to keep from falling off the cushion. Having found our upright, comfortable position, we sit and are breathed as we breathe. We don't know whether we're going to have a fast breath or a slow breath. Buddha's instruction was, "Just pay attention to what is happening." We spend much of our lives imposing the values of others on ourselves. In zazen, we release those impositions. Buddha said that if we are breathing a fast breath (and sometimes the breath does come fast) just notice it, be with it. When a slow breath is happening, instead of thinking, "Oh, look, I'm breathing slowly now," just allow it to be as it wants to be.

Before Kobun was chosen by Suzuki Roshi to join him in America to help create Tassajara monastery, he trained at Eiheiji monastery in Japan for three years and then was asked to teach beginning monks there. He accepted the assignment provided he could do so without using the heavy stick traditionally used to beat monks into submission, and is known to have used it only once. In San Francisco after his Tassajara assignment, Suzuki Roshi asked him to take over Haiku Zendo in Los Altos, and that is where I met him. He continued to teach Zen ritual forms at the San Francisco temple, but in Los Altos, his emphasis was strongly on zazen within the context of family lay practice.

He left us a definition of zazen: *Setsu nen zai shin. Setsu* means "yoga." Zazen is one of many yoga practices. *Nen* is "thoughts," like the *nen nen* in *Enmei Jikku Kannon Gyo.* Many thoughts, conscious thoughts. *Zai* is "let them stay," and *shin* is "heart-mind." First, our practice is body and the more at ease our body is, the more fulfilling our zazen is. This is the *yoga* of zazen. We spend so much time in our heads. We're talking heads, we're writing heads, we're thinking heads. Our intellect, our thinking is wonderful stuff. It's the glory and power of being human. But that's only one side. We sit zazen to embody the other side, to practice being human. *Many thoughts, conscious thoughts, let them stay, heart/mind.*

Ours isn't a concentration practice. We're not staring at a candle flame or focusing intensely on one spot. Kobun said zazen is "to be very mindful, to put all contents of your life together, not forgetting any, and not stressing any. Letting the whole thing work together. Not intensive sitting; it's broader, more basic."

Zazen practice brings us back to our only-ness, our aloneness, our oneness. It helps us face the sometimes difficult truth of how our life is going. Even when we discover mistakes and lies we've been hiding from ourselves, finally there's a tremendous freshness and a great relief in being honest. We see we're nothing special. We don't sit in order to achieve something or to have some fabulous experience. The heavens don't open up with violins playing, flowers don't rain down. Well, sometimes that might happen, but if you go to your teacher and say, "I understand the secret of the universe!" the teacher will congratulate you and send you back to your cushion. "Keep on sitting." Hakuin Zenji said that in our lifetime we may have maybe two or three big experiences and many, many small ones. His kind warning was don't get hooked by one big experience or you'll miss all those small ones that come later.

Perhaps sitting is as natural an impulse as the impulse a baby has to learn to walk. Even though there is no conscious idea in a baby's mind that "Now is the time for me to walk," still she makes every possible effort, even on very rubbery legs, to pull herself up at the edge of a table. She invariably loses her balance, falls down, hits her chin, cries. Still, she gets back up over and over, all unknowing, until she can triumphantly walk alone. Throughout our life, rolling over and crawling, walking, riding a bike, doing calculus, and developing spiritual intuition . . . we could say that we are grown as we grow.

The interesting thing about our zazen practice is that when we've been sitting for a long time, it begins to seem not so special. At the beginning of a sesshin, it feels almost too intense, and you wonder if you're going to survive. So many things come up. But as we open ourselves to it, we lose the compulsion to evaluate and repeat self-centered mantras like: "What is this to *me*, how does this enhance or denigrate The Great Me? Does it make me look good enough?" Instead, we begin to slip back before language. It isn't that we obliterate our mind when we meditate, and it isn't that we aren't aware; it's that we're more alive. When a bird calls out, it's us calling out. When it's raining, it's raining completely through us.

In life we're always headed somewhere, but walking meditation is a subtle moving version of zazen. We're not going anywhere, and that is a mercy. In walking meditation we're here, we're already here, we're arriving with every step. You'll find that your feeling about how you hold your body changes as you walk. If you put your mind on the soles of your feet, you directly feel where you are and experience the difference every single step is. You find all the creaks and cracks in the floor and the warmest spots and the coolest ones. All of that is you.

Thich Nhat Hanh said, "Find out how many breaths you take, or how many steps you take with every breath and just walk like that." Once, I did outside walking with him at Plum Village in the depths of winter. He stopped when something caught his eye, stayed with it for a while, and then went on. Going on, not going anywhere, being with the world, in and of the world, by it, and for it, we are walked as we walk, carried as we go.

Our life in zazen is like this, just being with the world. It's not always exactly pleasant. And yet, zazen has found us. We're not practicing to get anywhere. Our only activity is to return to the present, to be this *right now* place. When we exercise our returning muscle, it brings us back to the present moment over and over, even as our mind wanders off. Noticing and returning is the Buddha Way. In practicing this presencing, we can see, and see through, not once and for all, but moment after moment, as we live, as we are lived.

Eventually, in sitting we develop the ability to be with and see what's before us, without judging whether it's a good or a bad thing. We experience what it is, its so-called dharma nature. We see what shines from it, the light of it. We find truth and the law of things everywhere. We don't have to listen for it, or wait for it, but, as our minds quiet down, we begin to naturally appreciate, and be with, the garbage as well as the pristine mountaintop; to be with motorcycles, dogs, roses . . . .

This is where we meet the doubleness of life in what feels like a world of sharp edges, disappointments, and dashed expectations, though a world of beauty, bliss, and emptiness is promised. What does emptiness mean? This is the truth we seek as we make our way through our sharp-edged world, every now and then getting a glimpse of something beautiful. Sunset. Ocean. Newborn baby. Once, I was walking with my Tibetan friend Thrinlay when she stopped at a rose bush in glorious bloom. She quietly bowed to it, and dedicated its beauty to Buddha. Suddenly, we open up to be with where we are, not as a rote mindfulness exercise, but in a humble, whole-hearted way. A generous way. A saving-all-beings way. Often the Way of experiencing beauty is how we begin to find joy in our practice.

As Dogen said, to study the self is to forget the self and to be enlightened by all things, to allow them all in. We begin again with each meeting, even with simple things we've known forever. The old wooden spoon, the familiar shoe, are new each time, freshly, modestly. "Hello old bell, here you are!" Our things are a personal world for us in the impersonal world, a world that can seem rough and foreign, in which we often feel lonely, but only because we separate ourselves from it.

Martin Buber showed how this separation appears in the German language. In German you can use either of two words for the pronoun *you* in a way that you can't in English. In German you can address things and persons as *it*, and as Buber pointed out, when you say *it* to anyone or anything, your own person, your own *I* feels like an *it* also. Both become one more dispensable *thing*. On the other hand, when you can say *thou*, even to a stone or a flower, you are meeting your world as part of the whole of it, as Buddha. The *I* who says *thou* is a different *I*, is Buddha.

You can feel that, can't you? Depending on the word we use for the *other*, our understanding of and feeling for the world changes.

As lay practicers, we don't stand up from the cushion within a monastic tradition that surrounds us with bells, gongs, and clappers telling us all day long where to be, what to do, when to sit, when to chop onions, and when to dig the garden. If we lived in a monastery we would have constant support, a given schedule to follow. When we lay folk get up from the cushion, though, we're right away driving a car, or getting on a bus. We are plunged back into what feels like a fast and very different world. And yet the mind of zazen, of course, is ... I don't want to say "with us" because there isn't any *with*, it just is, as it is, *here* now, wherever *here* happens to be.

Often people will ask me how to keep their zazen practice ongoing, how they can stay awake in the chaos of everyday life. Mostly we lean on our intellect and ride on our instincts. We can be carried along with the flow, affected by the information that pours into us continually. Formed by what comes in, we become somewhat twisted if we're not very careful, because much of political and media information is intended to turn our minds in certain calculated ways. Much of Western culture is based on creating insecurity in us, or exacerbating an insecurity that we already feel. We're told that feeling bad about ourselves can be reversed. If we just buy a particular car we'll feel so much better! Feel terrible? Use this toothpaste! Such thinking harnesses our natural tendency to try to fall in line with everybody else, when all the while this marvelous integrity of us, this deep strong powerful integrity, is forgotten, or ignored.

It's important in our lay life to be organized and focused in order to sustain our practice. Having a time and a place set aside for meditation is essential, but also, by creating a particular time each day for gardening or cooking, drawing or music, we draw passion from our own skills and abilities. This type of practice includes our work in a shop or an office. Thus we can dedicate all our activities to benefit not only our own life and practice, but we can especially bring our skills and abilities into full expression for the sake of everyone's wellbeing and happiness.

So in vowing to save all sentient beings when we recite the Bodhisattva vows, we're vowing to take in whatever we encounter, to accept and to listen to the many truths constantly expressed around us, including, of course, many encounters we would prefer to avoid. Often the hard ones, the ones we turn away from, are those in which real teaching awaits us. Each of us has our own doorway calling for attention, places we must go to, places that need our awareness.

Old Ancestor, Hui Neng said: *In the best of paths there are no impure dharmas to avoid, nor are there any pure dharmas to seek. There are no beings to liberate, nor any nirvana to realize. No thoughts about liberating beings, nor are there any thoughts about not liberating beings. This is the best of paths.*

That's why old Chinese koans ask, "What is Buddha nature?" and in one, Joshu says, "It's the oak tree in the garden." That's what is present in that moment as the monks meet in a particular garden with a particular oak tree. It is what and where they are. What is Buddha? The tree, the bell, the striker, the clock. If we spend time with things, we feel them more keenly; they become part of our experience, familiars, friends. They are Dharma, truth, light.

In the beginning, when practice is new in our lives, study is not so helpful. Ideas buzz through our heads all the time. Adding more creates confusion. There is now a vast amount of excellent Dharma material available to us, unlike when I began, when there were three books. Maybe four? Five? Alan Watts; *Zen Mind, Beginner's Mind*; *The Three Pillars of Zen*. Material has been proliferating ever since. Contemporary teachers are publishing their Dharma talks, and countless translations of sutras, commentaries, and teachings are published. Even so, we have hardly touched the material that has accumulated in the last two thousand years.

Meditation is an experience of the body, it isn't an idea. We wouldn't study books about swimming before knowing what water is. We need to sit a while, need to know how to be in stillness and silence first. Only after considerable experience on the cushion do we study Dharma in books in order to confirm our experience.

Kobun translated the third Bodhisattva Vow as, *Dharmas are infinite. So there is learning and study.* As children in school, we were encouraged to study hard, but study in Zen is different; it is the study of the truth of things, of life as us, as all. Study, as well as sitting, is crucial for us at some point so we can speak as who we are and where we are, and connect in a truly authentic way with all who are waiting for a true word, an honest meeting.

When we begin to study, we ask ourselves questions of morality, of ethical behavior, that have been studied for thousands of years. We suffer with these questions. Those of us who have come to practice make an especially big effort to do the right thing, though not because our kindergarten teacher wanted us to be good. No, there's something in us that, in spite of all our confusion and bewilderment, maintains this ethical intention to do no evil, to practice good, to be with all beings.

Dogen says refraining from doing evil is the very first thing to practice and also the last. Good, he says, just doing good, attracts good faster than a magnet attracts iron. Goodness is an activity, not a moral imperative. It frees us. Before we take the Precepts, we chant a four-line gatha: *All my ancient wrong actions, arising from beginningless greed, hatred and delusion, based on mind, speech and body, I now fully avow.* This is honest acknowledgement of how things are, and how it's always been with us, without making a false promise that, "I'm never, ever going to be like that again." Having admitted, in full honesty, our human nature, we are free to take refuge in the Three Treasures.

Buddha said that we come into this world with the possibility within us of every good and every evil, or all wholesomeness and all unwholesomeness. The Precepts don't come from some bearded parent-in-the-sky trying to force us into obedience like bad children, but arise from our true goodness. As we practice the Precepts, we stay awake to our doings, notice our errors as they arise, and make amends as we can. We will never achieve anything like perfection in our lives, and that isn't the point. The Precepts enable us to honestly recognize our human nature as Buddha nature, "splashed with mud and soaked with water," as Dogen said.

Buddha's teaching is that from "beginningless beginning" we have the means to understand and cultivate the generosity, loving kindness, and awakening that can flourish in us and to see through the greed, hatred, and delusion that blindly drive us. These are called the six causes of action, actions arising out of unwholesomeness and wholesomeness in our attitudes of mind.

Action is another way to speak of karma. Not the "my karma" and "your karma" of New Age speak, but a description of how things are vastly interconnected and deeply affect each other. Sometimes I see this as millions and billions of vectors—arrows of energy—long ones, short ones—all converging and de-converging in innumerable ways in an enormous dynamic that can never be traced back to our personal karma in any precise way. It's too vast for us to know. But we can, from this place, know ourselves as a convergence of the many energies we call "the universe," and our life as a continual expression of these energies.

Our actions, then, arise out of the unwholesomeness or wholesomeness of our attitudes. They're not something we have, but something we are and do. Though we can't directly cut off our negative tendencies and projections, we can begin to study and understand them, and to honestly acknowledge how it is with us. Much of our sitting practice is involved with that work, as we sit without intention and simply accept what comes and goes in our meditative abiding, upright and aligned.

The Three Poisons—greed, hatred, and delusion—are sometimes called the motor that turns the Wheel of Life. The Wheel of Life refers to the samsaric world, the world that often seems so bleak and difficult and has so much suffering in it. There's a mandala that describes the Wheel's meaning. In its center are a pig, a snake, and a cockerel. The cockerel represents greed, the snake represents anger, and the pig represents ignorance. Each is biting the other's tail in a clockwise circle. They're the central engine that turns the Wheel of Life, including everything that creates trial and tribulation for us. The Wheel of Dependent Origination encircles this central engine and shows human life from painful birth, through many life-sufferings, to old age and death. This Wheel sits in the fangs and claws of a monster, Time. And then, above, Buddha sits at ease in the sky, together with the moon. The whole mandala is a metaphor for our life/mind in terms of unwholesome, self-centered, delusional action, replete with the possibilities of generosity, compassion, and the full light of wisdom.

So, we don't need to say, "Alas, life is a complete disaster!" Actually life is quite amazing. It's quite spectacular. By practicing sincerely with the inherent wisdom/compassion of the Precepts, unsticking ourselves from our endless delusions and illusions, not being caught for too long by any of this, we see that this very world of samsara is nirvana itself in which we live wholly and completely, fulfilling every moment. The Precepts are aspirations, direct reminders in the midst of our activities of just where and how we actually are. And more than anything, they're Truth, the truth of our own being.

The basis of our lives is what Dogen called "good doing," though often when we are entangled in ignorance, we imagine a precarious self where no self actually exists, and desperately try to protect it. When we become confused, when we are hurt, our first impulse can be to project our pain onto someone or something else apparently out there.

The poet, Charles Bukowski, wrote that when he was a little boy, after he'd had a terrible day at school and had been beaten up on the way home, he arrived to find his parents drunk and fighting. He went to his room, closed the door, and walked over to the window where a spider was hanging in its web. He stared at the spider, then fiercely smashed it. After this he felt great relief, but he remembered the experience for the rest of his life with horror and shame.

There's also the famous Buddha story of Angulimala, who was so traumatized when his mother was murdered that he decided he would murder a hundred people to pay for her death, and would take a finger from each victim and wear them on a necklace. Angulimala means "one hundred finger necklace." By the time Buddha arrived in his area, Angulimala had already dispatched ninety-nine people and was the terror of the district. When Buddha said he was going to take a walk out that certain way, people said, "Don't go out there. That's where Angulimala is." The townspeople told Buddha the story, but he said, "I think I'll go out there anyway." He strolled along that road and Angulimala jumped out and cried, "Stop!" but Buddha kept walking. Angulimala started running after him but he couldn't catch up and he kept calling "Stop! Stop!" Finally, Buddha turned around and said, "I have stopped, Angulimala, how about you?" The projection fell away and Angulimala became one of Buddha's disciples. He had a very short and difficult life, they say, because of the terrible karma he had created. But he dropped the projection, the blame, the misunderstanding.

Of course, Angulimala couldn't stop by himself. He was lost in his anguish and his pain. It took a good friend to come along and bravely help him. We need each other just like this. As a community, we need to know how to recognize when help is needed, and be willing to reach out. Without community, we can't deal with our pain.

And as we're willing to help, we inevitably feel the other person's pain. If we think, "I can't bear it, my life is already too hard," it helps to remember the Tibetan practice of tonglen, where you breathe in one another's pain and exhale loving kindness. Although it seems counterintuitive—you imagine that you'll get really depressed—in fact, you experience joy. The more we're willing to feel for others, the more we free ourselves of our own suffering.

If we're full of opinions, full of our own ideas, how can we understand our misperception of self? Well, we have a practice. We are a practice. And this practice is itself the Way. It's hard to "be good." It's very hard to even dream of keeping the Precepts in the sense of not actually killing, not stealing, not lying. Every word we speak is far from the actual truth;

every wipe of our brow kills. But we're making efforts toward knowing and speaking the truth. Our deep wish is for life to be wholesome and safe for everyone. We can read the paper and be upset by the "badness" in our world, but everything starts with us. The starting point is the one point of zazen, where we sit down, drop our ideas and opinions, and become a living, breathing Buddha, a life that is and means to be.

In our culture, especially, we struggle with issues of self-esteem. We've been taught to mistrust ourselves, doubt ourselves, fear what we might discover inside us. The opportunity to actually sit down and experience ourselves is intimidating in the beginning. We don't know what's going to come up. As time goes on and we go deeper into our practice, we see that all so-called good and bad is present in us as seeds of possibility, seeds of action that we can become familiar with and cultivate, or not. We cobble ourselves together as a self, and as we sit, we begin to see the different layers, shards, and leftover pieces stuck together creating a "me" that we hope is fixed in place. As we sit further, we become more simple, more present, more deliberate, and more honest. We don't have to project, because we're not protecting any fixed idea. There's really no fixed self to protect in that way.

Kobun would say, sometimes with tears in his eyes, how grateful he was for zazen. When we come, frazzled and scattered, to sit in a quiet room, our faces begin to smooth and our eyes to soften and shine. Our minds become less pressed, less oppressed, all by apparently doing nothing. Buddha means *awakened one* or *awakening*. Buddha nature is wisdom and compassion—not shown through fancy dramatic gestures, but through living selflessly, generously, lovingly. We give each other these gifts as we sit together, as we breathe and work together.

We've lucked out, haven't we? We found and were found by the black cushion, found by the quiet chair. A way was found to stop.

Myoshin Kate McCandless *is a resident teacher of Mountain Rain Zen Community in Vancouver, BC, Canada along with her husband Shinmon Michael Newton. They were ordained in the lineage of Shunryu Suzuki Roshi by Zoketsu Norman Fischer and received Dharma Transmission from him in 2011. Myoshin has worked as an organic farmer, a teacher of English as a Second Language, a hospice/bereavement counselor, and as a translator. Her recent translation,* A White Tea Bowl: One Hundred Haiku from a Century of Life *by Mitsu Suzuki, wife of Suzuki Roshi and edited by Kazuaki Tanahashi, was published in honor of the poet's 100th birthday.*

The State of No Mistakes

Myoshin Kate McCandless

"Have you ever been anxious about making a mistake in the zendo?" I ask, and nearly everyone responds with laughter or a raised hand. The precise forms of Zen practice can be quite daunting. It seems there's a right way to everything: bowing, ringing a bell, striking a drum, walking around the zendo, even holding a teacup. These elements are wonderful mindfulness aides, elegant and economical ways to practice Zen in motion. And yet they seem designed to push our buttons.

We may think, "I came here to learn meditation. What do all these rules have to do with it?" Or "Everyone else seems to know what to do. They must think I'm an utter klutz." Or "Well, I really blew that. How embarrassing!" These forms put us face to face with our conditioned reactions to making mistakes. Shame and anxiety are common, sometimes masked by rebelliousness and resentment toward whoever seems to have set us up for failure by adopting and maintaining these forms in the first place.

However, we can learn that when we make mistakes in the zendo, we are supported by Buddha, Dharma, and Sangha. Within the container of our practice we can learn to treat our mistakes, and those of others, with patience and kindness. We begin to appreciate that even our most dreaded blunders can be tender, beautiful expressions of our sincere practice. We begin to realize that there really are no mistakes and to extend this realization into our daily lives.

There's a wonderful old Zen story about mistakes: Zen Master Dongshan and his dharma brother Shenshan, who lived in ninth century China, were traveling together on pilgrimage when they came to a rushing river they had to cross. We can imagine this being a mountainous part of China, and the fast-flowing river icy-cold, full of slippery mossy rocks. I have crossed such streams hiking in the mountains here in Canada. It can be pretty daunting.

Dongshan said to his friend, "Don't make a mistake or you'll fall into the river."

Shenshan replied, "If I make a mistake, I won't live to cross the river."

Then Dongshan said, *"What is the state without mistakes?"* Perhaps he caught his friend's eye.

We can imagine Shenshan smiling as he answered, *"Crossing the river with you, elder brother."*

Have you ever been faced with a dangerous crossing in your journey through life, when you froze, afraid to make a misstep, afraid to get it wrong? When it felt like if you slipped, you'd be swept away, obliterated, pummeled by the rocks of judgment, shame, and humiliation. Maybe you didn't have a dharma elder brother or sister to call forth your inner clarity, as Dongshan did for Shenshan.

If we look deeply into our experience of making mistakes, perhaps we, too, can find the state of no mistakes. Let's start by defining our terms. One dictionary definition of a mistake is *a misunderstanding of something's meaning.* This would be, for example, what Suzuki Roshi in *Zen Mind, Beginner's Mind* (1970) calls the mistake of practicing zazen with a "gaining idea," with the ideal or goal of enlightenment, or for the pleasurable states one can experience in meditation. When we get caught in a fixed or one-sided idea of what Zen practice is, we can easily convince ourselves that ours is the way to true enlightenment. We look for the weaknesses in other practices or traditions, believing we've found the very best, until we come up against the challenges in our own practice. Then we become disillusioned and discouraged. We suffer from our mistaken understanding.

The other dictionary definition of mistake is *something done wrongly due to ignorance or inadvertence,* or, we might add, inattention. We have all observed the effects of lack of mindfulness in our lives. Mistakes of inattentiveness can have serious consequences. Multi-tasking while driving can be lethal.

Many of our minor mistakes don't really do any harm, except perhaps to our pride. It's good to cultivate a sense of humor towards them, even a certain delight. Sometimes a mistake is like a good joke on us; we can smile and let it go.

But when our mistakes do cause harm, we have to sincerely examine our intentions. Sometimes even if we didn't intend to do harm, we have to take responsibility for our actions. We may have to say, "I'm really sorry. I didn't realize how much this means to you." Or, "I was distracted. I wasn't paying attention." Sometimes we have to make amends, to re-build trust, even when we meant no harm. It's not easy to do this when we're feeling unfairly blamed, when we feel the other person is being over-reactive. It's so easy to get hooked, and become defensive and self-justifying.

Then there are harmful actions done out of a self-centered motivation, out of greed, hostility or envy. I have a hard time calling such actions mistakes, although they are often spoken of that way in popular discourse. From former President Bill Clinton when he technically did not have sex with intern Monica Lewinsky to Canadian rapist and murderer Paul Bernardo, public figures have referred to their past behavior as "mistakes." It's disturbing when harmful acts are brushed aside as though they were inadvertent missteps or errors on a math test—simple miscalculations.

I raise this issue of language to show how we can use words to distance ourselves from our self-centered motivations and to avoid taking responsibility for our harmful actions. I've used particularly repellent examples to make the point, but who among us has never squirmed to get ourselves off the hook of blame or accountability, even for minor infractions.

The state of no mistakes is definitely not a state of disregard for morality and the wellbeing of others. We need to be scrupulously honest with ourselves when our actions, even with our best intentions, are contaminated by self-clinging, by greed, aversion, or ignorance. This can be a very subtle investigation.

At our zendo, once a month on the full moon, we follow the ancient practice of reciting the Bodhisattva precepts. The ceremony begins with chanting the verse of repentance or purification:

> All my ancient twisted karma
> From beginningless greed, hate and delusion
> Born from body, speech and mind
> I now fully avow.

We look into the deep roots of our suffering, we take refuge in Buddha, Dharma and Sangha, and then we renew our vows to speak and act in ways that are non-harming and of benefit to others. We pause to reflect on what points of right conduct have been problematic for us in the past month.

In this way, our mistakes can hone and refine our practice. They help us deepen our understanding of Right Speech and conduct, of the subtleties of the precepts. We need to feel the pain of having caused harm—but without clinging to guilt.

A Buddhist understanding of karma—cause and effect—recognizes that causes and conditions have led to our acting in a particular way. It supports us to see deeply into our karmic life, take responsibility for our actions, and renew our vows again and again. Responsibility without guilt.

When we are governed by guilt and fear, anxiety arises around making mistakes. We can defend against that anxiety in different ways. One common way is to inflict upon ourselves and others a rigid and judgmental perfectionism that only serves to create more suffering. Another way is to fling ourselves into dangerous or difficult situations with a kind of reckless abandon or rebelliousness. Or we can give in to nihilistic despair: "I can't do anything right, anyway. I'm just no good. So it doesn't matter what I do."

Our practice is to clear away the obstructions to our full engagement with the world around us, to express a deep caring for others that is free of self-clinging. Of course, there are those who are seriously impaired when it comes to empathy or a sense of conscience. These people are sometimes labelled as sociopaths or psychopaths, or as having narcissistic or antisocial personalities; however, most of us have a functional sense of conscience and a capacity for empathy, but aversive mind-states and limited views get in our way.

Let's go back to Dongshan and Shenshan to see what their wonderful dharma friendship has to offer as example. On one occasion, Dongshan came upon Shenshan doing some mending.

> *"What are you doing?" Dongshan asked.*
> *"Sewing."*
> *"How are you sewing."*
> *"One stitch after another," said Shenshan.*
> *"We've been travelling together for twenty years! How can you say such a thing?"*
> *"What would you say, Elder Brother?"*
> *"Each stitch is like the earth spewing flame."*

This is reminiscent of Dogen Zenji's saying that we should sit zazen as if our head was on fire—with a vivid urgency. And yet Dongshan and Dogen are not recommending that we sew or sit zazen with a feeling of panic or crisis. The image comes to mind of the Buddhist deity, Fudo

Myo-o, or Unmoving Heavenly King, very popular in Japan. He sits or stands with a fierce expression, in a ring of flames, with sword ready to cut through delusion. His name "Unmoving" does not mean a state of paralysis or rigidity, but a dynamic readiness to move in response to each moment's awareness. This is where we find the state of no mistakes.

These two stories about Dongshan and Shenshan are not found in the classic koan collections the *Blue Cliff Record*, the *Mumonkan*, or *Gateless Gate*, and the *Book of Serenity*, but come from Dogen Zenji's collection of three hundred koans. I've lightly adapted the stories from two translations: *Master Dogen's Shinji Shobogenzo: 301 Koan Stories*, (Nishijima, 2003), and *The True Dharma Eye: Zen Master Dogen's Three Hundred Koans* (Loori/Tanahashi, 2005). I'm glad Dogen chose stories about these good friends, who don't hit and shout, but just kept on travelling together, playfully testing each other, continually reminding each other not to get stuck in the perspective of the absolute or the relative.

In Buddhist thought, these perspectives are called the Two Truths, the truth of oneness and the truth of particularity, simultaneously true. John Daido Loori, in his commentary on the sewing koan, says: *In cooking, eating, sewing, and sweeping, you should realize the meeting points of enlightened reality and mundane reality in what he calls the dharma dance of the sacred and the mundane.*

In this dance, every step, every stitch is aflame with life. This koan evokes the practice of hand-sewing the Buddha's robe, whether the *rakusu*, or the priest's *okesa*. When people sew their *rakusu*, all manner of conditioned reactions arise. Sewing seems to be one of those activities where we struggle with our ideas about ourselves and our ability to get it right. Some of us expect to be able to do it really well and are frustrated when it comes out less than perfect. Others are convinced they are hopeless.

Maybe we'll need to take apart and re-do sections any number of times. Can we make a mistake and correct it with equanimity? Or do we sulk and grump? "I'm just no good at this, and that's all there is to it!" When is it best to take the stitches out, and when should we be happy with our best effort, just as it is? The answer is different for each person.

Recently I read a wonderful book called *The Paper Garden: Mrs. Delaney Begins Her Life's Work At 72*, by poet Molly Peacock. It's an unusual book: a biography of Mary Delaney (1700-1788) who, after the death of her beloved second husband, began her life's work as an artist at the age of 72, eventually creating over three hundred paper collages of flowers. They are vivid, sophisticated in design, and gorgeous. The book is partly a memoir, as the author weaves in her own parallel experience and finds affinity with Mrs. Delaney and partly a reflection on the creative process in art, craft, and women's lives. Some pertinent thoughts on perfectionism:

> *Great technique means that you have to abandon perfectionism. Perfectionism either stops you cold or slows you down too much. Yet, paradoxically, it's proficiency that allows a person to make any art at all; you must have technical skill to accomplish anything, but you must also have passion, which, in an odd way, is technique forgotten. The joy of technique is the bulging bag of tricks it gives you to solve your dilemmas. Craft gives you the tools for reparation. And teachers give you craft, for a good teacher urges you beyond your childish perfectionism. From there you proceed into the practice that eventually becomes expertise.* (Peacock, 2010)

A Buddhist teacher can give you meditation techniques, but likewise urges you beyond your childish perfectionism. Steady practice over many years leads not so much to expertise, but to freedom from hindrance and fear; it brings the suppleness of an unobstructed mind. Not that Zen masters never make mistakes. *A Zen master's life is one continuous mistake.* This popular quote is sometimes attributed to Shunryu Suzuki Roshi, sometimes to Dogen Zenji. It's actually a paraphrased version of a passage from *Zen Mind, Beginner's Mind*, and refers to a phrase used by Dogen Zenji, *shoshaku jushaku* in the Japanese, which means one mistake after another. So perhaps we should say, "A Zen master's life is one mistake after another." Such a life of ongoing practice and sincere effort is the state of no mistakes.

Molly Peacock continues: *Sometimes a blunder shifts the observer into greater tenderness of observation . . . . When invention fails and you are overcome by what you may have ruined, knowing how to reconstruct releases the energy to fix the flaws and go on. Craft dries your tears.* What a beautiful depiction of the utility and dignity of failure! What we can aspire to, when we make mistakes, is to make reparation with grace and humility, and our Zen practice supports us to do that.

In our journey through this human life, we will make missteps, mistakes, misdeeds. Our karmic conditioning is strong, and there are causes and conditions far beyond our control to which we must respond. We will inevitably be hurt and hurt others. Even after decades of practice, occasionally we'll be clumsy or absented-minded in the zendo, especially as we grow older!

When we navigate the difficult and dangerous crossings of our lives, all we can do is make sincere effort in each moment. That does not mean that we can always avoid getting our feet wet; but neither paralysis nor recklessness does any good. The best we can do when we slip out of balance, become entangled, and stumble is to right ourselves, re-align ourselves with our best intentions, make amends if need be, and keep going. It definitely helps to have good travelling companions who can remind us when we get stuck in our fears and narrow judgments.

For living with mistakes, whether mine or those of others, I've found no better way than moment-to-moment awareness of breath, body, and mind. When we stop and breathe, we can bring awareness to mind/body states that contaminate our best intentions and lead to harmful speech and actions. We can open up space to reset our inner compass and turn our words and actions in a more beneficial direction. When we do slip, we're less oblivious. We're aware of the consequences of our mistakes, and we patiently do our best to learn from them. When we can live in this way—whole-heartedly practicing—our mistakes, and those of others, take on a certain poignant dignity. We can live in the state of no-mistakes, even as we make one mistake after another, just like the old friends Dongshan and Shenshan. May we be such travelling companions to each other on our pilgrimage through life.

Works Cited

Dogen, Eihei. *Master Dogen's Shinji Shobogenzo: 301 Koan Stories*. Trans. Gudo Nishijima. Tokyo: Windbell Publications, 2003.

Loori, John Daido. *The True Dharma Eye: Zen Master Dogen's Three Hundred Koans*. Trans. John Daido Loori and Kazuaki Tanahashi. Boston: Shambhala, 2005.

Peacock, Molly. *The Paper Garden: Mrs. Delaney (Begins Her Life's Work) At 72*. Toronto: McLelland & Stewart, 2010.

Suzuki, Shunryu. *Zen Mind, Beginner's Mind*. New York/Tokyo: Weatherhill, 1970.

Etsudo Patty Krahl *is a Founding Teacher of Siskiyou Sansui Do, Mountains and Waters Way, also known as Ashland Zen Center in Ashland, Oregon. She received the precepts in Shukke Tokudo in 1994 from her teacher Keido Les Kaye, Abbott of Kannon Do in Mountain View, California. In February 2004, Keido Roshi bestowed Dharma Transmission in the lineage of Shunryu Suzuki Roshi in ceremonies at Kannon Do and San Francisco Zen Center. In October 2004, she was recognized by the colloquy of North American Soto Zen teachers at Dharma Heritage ceremony thru the Soto Zen Buddhist Association.*

Since training at Kannon Do and Tassajara Zen Mountain Monastery, Etsudo has been practicing and teaching beginner's mind with co-founder Jintei Harold Little at Ashland Zen Center, founded in 1993. Ashland Zen Center offers non-residential temple-based training opportunities with teachers, priests, and a sangha to those meaningfully engaged in work and family life. The practice schedule includes regular zazen four times each week, work practice, services, one-day sittings, sesshins and extended retreats.

Notes from the Frontier

Etsudo Patty Krahl

June 26, 2013

Eido knocked on the door today (via e-mail) and asked me to write an essay for Temple Ground Press' new book giving voice to women teachers, known and unknown. I fall into the latter category and am happy to be here. At first I balked. Siskiyou Sansui Do, aka Ashland Zen Center, is a small dharma center in an old yellow house and barn in a small college town lost in the Siskiyou Mountains of Southern Oregon. I am lost there, too, and see no need to be found. She Who Must Be Obeyed chimed in "Summer in the Rogue Valley of southern Oregon is a time for work practice . . . painting, gardening, canning . . . not writing," and "There is no shortage of Zen authors out there. Why do they need this nobody's voice?" I teach most often by contact rather than with words. The mountains and rivers, the blueberries and tomato worms, these are the things that inform me. I share them with students, and they share themselves with me. Winter, we sew Buddha's robes or study around the fire, fill the frozen bird feeders, and sit zazen together; spring, we cut peonies for the altar, plant berry starts, weed, and sit zazen together; summer, we paint the tool shed, string cable for the deer fence, put up our tea booth in the park for the Fourth of July, and we sit zazen together; autumn, we harvest bushels of apples and fill the pantry with quarts of applesauce, walk the Rogue River trail bearing witness to Fall's brilliant display, stock the wood shed with dry bark and kindling, and we sit zazen together. We turn compost and sit together. We repair the irrigation system and sit together. We clean the zendo and sit together. We rake mountains of sycamore and cottonwood leaves and sit together. We chant the Buddhas and Ancestors and we sit together. We screen the crawl space to keep the skunks out and we sit together. What else is there?

> *It's enough*
> *To be alive*
> *To see the sea*
> *And sky and*

Watch the changes
To sit, talk
Joke and create
Love feel
The air ground
Sun yourself
And not
Have to
    Be somebody.
          –B. Gunther

July 9

For years I have taught the dharma through the body, simple and straightforward, like the Chinese Zen Master wrote more than a thousand years ago: *Magical power, marvelous action! Chopping wood, carrying water.* I'm not sure what I can offer to the greater circle when there are such accomplished teachers on Dogen, Nagarjuna, the *Lotus Sutra.*

But good teachers are skillful. They sneak up on you from the side, widening your field of vision and readying your mind. *Such a book helps to encourage teachers toward their own publication for the sake of their Sanghas, provides an historical record of Dharma teaching for our times, helps students to connect with teachers with whom they might wish to practice and train, influences newcomers to the Dharma, and is helpful to those who are not in proximity to teachers or centers*, Eido's invitation reads. Turning words: *for the sake of their Sanghas and helpful to those who are not in proximity to teachers or centers.* Hmmmm! Beyond the gates of the large residential training centers, traditional Zen practice of chopping wood and carrying water isn't very sexy or even particularly popular these days. People seem more interested in books, talks, cyber sanghas and the refuge of retreats. Isolated in the mountains without the dazzling workshops and visiting circuit teachers, our group remains small. Small is good. Small is intimate. But our sangha is aging and could use new blood.

What would Suzuki Roshi do? I never met Suzuki Roshi. He died before I found the Way to practice. I've read what others have published of his teachings and have heard many stories about him. Practicing at any of San Francisco Zen Center's facilities, one absorbs him through osmosis. I understand through his students that his main teaching was silent, impressing them with how he did what he did. But mostly, I know him through my own teacher Keido Les Kaye Roshi, his character and his constancy. He *is* Zen at Work, not just its author. Seasons come and seasons go at Kannon Do; students come and students go, but he is always there sitting zazen at five-thirty in the morning. If the irrigation system needs fixing, he fixes it. This is Zen practice, the extension of zazen into the activities of daily life. Nothing exciting ... no sizzle here. Just ordinary, plain presence from which right effort, right action blooms and returns.

When Les invited me to Kannon Do to lead a month-long practice period as *Shuso* (head student), he absented himself often, conveying his trust in the dharma and me. But he and Suzuki Roshi were always there right under my knees on the tatami mat in front of the altar. It was the original bowing mat from Suzuki Roshi's early days in Los Altos at Haiku Zendo, a made-over garage in the house where my teacher still lives today. Those years of daily bowing, knees hitting grass mat again and again and again, had left indentations. It made standing in front of the altar precarious, unsteady, a bit off-balance. But the instant you laid your self down, the knees sank into the dharma grooves of fully embodied practice ... Suzuki's knees, Keido's knees, Etsudo's knees. Not three sets of knees, just knees, bodies bowing. This very body, this very spot.

One of my favorite stories about Suzuki Roshi is published in David Chadwick's *Zen is Right Here*:

> *One day at Tassajara, Suzuki Roshi and a group of students took some tools and walked up a hot, dusty trail to work on a project. When they got to the top, they discovered that they had forgotten a shovel, and the students began a discussion about who should return to get it. After the discussion had ended, they realized that Roshi wasn't there. He was already halfway down the mountain trail, on his way to pick up the shovel.* (Chadwick, 2007)

Time to pick up the ax and start chopping. Guided by clear self-reflection, by buddha-mind, all activity is the same activity. Bowing deeply, I embrace the notion that *giving voice* would be of benefit to our heartfelt community and accept Eido's kind invitation. Submission deadline for the article is November 15 ... I vow to become it!

August 19

Weeks of painting behind us, I treat myself one morning to a Starbucks. So have many others, and I take my place in the long line. Several of the locals are visiting with one another as they wait and I feel a tap on my shoulder. Turning around, I see the familiar face of a woman who is active in our local Peace House. She says, "I know you haven't seen me for a while at the zendo, and it occurs to me that you might wonder why people come and sit for a while and then one day you don't see them again. Would you like to know why I quit coming?" I greet her and assure her that I would like to know. "Well," she says, "I really like to come and meditate in the morning with others, even though I'm not crazy about the traditional forms and all, but I was willing to overlook that. Then one morning I was the last to leave and you and Harold (Jintei Harold Little, co-founder of Ashland Zen Center and my husband) were putting all the cushions away and you asked me if I'd like to help put things away, too. I am a busy person with a job and a family. I come to the zendo to find some peace and quiet, not to do more work. I just don't need more people wanting something from me. I hope you understand." I thank her for sharing her feelings, but before we can talk further, the barista asks for my order. One plain bagel, hold the cream cheese and a black decaf coffee, but make mine full-bodied, please. I turn to invite her to sit with me, but she has ordered hers *to go* and is already gone.

This is not a new experience for me. Our group is small and wholehearted. It is a seedling of twenty years of practice here in this community of twenty thousand people. Will it survive along the Way, even thrive? Don't know. Doesn't matter. When my great grandmother started out with the other pioneers from Missouri to reach the promise of the Pacific Northwest, she trusted that everything she needed to make the journey was already given. She stood up in the middle of not knowing and hitched her wagon. Her party made it as far as Fort Laramie on the South Platte River of Wyoming before winter blizzards stopped them. That's where she homesteaded. I once read a line from a woman's journal kept during those difficult weeks and months along the Oregon Trail: *The cowards never started; the weak died along the way.* It takes tremendous courage to attempt the impossible.

Reminds me of another trail, another path of courageous beings that set out to do the impossible: the Bodhisattva Way. Who is the Bodhisattva? What is she doing? Where is he going? In Zen temples all over the world, the four great Bodhisattva vows are chanted daily. They are: to benefit an infinite number of beings; to rid ourselves of infinite delusions; to do infinite good; and to become this infinite vow. Here in this temple, we chant: *Beings are numberless, I vow to free them. Delusions are inexhaustible, I vow to end them. Dharma gates are boundless, I vow to enter them. Buddha's Way is unsurpassable, I vow to realize it.* These are heroic vows, impossible to fulfill. They are aspirations, inspirations to grow up, fully mature, and give oneself away to all of life—to serve. For some who grew up in the flower child era of the sixties and seventies, got lost in the eighties and nineties, or found themselves in the "whatever" never land of the millennium, well, this life of vow can seem less than desirable. Some have a strong case of Peter Pan, an adolescent boy who mistook pleasure for happiness. His vow was to never grow up, and, of course, his helpful friend Wendy assisted him in remaining caught in childishness by being his caretaker. This stunted development focused on the self is at the root of our unhappiness. Its antidote is the Bodhisattva Way, a life of cultivating self-awareness through zazen practice and extending it through selfless service. It is powered by remarkable efforts and inconspicuous kindnesses. It answers the question, "How?" with vow. And because these vows can be practiced, embodied, but never fulfilled, one can finally come to rest here in the midst of their inexhaustible nature.

Some years ago, my mom called while I was writing a talk about the Bodhisattva's life of enthusiastic effort and vow. She was eighty-six at the time and had a hearing aid. We had a new phone system with a volume control. She mistakenly had her aid turned down and I mistakenly had the volume turned down on our new phone system. Before we realized it and corrected the problem, she asked what I was up to. I said I was writing a talk on a life of vow. "A life of what?" she asked. "A life of vow," I said. "What?" Again, "Vow!" I said. Meanwhile I hear her dog barking in the background. "You mean Bow?" she said, "like bow-wow?" "No! Vow!" I said again with emphasis. "Spell it!" Mom said. I did. "Oh! Wow!" she said, "you mean Wow? A life of Wow?" "No," I said loudly, "VOW!" "Spell it again," she said. I did. Then there was a silence. Finally, she said, "Well, that sounds pretty dry, but I guess you know what you're doing!" I always listen to three people: my mother, my teacher, and my husband. They've never failed to give me wise and humorous council.

Not all are drawn to the Bodhisattva Way, and not all who are drawn call themselves Buddhists. Harold and I met a man at Immigrant Lake when we were walking our dog Emma. We watched him working with a 15-foot pole saw on a mighty oak tree as we walked along the dam toward the knoll. When we got near him, I asked him what he was up to. He told us he was cleaning mistletoe out of the old tree. He had loppers for pruning and a ladder in his truck for reaching the topmost branches. He showed us the parasitic thick yellowish-green leaves and flowers that would turn into the red mistletoe berries next winter. The clumps were everywhere amongst the branches of the old oak, and I asked if the mistletoe was about to kill the tree. He assured us that the mistletoe couldn't kill an oak, but that it could weaken it and leave it vulnerable to other fatal diseases and conditions. He said, "I just want to make sure that the old oaks will flourish around the lake, so I made a resolution to work away at them little-by-little, removing the mistletoe." I asked if he worked for Jackson County Parks or the State Forestry. He said, "No. Nobody else was taking care of the trees out here, and I just like to see things thrive. I could see that the oaks needed some help and I wanted to give it to them. Besides," he said, with a waving gesture toward the lake surrounded by hundreds of old oak trees, "who wouldn't want to spend their time here?" Indeed. So every few days, he took his dog to the lake along with a pole saw and a ladder and whittled away at the mistletoe . . . freeing all beings . . . saving all beings. I smiled and we walked away. He called after us, "You'll see a difference when you come back this way from your walk. Even a little effort makes a difference, you know."

That was in March 2000. We have seen the Mistletoe Man alone at his endless task on many such cold and wintry days over the past thirteen years. His old dog died, and there is now a young pup bounding playfully at his feet. The trees he cleaned so carefully a decade ago are sprouting young parasitic shoots of mistletoe again, yet he continues on: unwavering resolution to practice giving, patience, enthusiastic effort, ethical conduct. You don't have to look very far to find the Bodhisattva spirit. It comes from the one who says, "Yes!" to whatever request comes their way. And when this Bodhisattva spirit is full blown and mature, it joyfully does whatever needs doing without anyone asking at all. Look for it. Listen for it. Ask for it. Attend fully to this unwavering resolution. Let it fill your every thought and deed with inspiration, with aspiration. May you become Buddha's Way.

Still sipping the last of my coffee at Starbucks, I notice something printed on the side of the cup:

The Way I See It #8
If you want to cheat death,
It is not how much you earn
Or how good you look.
It's in every small act of kindness
You share with someone else.
That is how you live on.
      –Mitch Albom, radio host and author of
      The Five People You Meet In Heaven

The teachings are everywhere, alive and well, right here at Starbucks.

September 10

[Ed. note: Some names in this story have been changed.]

Labor Day is over and the school bus winds its way once again up our street. Summer is waning, turning fall. The article for Eido idles in the soft drive. Harold loads the cooler and bags into the car and we head for Idaho to visit his daughter before the snow flies. Think we'll ramble some, too. Montana's Waterton-Glacier International Peace Park is in our sights, and we drive, grateful for this time together on the road and in the wild. Maybe these two monks from Oregon will get lost along the way . . .

Many Glacier is pristine, even after a belly-full of summer tourists. The season is changing quickly at this higher elevation, the glacial ice diamond-like in the sunrise. The National Park is winding down, due to close at the end of the week. We've lucked into the last two tickets for boat rides across two high lakes that will land us at the trailhead to Grinnell Glacier. Neither of us can hike the long distances of our youth, and we're happy for the chance to cut six miles off the round-trip hike by boating across the first lake, hiking a quarter-mile to the second lake and boat ride, and then hiking one mile to the small lake below the glacier that connects with the trailhead.

We're joined on the boat by a group of fifteen photographers, two fifty-ish brothers and their father, another couple, and the two college women, summer employees of the Park Service, who enthusiastically drive the boat and share the history of Many Glacier with us. Assembled from California, Canada, Japan, and Minnesota, the group glows with anticipation of the day's unfolding. I notice the tall man with the red-tipped white walking staff boarding the boat with great difficulty, each step carefully placed along the plank. He falls into his seat with a sigh of relief, and his wife settles in next to him, reassuring and encouraging him with kind words.

The morning is breathlessly still, the lake a perfect mirror for the mountains, and we're so happy to have this rare time away. A bull moose lingers in the shallows beside the dock on the far side of the lake. We slowly disembark, watching again as the big man navigates the boat ramp and dock. He is at least six-foot four, maybe more, and a solid two hundred twenty-five pounds. His disability, I learn later, is Parkinson's disease, and at sixty-two he is twenty-plus years into the early onset diagnosis. His name is Bo, and his diminutive lady friend is Sally.

The group of photographers hurry on up the trail to the next boat; Harold and I hang back to enjoy a slower, more silent hike. Bo, ahead of us, forges on with determination, repeatedly veering to the right with a jerky gait, while a slim Sally tries to steady him by holding his back belt loop. The Parkinson's, a progressive form of paralysis marked by tremors and loss of flexibility in the muscles, has clearly weakened his body, but not his spirit. And then it happens. One misstep and he is tumbling into the thimbleberry and salal that border the trail. Harold hurries ahead to help, and Sally repeats instructions from Bo's physical therapist to get him back on his feet. After several attempts, he is standing again, and with a nod to Harold, continues his slow deliberate march toward the second boat. Sally chatters encouragement with each step, but Bo doesn't speak or even seem aware of her at times. He just plows ahead, unsteadily and deliberately, until Harold, of average height and build, takes up a position on his listing right side, guiding Bo, and sometimes bearing Bo's full weight. They make their way with great effort, the boat waiting for them, and Bo sinks into the bench seat red-faced and spent. Sally straightens him up, but the fatigue leaves him bowed, head in hands. It is clear that he has done his utmost.

A second beautiful boat ride across another crystal clear blue lake, and we ready ourselves for the one-mile hike to lake number three and trailhead. Sally suggests to Bo that they stay on the boat and head back, but he's not listening. With concern in her eyes, she looks at me and shakes her head. But he's off, staggering down the trail toward the swinging bridge, Sally now barking orders to "Dig in your stick!" and "Stand up straight or you'll fall again!" We lose sight of them and enjoy hiking with the Parks guide who points out different berries and bear grasses. Ahead, we hear a round of applause. The group of photographers has managed to assist Bo, leaning with both hands on his staff laid sideways between the cables, across the one-man swinging bridge. The helpers, now wet but happy from forging the stream in the man-to-man handoff of Bo on the bridge, return to photographing the waterfall. Hell-bent for the last lake, Bo moves unsteadily onward with Sally trailing. When we arrive, the guide circles us up for a short talk on glaciers. We all listen with interest, except Bo, who continues his now slow and unsteady gait ahead, listing badly to the right, until he falls into the shallows of this cold glacial lake. "No, no, no," escapes my lips as I foresee the inevitable, and Sally looks at me in despair. "There's only so much I can do," she said. "He has to find his own way."

One of the photographers, Tim, is nearby attempting the perfect shot, and he quickly steps forward, pulling Bo's arm to counterweight the fall. The two brothers and Harold quickstep to the scene, and all four men struggle to drag Bo back onto the rocks. He is wet to the hips, exhausted, and unable to be of much help himself. He sits spent on the beach, unspeaking. The Park guide and others continue as if nothing has happened, cameras clicking away. Perhaps they have lost patience and are now unwilling to sacrifice their plans to this foolish undertaking. But Tim, a Vietnam vet accustomed to "having your back," puts his camera equipment away and takes up a position on Bo's left side. He begins a quiet one-sided conversation, and his intent is clear: no man left behind. I suggest that perhaps they should start back since it might be slow going, and after resting a while, they begin. Harold and I exchange a silent understanding that our plans, too, have changed and, sorry to miss Grinnell Glacier, we retrace our steps back along what becomes the longest mile ever hiked. The trail narrows ahead, and Harold steps behind Bo and Tim, when suddenly Bo careens jerkily to the right propelling both Tim and Bo down the rocky ravine. Harold scrambles down the bank. I console Sally, who is now crying and unnerved. The two brothers once again appear, and drag Bo up to the trail, while Harold helps Tim up. The situation is deteriorating, and there is nowhere to go but forward. The four men haul Bo, now too exhausted to stand, to an old mossy stump and sit him down to rest. He can no longer hold himself up, but gestures to Sally for his pills. He takes several and stays there slumped over a long time. Meanwhile, concerned about the boat's departure, the group of photographers and guides continue on back to the boat. Now, we are an intimate party of five.

One mile, five thousand two hundred and eighty feet . . . think actual footsteps, one careening, lurching, reeling step at a time. Harold is now Bo's official right counterweight, bushwhacking through the brambles at the side of the trail, through the soggy creek beds, to keep Bo on good footing. Tim, carrying his own considerable camera gear, continues a litany of guidance and encouragement on his left flank, but Harold is the mule, bearing half Bo's weight. I now carry Harold's hiking stick, walk with Sally, hear the story of how they met, share the story of how we met; we calm one another with simple heartfelt conversation. Occasionally Bo falls again. No longer surprised, we all work together to right him, wipe off the dirt, clean the cut on his forehead, and sit him down to rest and hydrate. Eventually, the Park guide returns. The boat has gone on. She will radio ahead for another boat, she says. "Take your time." The four musketeers look at one another knowingly and smile. Water all around . . . we cheer. What boat? There is just this moment, just this next unsteady step, just this ragged breath.

Time beings later, we arrive at the first boat. Bo collapses into his seat. The two brothers and their father reappear, having taken a detour to see a grizzly foraging. We all breathe a sigh of relief, and let the old wooden boat carry us across the now choppy waters. Harold and I talk quietly, and he seems relieved that the brothers can now help Bo the last quarter mile to the next boat. We are ferried along in silence.

Reaching the other shore, the brothers and father disembark quickly and head out. We are back to the four musketeers and Bo. But now the musketeers are joined by the young Park guide and boat captain who chatter behind us about returning to college, plans for the Pacific Crest Trail adventure. The mule on the right, the vet on the left, Bo is virtually being carried down the trail. The oldest of the group at seventy-five, Harold sweats profusely and breathes heavily. He is exhausted, but intent on the task at hand. But even Bodhisattvas have limits. Knowing that wisdom and compassion are mutually supportive, I suggest to the two young guides that they spell him, which, after getting over the surprise of the request, they do willingly. Trading off, they get Bo to the final boat. Tim takes a seat in the back, as do Harold and I, returning to the anonymity of our initial launch. At the final dock, Bo pulls a hand full of wet, crumpled bills from his pocket and tips the guide. Someone runs up the beach to the lodge and reappears with a chair for him to rest in while Sally goes for their car. The mule and the vet disappear into the crowd that has gathered, the guides having radioed ahead for assistance.

Late in the day, sipping a cold pint of IPA on the deck of the Lodge, we spy Bo and Sally fly-fishing off the point. Astounded, we look at each other and laugh. Harold confides that he hadn't pictured the hike that way. He had been looking forward to our time alone together, the sights and sounds of the trail, the possible glacier sighting, glimpsing big horn sheep or mountain goats. "Things didn't turn out the way we wanted," he said, "but we had no choice."

Beings are numberless, I vow to save them.

October 11, 2013

I hear the pling of an e-mail falling into the box, a reminder from Editor Jikyo Wolfer that the clock is ticking. *The leaves are falling, it's getting chilly, even here in Washington, and the Dharma essays you are working on so diligently are due to me by November 15.* My own deadline for the article is October 31 when we celebrate Segaki, the hungry ghosts ceremony. If at all possible, that will leave November open to whatever arises. November is an important month in our home: Harold's birthday, our wedding anniversary, my birthday, Thanksgiving, and my brother's deathday, just to name a few.

Upon returning from Idaho, we learn that San Francisco Zen Center Abbot Myogen Steve Stucky and our student Donald Abel have both been diagnosed with advanced stage pancreatic cancer. We meet Donald alone at the zendo, share his tears and sorrow, express our own. Hearts are heavy here now. Brown sycamore leaves crunch underfoot as we depart.

All dharma, every body, every thing, every moment is in motion, constantly changing, birthing and deathing, coming and going, inseparably connected. Life is a verb—life-ing—and it runs silently through the mountains and rivers of this present moment that we share. At the center of all this activity is a place of stillness, a field of quiet receptivity, an unwavering continuum that informs and is informed by zazen. It is my home, both a place I return to and carry with me wherever I go. Not a philosophy or a notion, it is experienced through the body and is practiced intimately, warm hand-to-warm hand, in the ordinary actions of our daily lives. It is nothing special, but it is the Truth.

I would like to call my mother this year on my birthday, a tradition that I sorely miss since she died six years ago. I used to call and thank her for the gift of my life and we would love one another over the phone for a few minutes. She would always remind me that she was in the hospital that Thanksgiving Day giving birth to me, and that my Father was also in the hospital that same day with a heart attack. I've always chosen to believe they were not connected. But each birthday, over the phone with my mom or on my own, I stop and remember that we are connected, always have been and always will be. It's so easy to forget. But I know it's true, really true. And I can prove it. Reach down and put your finger in your belly button. See? The umbilical cord was attached there, one end to you and one end to your mother. And a snip of a cord can never make you separate. Neither can a skin bag. You are still connected and not just to your mother, not two, not one. You are connected to everything, and everything you ever needed was given to you at that moment of birth.

My birthday is also my brother Johnny's deathday. He died on my thirty-fourth birthday in 1984 of AIDs. He was thirty-five years old. It was his final gift to me. We are forever connected on this day—my birth, his death, but really not mine and his—just birth and death. No separation. He had a belly button, too.

His death at what seemed a young age has ever since called to me, reminding me not to spend my days and nights in vain. I am filled with gratitude for this human body, for this life. I am grateful to have been born, to have this human form. I am filled with thanksgiving. And I am aware that this form is temporary; that I will die.

In our marriage ceremony, we recite the Five Recollections:

I am of the nature to grow old. There is no way to escape growing old.

I am of the nature to have ill health. There is no way to escape having ill health.

I am of the nature to die. There is no way to escape death.

All that is dear to me and everyone I love are of the nature to change. There is no way to escape being separated from them.

My actions are my only true belongings. I cannot escape the consequences of my actions. My actions are the ground on which I stand.

Oh, my! These recollections ... so poignant, so wise. I am a temporary phenomenon. My actions are my only mark, the embodied Buddha being, the possibility to express the best of me right here, right now. They raise the question, "How does my life serve?"

This is the living koan. Am I awake to my actions? Do they serve to benefit others? Am I willing to walk intimately with everyone and everything in order to realize my own salvation, my own returning from the delusion of separateness? To enter the flow of life-ing wholeheartedly? To realize my limitations by being of service? To experience the frightening intensity of my feelings? To care? Will I have it, for better or for worse, for richer or for poorer, in sickness and in health? Will I have her, just as she is, "perfect" as Suzuki Roshi would say, while still needing a little work? It is an endless series of questions, puzzling and insistent, that can only be answered through the experience of this whole being. The brain-game that is often mistaken for "truth" cannot take me there. It is the realization of the impossible Bodhisattva vow, manifest through a curriculum of service, the mark of a life well lived.

Chop the wood, or there will be no fire; carry the water or there will be no drinking or cooking; write the article or there will be no book. Only nowadays, we are somewhat disconnected from these simple necessary acts. We seem to think we have a choice about whether or not we should have to chop the wood or carry the water. I wonder if our lives have become too easy, perhaps entitled. Have we lost contact, intimacy with our ordinary life? I get up and turn the thermostat off, put on a sweater. Non-residential practice leaves the responsibility, the ability to respond, with me. Just so.

One early autumn night a few years ago, our little friend Chelsey, who was living with us for a while, wanted to go spend the night with her sister, Samantha, who was living with another sangha family just around the corner. It was dark and cold, so I told Chelsey I would walk her over to Stacy and Ramana's house. She was glad, I could see. She had cut out stars of shiny gold paper and taped them to the ceiling of her bedroom because she was afraid of the dark. But when we got outside, she stopped and said to me, "But Patty, who will walk you home?"

I watch each of you at Ashland Zen Center from the corner of my heart. I wonder if you know how beautiful you are? I see the many ways that you take care of one another, and of Buddha's practice. I notice you cleaning the blinds or mowing the lawn when no one else is here; turning the soil in the garden to plant garlic before the ground freezes solid;

putting fresh water in the flower vases on 100-degree summer days, sifting ash, picking up the recycling, arriving early before zazen to plug in the tea urn so it won't make that distracting hissing sound during meditation; retrieving endless calls from the answering machine, preparing agendas and typing up minutes from innumerable Sangha meetings; giggling behind the curtain in the changing room; making bank deposits; baking tea treats; servicing the website; snaking the ever-problematic sewer line; planting a tree in the memorial garden; harvesting figs for sticky jam; collecting river rocks to line the paths; offering a kind word or a hug. In each small act of service, you are bringing light into the dark. Bodhisattvas, so beautiful to behold, practice shining, hand-in-hand with Buddha, walking each other home.

October 24

Autumn turning winter, pumpkin-colored leaves tumble from the Norway maple in our front yard, carpeting the driveway with yum! These are the butterscotch days. Steam rises from the roof next door as the early morning sun glints off the frosty crystals. Yesterday I saw city park crews tearing out the day lilies near the plaza and planting flats of pansies (from the French *pensée,* or heart's ease), as they do each fall. Come spring, they will look like Easter eggs, a solid mass of purple, white, and yellow. Meanwhile, they will sleep through winter in the cold and snow. When we first moved to Oregon, I couldn't believe the effeminate little flowers could survive the frozen months. They are "pansies" after all. And I was used to Wyoming winters, where only tubers buried deep in the earth would rise to bloom in spring. Filled with doubt, filled with hope, filled with not knowing, I planted my own seedlings, my own heart's ease.

Practice is just like that. By attending to this moment *as it is,* as Suzuki Roshi said—beyond preconceptions or doubts—pansies bloom. By taking care of my breath, by taking care of my speech, by taking care of the toilet, I remember who I am. This kind of simple practice, self-*less* rather than self*full,* can be of real benefit to a world such as ours. It can bring the heart's ease to the dis-ease of the human condition. It is so clear that greed kills. It is so clear that hatred kills. It is so clear that distorted self-centric thinking kills. So, how about it? Are we willing to plant pansies in the middle of not knowing? To make our best effort, though it may not suffice? To give it all we have and trust the rest to providence? I want to say "Yes!" in a resounding life of vow, responding appropriately and enthusiastically, chopping wood (or mistletoe), carrying water (or a fellow traveler), being of service and sometimes doing nothing at all right here in my small-town life—trusting snow to melt, spring to appear.

October 31

Strolling with Donald in Lithia Park this afternoon, big-leaf maples blazing golden in the waning light, we talked a little of many things, cabbages and kings. It is week three of his chemotherapy for the pancreatic cancer. He is nearing the end of his days, as we all are, but he knows it. He told of how this cancer is a teacher for him. "I've noticed that my anger and pettiness are gone now. It's not that they went anywhere, really. But they just aren't here now," he said. "I wrote a haiku to express it," he said quietly:

> *The Way of all things*
> *A single leaf falls*
> *Yet every leaf falls.*

His call deserved a response:

> *A single leaf falls*
> *The whole works.*

He thanked us for getting him out of the house on such a beautiful day, for the hot chocolate, and said quietly, "I am happy to be here." Me, too.

November 11, Veteran's Day

A gentle reminder from Jikyo, the editor, arrived regarding the November 15 submission deadline. Though filled with resolve, I have missed my personal timeline and am putting the final touches on these notes. Big mind in front of small mind often requires letting go of arbitrary agendas. There is no such thing as being late in Buddha mind, only being.

Many who have offered a life of service are well-known: Martin Luther King, Mahatma Gandhi, Mother Theresa. Most are not. A few years ago, friend and student Mike invited us to a Pow Wow at the veteran's domiciliary in White City. Mike, himself a veteran, is head of the laboratory there, and he knew we'd appreciate the humbling ceremony of recognition and gratitude. Native Americans from many tribes gathered from near and far at the hospital on the day after Memorial Day to acknowledge those who served their country, living and dead. Out in the field, they formed a huge ecumenical circle of human beings and invited all who had served to form a circle on the inside. Then, walking silently in opposite directions, drums beating a steady relentless rhythm, each man and woman who had served was thanked with a warm handshake by each and every person in the circle of tribes. Grown men wept, some of them knowing the gratitude of their fellow man for the first time. Races disappeared, no red, no brown, no white, no black... just humans being, buddha beings.

Fifteen years ago, Harold and I were taking a little time off with our dharma sister Misha. She had driven up from the hustle and bustle of the Bay Area, and we were reveling in the solitude and quiet beauty of Diamond Lake together, camping, cooking, and walking the trails. As the canoe glided between the sedges along the shoreline, she told of her school kids pretending to be Indians on their school campout, and we playfully began giving one another silly names. Harold, who is a quiet, grounded mountain in my life, was named "Talks to no one;" Misha's handle was "Has to say something;" Mine was "Say no more."

Postscript

Deadline realized; lifeline realized. Thank you, Eido, for the invitation and the encouragement. I'm thinking of changing my Indian name: Happy being, here now.

Works Cited

Chadwick, David. *Zen Is Right Here: Teaching Stories and Anecdotes of Shunryu Suzuki*. Boston: Shambhala, 2007.

Gunther, B. This untitled, handwritten poem was a gift to the author from her mother some forty years ago.

Kaye, Les. *Zen At Work: A Zen Teacher's 30-Year Journey in Corporate America*. New York: Three Rivers Press, 1997.

Byakuren Judith Ragir *is the guiding teacher at Clouds in Water Zen Center in St. Paul, MN. She studied with Dainin Katagiri Roshi for seventeen years and received Dharma Transmission from Joen Snyder O'Neal in the Katagiri lineage.*

Does Time Fly By?

Byakuren Judith Ragir

Most all of us feel that our lives are too busy. This is our predicament. The American mantra is "I'm too busy. I'm too busy." Maybe that's why we are all here at a Zen center—to find out how we can take back our lives. There is no escaping the busyness of our lives. Even on vacation, my mind finds a way to feel busy. Case 21 of the *Book of Serenity* is a koan that directly points to the bondage we feel to our stories and timelines.

> ### Case 21: Yunyan Sweeps the Ground
> *As Yunyan was sweeping the ground, Daowu said, "Too busy."*
> *Yunyan said, "You should know there's one who isn't busy."*
> *Daowu asked, "Is there a second moon?"*
> *Yunyan held up the broom and said, "Which moon is this?"*
> (Cleary, 2005)

The first part of the koan sets up our usual dilemma of duality. Are we busy or not busy? Are we deluded or free? Are we in time or timelessness? Do we have an evaluation of which side is better? Do we stick to one side or the other?

Zen practice encourages us to sit in the middle of the foci of duality. It's neither one nor the other. We seek to express the simultaneity of busy and not busy, or time and timelessness, in this very moment. The function of the opposites is a process of dynamic exchange. The closer we can stay to this hot fire of the Now, the less we will be dragged down by our ordinary sense of *busyness*.

In a commentary on an excerpt from Dogen's "Being-Time" in *Each Moment is the Universe* (2008), Katagiri Roshi, my first teacher, writes about the mutually assisting aspects of busyness and stillness. He says that you can't stay with busyness for the twenty-four hours of the day or you would go crazy. So this busyness itself has the great power to emancipate itself. When we're exhausted with work, we truly want to be quiet. We want to return to no-time or stillness. But we also can't stay in stillness forever or we would die. So stillness very naturally births into activity. Stillness rejuvenates us for activity. Activity allows us to want stillness. And so it goes, sitting in the middle of the process of activity and stillness renewing each other.

Our practice and the understanding of Buddhist principles can soften up the chronic stance that we are always too busy. How can we take care of time without going crazy? As we investigate what is actually happening in the moment, we see that its appearance is not what it actually is. As we let go of our false impression that we can control things and begin to enter *always changing*—we can have a new view on how to take care of our life.

I feel that working with a deeper understanding of time can be a complete avenue to awakening. We know that one of our primary admonishments is to *live in the now* but what does that mean exactly?

Buddhist practice begins by deconstructing our concepts of time and space. In order to understand what's really going on, we have to deconstruct what we *think* is going on. This does not mean that we abandon or annihilate the story of our lives. We still have our personal development and we still have relationships with our loved ones, etc. But we learn a different way to take care of our lives by transforming the basis of operation in our minds. We develop a new view that has a different sense of what time or space is. The details of our life remain exactly the same, but we see our life from a new angle.

Dogen Zenji is a thirteenth century Zen teacher and writer, who is very important in my lineage and in Soto Zen. He puts forth this question: how can we take care of constructed reality from the view of negation? Negation comes from the teaching that everything is impermanent and empty of inherent existence. His answer to this question is somewhat unusual in Buddhist thought. Dogen emphasizes a practice that is very personal and subjective rather than impersonal and objective. He teaches that time and space come to being and intersect in this very moment. Through the unique temporal conditions that arise right here and now, we meet the bodhi-mind. He calls this intersection *Being-time*, which is one of the fascicles of his major work, *Shobogenzo, Treasury of the True Dharma Eye*. If you can express being-time in your life, then you can take care of your life in a very practical way, but you are still coming from emptiness or coming from a huge universal perspective.

Each moment is the totality of the universe. This teaching of Dogen's was influenced by the Hua-Yen school before him, which studied and expanded on the Buddhist understanding of time. The Hua-Yen school especially emphasized the simultaneity and mutual identity of opposites. All things in multi-dimensions interact and interpenetrate without any obstructions. All the ten directions and all the ten times are expressed in the creation of a moment. The microcosm and the macrocosm express themselves together. The inside of a so-called *Being* and the outside of the so-called *environment* are interconnected. They have a mutual identity. For example, the one who isn't busy is not opposite to the one who is busy. These two sides mutually assist each other in dynamic functioning and they function as one complete whole. These Hua-Yen teachings were the forerunners of the term *Being-time* in Dogen's language. The multi-dimensional crossroad of time and space includes all time—past, present, future, and all directions.

This whole predicament of seeing mutuality would be so much easier if we could find the Now; but we cannot find it, at least through consciousness. Perhaps it can be felt, or experienced through awareness, but not through our discriminative thinking. A thought, the scientists tell us, takes 500-2000 milliseconds to conceive. So we really cannot catch an experience through our discriminative thinking. It comes to our perceptions 2000 milliseconds late! A one-pointed mind or concentrated mind can be still, without thoughts and naming, so perhaps this can help us just *be*. Maybe through non-verbal awareness, we can become closer to experiencing the Now. But still this non-verbal awareness takes a little time, less than 7 milliseconds, to perceive. So we are closer, but it is not a bull's-eye. We cannot grasp the true Now. Perhaps the true Now, as the ancient ones tell us, lacks inherent existence!

In his commentary, Katagiri Roshi calls this moment the *pivot of nothingness*. It is both very dynamic—the opposites creating each other or polarizing around each other (the pivot)—and very silent with no activity (nothingness). This is an example of the simultaneity of pairs of antitheses: activity and no activity. It is similar to the famous quote from the Heart Sutra: *Form is emptiness and emptiness is form.* Can we let go of our discriminating minds enough to understand this in a non-dualistic way?

The basic Buddhist teaching of impermanence challenges our minds that want to construct solidity, permanence, and linear time. In order to understand Buddhist Time, one has to understand impermanence, which enables us to enter timelessness. In Buddhist thinking, the creation and destruction of the moment is so fast that it is beyond what we can conceive. The *Abhidharma* (the commentary on sutra teaching which could be called, in modern times, Buddhist psychology) calls this moment a tanji. In this tanji, everything is born and annihilated in 1/62nd of a finger snap. In quantum physics, a moment (sometimes called a "jiffy") is 10^{-43} of a second. Dogen writes that there are 6,400,099,090 setsunas or moments in one 24-hour period and in each of these moments our five skandhas appear and disappear repeatedly. Our minds certainly can't catch the tanji; it's just too fast. Katagiri Roshi says: *The real state of existence is coming and going at **super-speed**.* Considering this super-speed, a stimulating question arises. How do we follow the instructions to be in the present moment when the present moment is too fast to catch or doesn't really exist?

For understanding's sake, we verbally return to a dualistic concept of the relative and absolute truth. To correspond with that teaching, there are two kinds of time in Buddhist understanding: flowing time and stopped time or, in another translation, the stream of time and the eternal present. Flowing time is what we are greatly familiar with. It is developmental time, clock-time, and from this time we construct our stories. Most of us have very little familiarity with the eternal present. I think that is why we come to practice, why we meditate, and why we end up at a Zen center. We need to become more familiar with and be able to use the eternal present in our life. It is the way to find freedom from the burden of our schedules and historic selves. Even if we are estranged from our sense of eternal time, we CAN cultivate our connection with timelessness, especially through zazen. Even though eternal time is all around us and interpenetrating everything, we have to practice to re-awaken it in our consciousness. It's very important to do this because, as Dogen says, *time is just flying by* if we don't. We feel as though we are overwhelmed by life's schedule and we are hanging on by a thread to the coattails of time. In order to find freedom, we need to have some experiential knowledge of the *one who isn't busy.*

If you can learn to live in the intersection of time and space, your sense of being and your sense of time become one, and at that moment, you can experience your life in a different way. When I'm able to be at that place, my day slows down and becomes more vivid. However, it's difficult to live like that mainly because we don't trust life. I have a kind of silly assumption that if I don't get my "to-do" lists done, the world is going to fall apart. I don't trust that I can go into timelessness and expand my experience of multi-dimensionality without either me or my life falling apart. I think I have to, somehow, control my life and cling to the time constructions that I have created. Our practice teaches us that this understanding is not true! This is why we need Sangha and community. We need to remind each other that we will not fall apart if we let go.

In "Uji, Being-time," Dogen writes:

> *Do not think that time merely flies away. Do not see flying away as the only function of time. If time merely flies away, you would be separated from time. The reason you do not clearly understand the time being is that you think of time only as passing. You fail to experience the passage of being-time and hear the utterance of its truth because you only learn that time is something that goes past.* (Tanahashi, 2013)

We are running around but not experiencing our life. There is no savoring. This is very dissatisfying as Buddha reports in the First Noble Truth. We rarely get the nurturance of the eternal present in this scenario. We are not *being* the moment.

Dogen: *"The going and coming of life is obvious, you do not come to doubt them. But even though you do not have doubts about them **that is not to say you know them**"* [emphasis added] (Waddell/Abe, 2002).

With ordinary perception, we just see time in a developmental, linear way. We really have no doubt about sequence. The sun rises and sets. We are born, have a childhood, adulthood, get sick and die. We do not doubt what is obvious to our eye. What is obvious to me in my life right now is that my children are grown and have left the house. How their childhood flew by! But if we only experience life as flying by, we don't have real intimacy with that which is actually happening. Did I savor each moment of the times my children were with me? Can I *be* the moments of grief, now that the children are gone? If we start to penetrate each moment, to be devoted to each moment as life itself, then we can savor our life and its mystery. We can come to really *know* this moment as an independent time.

Dogen continues:

> *Every entire being in the entire world is each time an independent time, even while it makes a continuous series. Inasmuch as they are being-time, they are my being-time. My self unfolds itself through out the entire world. Self, the world, and time arise enlightenment simultaneously.* (Tanahashi, 2013)

We think ordinarily of time as something outside ourselves, an external flow, that passes us by. We think that we enter *time* when we are
born and leave *time* when we die. Dogen instructs us that this is not
so. Time is not an impersonal current. It actually arises from us. Our
so-called *self* is an expression of time and an expression of the eternal
source in every moment.

Dogen writes: *Such is the fundamental reason of the Way—that our
self is time* (Waddell/Abe, 2002).

Our self and the environment are interconnected. This, of course,
is one of the most basic Buddhist principles—co-arising or inter-being
or interdependence. Through understanding, we are opening up all our
limited views. Self is expanded to include everything that arises simultaneously with us. Time is expanded to include past, present, and future
that extends out or is expressed by this very moment. This moment is the
source. *Each moment is the universe,* as Katagiri Roshi's book title says.

Dogen writes that *each moment is an independent time, even while
it makes a continuous series.* This is a delicious phrase to contemplate.
It is a true expression of the historic and the universal arising together.
It merges the idea of flowing and stopped time. Each moment is both
an independent time and a moment in a series. Dogen calls it continuous and discontinuous time. Continuous time is an acknowledgement
of cause and effect or karma. Every moment is a result of previous influences. The future is a result of our actions today. Discontinuous time is
an expression of the eternal source that is always arising. Each moment
is a complete unit of birth and death in 1/62nd of a finger snap. Or being
more exact, in this *super-speed,* there is no differentiation of arising and
destroying, and therefore the center is empty or still. Actually, the idea
of arising and destroying dissolves. It is just bodhi-mind. It is the hole in
the doughnut or the nothingness in the center of the pivot. It is eternally
present and non-productive.

Waddell and Abe translated this as *seriatim passage.* It reminds me
of other oxymorons that Zen uses like the gateless gate. *Being-time has
the virtue of seriatim passage* (2002).

Seriatim means in a series, one after the other. There is also a frame
or a cipher, which is the gate or the passage of the present moment.
Each moment is an independent, discontinuous time. People often balk
at the idea of discontinuous time—the idea that each moment is the
whole creation or *non-creation* itself. I think Dogen emphasizes the discontinuous time to allow us to break through our long held belief of

continuity and life span. But he never abandons continuous time either. Continuous time represents the ancient law of karma. He affirms developmental time. Linear time is part of obvious time. We do not get younger or, as Dogen says in *Genjokoan: ash does not turn back into firewood* (Okumura, 2010).

CAUSE → EFFECT

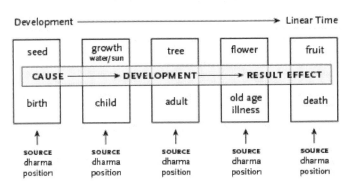

TIMELESSNESS

This chart from a lecture by Shohaku Okumura Roshi illustrates the relationship between developmental (cause and effect) time and the source arising fully, wholly, and discontinuously in each moment. The phrase *dharma position* is used to break through our concept of flowing time and allow us to realize that every moment is fully complete and is the source itself. Each moment, good or bad, like or dislike, has its own integrity as a dharma position. Each dharma position dwells in its own unique suchness.

As previously mentioned, we don't doubt linear time. A seed if given the conditions it needs—sun and water and good soil—will grow into a tree; a tree will flower and bear fruit. Practice helps us to appreciate and see that each moment is whole and complete unto itself. Each moment is exactly what it is and, as Katagiri Roshi repeatedly said, *Each moment is Buddha.*

Dogen writes more about the integrity of each moment in another *Shobogenzo* fascicle called "Bussho" or "Buddha-nature." In this fascicle, he expounds on the instruction that each dharma position expresses the source itself:

Buddha said, "If you wish to know the Buddha-nature's meaning, you must contemplate temporal conditions. If the time arrives, the Buddha-nature will manifest . . . . The way to contemplate temporal conditions is through temporal conditions themselves." (Waddell/Abe, 2002)

Dogen is really saying the same thing that Okumura Roshi said in his chart. The way to know the source, or Buddha-nature, is to completely penetrate into the temporal condition that is arising. The source and the temporal condition are exactly one. Dogen writes a beautiful pointer expressing this merger:

"Look!!! Temporal conditions!!!"
It is the Buddha-nature's emancipated suchness.
It is
"Look!!! Buddha! Buddha!!"
It is
"Look Nature!! Nature!!!" (Waddell/Abe, 2002)

Dogen ends this section of "Bussho" with: *There has never yet been a time not arrived. There can be no Buddha-nature that is not Buddha-nature manifested right here and now.*

So given that all this is true, Katagiri Roshi often presented a conundrum of our existence: how can we live in a world of ever-changing impermanence and still take care of our lives? How do you take care of this moment? He taught that we can simultaneously touch the source of existence and bloom the particular flower of the moment. Katagiri Roshi writes: *Just live right in the middle of the flow of change, where there is nothing to hold on to. How? Just be present and devote yourself to doing something* (2008).

The way Dogen puts the same admonition in "Uji, Being-time" is to *penetrate exhaustively each dharma position or independent time, each moment* (Waddell/Abe, 2002). Nishijima and Cross translate the same phrase as *vigorously abiding in each moment* (1994). Katagiri Roshi unpacks this by saying: *practicing with full commitment to the moment, leads you to that which you seek.* Our seeking gets resolved in our *being.* Enlightenment becomes *one continuous line of immediacy* ("Daigo" Nishijima/Cross, 1994).

The koan of Yunyan sweeping the ground explores this human enigma. The koan explores the same question: how can we bring our daily life and emptiness together? In the koan, Daowu and Yunyan work with the duality between busy and not busy, form and emptiness. Are they split into two?

Daowu asks, *"Is there a second moon?"* Are there one moon or two moons? Busy or not busy? Yunyan holds up the broom and says, *"Which moon is this?"*

Ah, what a terrific comeback! Everything is included in his sweeping. Everything, the sacred and the ordinary, busy and non-busy, are dynamically working in the present moment of sweeping the ground. He holds up the broom. The present activity is one and many!

The commentary to the koan continues: *Good people, as you eat, boil tea, sew and sweep* (or we moderns could say, as you do your email, listen to your answering machine, vacuum, load the dishwasher, put birdseed out, make the budget, drive the car) *you should recognize the one not busy—then you will realize the union of mundane reality and enlightened reality* (Cleary, 2005).

This is the biggest lesson I learned from my teacher Katagiri Roshi— the two realities merge in the present moment, and the practice is to be here and feel that merger as we're living our life. The sacred and the ordinary come together in the activities of our life, moment after moment after moment—One Seamless Reality.

In *Eihei Koroku*, Dogen writes:

> *Who sweeps the ground and also sees the moon?*
> *Holding up the moon, her sweeping is truly not in vain.*
> (Leighton/Okumura, 1995)

To have a direct mind is to do all our activities as holding up the moon, connected with the universal perspective, and therefore, nothing we do is in vain. That eases my soul. Nothing I do is in vain. Nothing is just trivia and wasting my time. I can take care with even the smallest thing like putting the paperclip back in its magnetic box. When I can receive life as a whole, then each moment, extraordinary or ordinary, is enough.

Another commentary in the Book of Serenity: *Yunyan was empty-handed, yet holding the broom.*

I have extreme gratitude for and bow deeply to Katagiri Roshi and Okumura Roshi who unpacked Dogen for me. All mistaken views are my own.

Works Cited

Book of Serenity, One Hundred Zen Dialogues. Trans. Thomas Cleary. Boston: Shambhala, 2005.

Dogen, Eihei. *Dogen's Extensive Record: A Translation of the Eihei Koroku.* Trans. Taigen Dan Leighton and Shohaku Okumura. Boston: Wisdom Publications, 1995.

---. "Uji" and "Daigo." *Master Dogen's Shogobenzo.* Trans. Gudo Nishijima and Chodo Cross. London: Windbell Publications, 1994.

---. "Uji." *The Heart of Dogen's Shobogenzo.* Trans. Norman Waddell and Masao Abe. Albany: State University of New York Press, 2002.

---. "Uji." *Treasury of the True Dharma Eye: Zen Master Dogen's Shobo Genzo.* Ed. Kazuaki Tanahashi. Boston: Shambhala, 2010.

Katagiri, Dainin. "Commentary on an Excerpt from Dogen's 'Being-Time.'" *Each Moment is the Universe: Zen and the Way of Being Time.* Boston: Shambhala, 2008.

Okumura, Shohaku. *Realizing Genjokoan, The Key to Dogen's Shobogenzo.* Boston: Wisdom Publications, 2010.

Domyo Burk *is the teacher and director at Bright Way Zen Center in Portland, Oregon, and administrative director of the Soto Zen Buddhist Association. She trained as a priest at Dharma Rain Zen Center under Gyokuko Carlson in the lineage of Jiyu Kennett, and received Dharma Transmission from Rev. Carlson in 2010. She is the author of* Idiot's Guides: Zen Living, *a comprehensive but accessible introduction to Zen practice and teachings.*

Longing for Enlightenment

Domyo Burk

Longing for enlightenment, like any desire, can cause great distress and can become an obstacle in spiritual practice. This spiritual longing can also become a force that propels us along a difficult path and drives us to investigate the deepest and scariest spiritual questions, so I heartily encourage it.

When I first started Zen training, I experienced three or four initial honeymoon years, when I was thrilled with my discovery of Zen and used it to transform my life. I imagined I would continue to "succeed" at Zen as I had succeeded at many other things, but I soon began to encounter teachings and practices that would not yield to my habitual method of investigation. I longed to understand what I could not understand, to master what I had not mastered, and to become something I had not become—at least not yet.

For the next seven years of my Zen training, I was in an almost continual state of anguish due to my spiritual longing. This longing was aroused and inflamed by chants like this part of the *Hsin Hsin Ming*, or *Faith In Mind*, by Chinese Zen ancestor Seng Ts'an, which we would chant daily at the meditation retreats I attended:

> *The Way is perfect like great space,*
> *Without lack, without excess.*
> *Because of grasping and rejecting,*
> *You cannot attain it.*
> *Do not pursue conditioned existence;*
> *Do not abide in acceptance of emptiness.*
> *In oneness and equality,*
> *Confusion vanishes of itself.*
> *Stop activity and return to stillness,*
> *And that stillness will be even more active.*
> *Merely stagnating in duality,*
> *How can you recognize oneness?* (Yen, 2006)

This chant felt like a taunt after several hours of seated meditation during which I might not have experienced a single moment when I was not choosing and rejecting, striving and entangled. There was rarely a moment that seemed *perfect like great space, without lack, without excess,* and if there was, it was fleeting and impossible to re-create. I tried to *stop activity and return to stillness,* but I only became more agitated. I felt like I was *stagnating in duality*—helplessly, cluelessly. Seng Ts'an seemed to be telling me "It" was so close, so accessible ... which only made me a bigger idiot for not being able to discover it.

The *Hsin Hsin Ming* was not the only teaching that aroused my longing while causing enlightenment to seem far from my grasp. Even the simplest of our chants, Dogen's instructions for zazen, "Fukanzazengi," told me that if I learned to *take the backward step that turns the light and shines it inward ... body and mind of themselves will drop away, and your original face will manifest* (Sotoshu Shumucho, 2001). What was my original face? Would I see it only after a dramatic awakening experience? Why couldn't I get my body and mind to drop away, no matter how hard I tried? Nothing in my life mattered more to me than discovering my original face. I would have sacrificed just about anything to do so.

My unrequited spiritual longing led to real despair. Such suffering may seem trite to those who have never experienced it, but perhaps this poem I wrote during this period of angst can communicate some of the pain of it:

Daffodils
On the day of my deepest desperation,
there is not the slightest sympathy
in the gleaming yellow of the daffodils.
They simply wait
for my return.

To me, life without the realization I longed for seemed bleak and pointless. I lost my taste for everything else, so there was no distraction or solace to be found. I was on the outside looking in, separated from my original face, from unity, from the One, from Buddha-nature, from those who *knew.* I still vividly remember the brilliance of those daffodils in the spring sunshine, beaming despite my suffering. The daffodils and Zen masters seemed to murmur together about the great mystery of life, just out of my hearing. They all looked down on me in pity, saying to each other, "Oh, it is so obvious, doesn't she see it?"

During this period of acute longing, human beings were divided into three factions in my mind: those who understood The Great Matter, those who didn't but were trying to, and those who didn't care. I despised and pitied the last category and burned with envy toward the first. I imagined that those who had experienced awakening or were empowered teachers had not only gained a badge that set them apart from me, they had made sense of their lives. I was drawn to them because I wanted their understanding, but I resented them too. Nothing they had offered so far had triggered my awakening. They seemed to keep repeating the same maddening lines about how it was right here, right now, so there was no need for such angst and struggle.

For each of us, our deepest spiritual longing takes a different form or attaches itself to different words, and this form can change over time. Sometimes what I wanted most was to know I was fundamentally okay—acceptable, worthy, lovable. At other times I longed to be able to speak and act freely and spontaneously as my "true self," free from the constraint of self-consciousness. I also craved understanding. I wanted to know for myself what the masters were talking about.

I persisted because my longing was stronger than my despair.

Two Camellias
Even after all the effort,
the grief is not gone.
Having tried everything,
having mastered nothing,
there is no hope even
for temporary relief. And no one else can help.
(Consumed as they are by their own struggles, or,
victorious,
their encouragements
echoing across the abyss
that separates sanity from despair.)
And yet it seems there is some shred of faith left:
on an aimless barefoot walk in the cold rain,
careless of broken glass
and unyielding pavement,
stooping to pick up two fallen camellias,
cradling pink rain-dropped petals
all the way home,
finding a shallow glass dish
and filling it with water,

setting the camellias afloat in it —
poignant,
superfluous
hope.

The terrible irony of spiritual teachings that arouse spiritual long-ing is this: the Buddha's first teaching is that craving is the very cause of dissatisfaction! But while it may seem relatively straightforward that we should let go of our desire for worldly things like fame, wealth and plea-sure, how can we awaken if we let go of our desire to awaken? Should we really just give up our desire for liberation and enlightenment?

The answer is a paradoxical *yes* and *no*—typical of Zen. *Yes*, because to realize what the Zen masters are talking about, we have to let go of any idea, let alone any hope, of enlightenment. *No*, because until we un-derstand what the Zen masters are talking about, we don't know what it means to let go of any idea of enlightenment. It's no use to pretend to be enlightened before we are. It doesn't help to anticipate the final answer and try to avoid going through the process to arrive there. Ideally we don't give up our spiritual longing until we are truly satisfied; it keeps us motivated, searching, and practicing.

After all, Zen Master Dogen made an arduous and dangerous trip to China in the thirteenth century because of his spiritual longing. He wasn't fully satisfied with the Buddhist teachings and practices he encountered in Japan, so he traveled to China, where he encountered Rujing and achieved the understanding he longed for. Later Dogen wrote in "Fukanzazengi": *Why leave the seat in your own home to wan-der in vain through the dusty realms of other lands? If you make one mis-step you stumble past what is directly in front of you* (Sotoshu Shumucho, 2001). This sounds very wise, but hindsight is 20/20. I sometimes wonder if Dogen heard a teaching exactly like that from one of his Buddhist teach-ers before he left for China, but nevertheless had to make the trip to truly understand it.

Another poem from my years of junior training describes my feel-ings better than any prose can.

Aspirations
Is an aspiration still an aspiration
when you stop believing you can attain it,
when you stop believing it can be attained?
Just one of billions —

a number beyond imagining —
and full of rot,
sainthood recedes like a puddle of water
in a hot pan.
I, for one,
had soup for lunch,
stooped to caress a cat on the sidewalk,
and drew easier breath
under the yellow-garland cottonwoods
on the riverbank.
What have I to do with saints? Their
insight and perfection,
their principles and influence?
And yet, I'm not ready to fold up
in my stacks of linens
or drown in my dishwater.
Those sages agitate my living
like a mosquito near my pillow in the night.
I keep going forward,
more and more hopeless but
unable to ignore that sound.

Before we awaken to our true nature, our spiritual work is like polishing a tile to make a mirror. This image comes from an ancient Zen story about the interaction between a Zen teacher, Nangaku, and his student, Baso. Baso had been sitting constantly in zazen for ten years. In his *Shobogenzo* fascicle "Kokyo," Dogen writes: *We can imagine what it is like in [Baso's] thatched hut on a rainy night. There is no mention of him letting up on a cold floor sealed in by snow* (Nishijima/Cross, 1994). Can you imagine this kind of dedication fueled by anything other than spiritual longing? Dogen continues:

> *Nangaku went to visit Baso and asked him, "What is the aim of sitting in Zazen?"*
> *Baso answered, "The aim of sitting in Zazen is to become a Buddha."*
> *Nangaku then picked up a roof tile and started rubbing it against a rock. Baso asked him what he was doing. Nangaku replied, "I am polishing a tile."*
> *Baso asked, "What is the use of polishing a tile?"*

> *Nangaku said, "I am polishing it into a mirror."*
> *Baso asked, "How can polishing a tile make it into a mirror?"*
> *Nangaku answered, "How can sitting Zazen make you into a Buddha?"*

At one level this story points at the folly of our efforts in spiritual practice when we are still stumbling past what is directly in front of us. Sometimes people in Zen practice have an idea about what the result of the practice will be. When the master sets them to polishing a tile, they assume he knows what he's talking about, and they earnestly and busily go to work. Later, when they get frustrated, they think the master has made a fool of them, and they become angry. They may even think they have solved the riddle of Zen practice by saying, "Forget this tile-polishing! There's nothing to get, I had it all along, and the test was just to see how long I would go about this foolish business." But this is not a real answer. This may make a person's life easier, but it won't really satisfy their spiritual longing.

At deeper level, earnestly and diligently polishing a tile is sacred activity even if you can't make a mirror out of it. In his compassion Dogen writes in *Kokyo*:

> *For several hundred years, since ancient times, most people interpreting this story—great matter that it is—have thought that Nangaku was simply spurring Baso on. That is not necessarily so . . . the making of mirrors through the polishing of tiles has been dwelt in and retained in the bones and marrow of eternal buddhas; and, this being so, the eternal mirror exists having been made from a tile . . . . Tiles are not dirty; we just polish a tile as a tile. In this state, the virtue of making a mirror is realized, and this just the effort of Buddhist [ancestors].* (Nishijima/Cross, 1994)

When we just polish a tile as a tile—when we just sit zazen—ironically our goal is realized. But this is not easy. Most of the time we keep on sitting zazen in order to become a buddha, which is a mistake, but there is no way to correct that mistake without continuing to sit zazen and trying to become a buddha.

The mistake is that we are looking somewhere else for the object of our longing. We can't help it; it's the habit of a lifetime, or longer. Even looking within ourselves for the answer doesn't help, because that is still looking somewhere else. We have to stop any looking whatsoever. When someone asks you to show your original face, you cannot hesitate for an instant, wondering where it is or whether you can manage to show it. It is not that you find your original face and hang onto it for such occasions, holding it up with confidence and saying, "Here it is! I found it last October!" Rather, it is that you are no longer tempted to leave your reality to look for the answer. It is just you meeting the challenge before you, bare and undefended. And what is this, if not your original face?

Although we need to stop looking, we should not stop longing. This is just giving up. Our heart needs to be filled to the brim with spiritual longing as we finally stop looking. Usually we can only do this when we have spent a great deal of time and energy desperately polishing a tile, and we finally give up that technique out of sheer exhaustion. In the meantime, polishing away, we keep our longing close enough to motivate us, but at enough distance that we don't get burned out by it. In the "Precious Mirror Samadhi" Dongshan says: *Turning away and touching are both wrong, for it is like massive fire* ... (Sotoshu Shumucho, 2001). Before and after the realization we are longing for, there is no effective position we can permanently adopt and then stop responding to what is most needed. Our practice is a dynamic process.

A moment of transformative and satisfying insight into the nature of self is deeply personal and intimate. While it has nothing to do with the details of our conventional selves, it has everything to do with the being who sits on our meditation seat, longing and wondering. That being is just like the disciples in the *Lotus Sutra* who went up to Shakyamuni Buddha and asked, one by one, for their personal predictions of Buddhahood. Essentially, each one stood before the Buddha and asked, "You mean me? Me too?" To stand like this—vulnerable, empty-handed, filled with longing—takes courage. When we arrive here, our hearts and minds are completely open because none of our efforts have appeased our longing. This is one step away from claiming our birthright and allowing our Buddhahood to come to pass. We still don't think we know how to achieve Buddhahood, but asking for our prediction of Buddhahood betrays that, at some level, we suspect it's possible for us to realize it.

Absorption
Luminous moon,
how many anguished hours have I spent

gazing into the heavens,
longing for your bright secret?
All the while bound
to the low and heavy earth
with the weight of my passion?
You are beaming with relief
like a proud parent
as I make the daring leap, call out:
Hey, moon!
How wonderful that we ended up
in the same night sky!

As I left my first husband to absorb myself in Zen practice (not something of which I am proud), he warned me that I wasn't going to find what I was looking for. The gratitude I feel for the Dharma, my teachers and my sangha is infinite, because I *did* find what I was looking for. For a long time it looked like my first husband was right, but eventually my true heart's desire was met. I found out who I was, and experienced first-hand how I am luminous, complete, and free of any need to justify my existence. And the same is true of everyone and everything else.

Works Cited

Dogen, Eihei. "Fukanzazengi." *Soto School Scriptures for Daily Services and Practice.* Consensus translation. Tokyo: Sotoshu Shumucho, 2001.

---. *Master Dogen's Shogobenzo.* Trans. Gudo Nishijima and Chodo Cross. London: Windbell Publications, 1994.

Liangjie, Dongshan. "The Precious Mirror Samadhi." *Soto School Scriptures for Daily Services and Practice.* Consensus translation. Tokyo: Sotoshu Shumucho, 2001.

Yen, Master Sheng. *Faith in Mind: A Commentary on Seng Ts'an's Classic.* Boston: Shambhala, 2006.

Acknowledgements
A previous version of this essay was posted to the Bright Way Zen blog (brightwayzen.org) on September 15, 2012 and mirrored by Sweeping Zen (sweepingzen.com).

Shinshu Roberts *ordained in the Soto Zen lineage of Shunryu Suzuki and received Dharma Transmission from Sojun Mel Weitsman. She holds Kokusaifukyoshi (teacher qualification) from the Sotoshu in Japan. Along with her partner, Daijaku Kinst, Shinshu is cofounder and teacher at Ocean Gate Zen Center in Capitola, California.*

Practicing in the Middle of Our Life

Shinshu Roberts

Eihei Dogen, the 13th century founder of Soto Zen in Japan wrote a text called "Guide-lines for Practicing the Way." This lecture is part of a series given on that text in 2013 at Ocean Gate Zen Center by Revs. Daijaku Kinst and Shinshu Roberts.

In the Buddha Way you should always enter enlightenment through practice.

In the Buddha Way is practicing the Dharma with all beings. *You should always enter enlightenment through practice* is realization expressed through daily practice. Combined practice and realization become one idea: practice-realization. We do not practice to become enlightened; rather our practice is an expression of the enlightened mind. The only way we can express enlightenment is through our actions. It is a misconception to think enlightenment is something we get or attain. Enlightenment is an expression of our true nature. This true nature is actualized by our actions; moment after moment. It cannot be understood as something once attained and never lost. Realization is practice. It is our everyday life. In Dogen's fascicle called "Mystical Power," he quotes Ho-on who said that carrying water and chopping wood are examples of mystical powers. These are examples of appropriate responses to everyday activity.

It is unheard of that without studying someone should earn wealth or that without practicing someone should attain enlightenment.

Since practice itself is the actualization of the enlightened mind, studying practice is the source of our wealth. It is a study of the nature of the self, which is to say the nature of reality itself.

In Zen there are no written tests, just each moment's response. Making an effort moment after moment requires deep dedication to the Dharma. What is required is a sincere heart and a steady effort as we deeply engage the Buddha Way. This process begins when we take responsibility for our lives. We look to the teachings of Zen masters for inspiration, we look to the teachings of the Buddha for wisdom, we look to our own teachers for guidance, and we enact practice in our day-to-day life.

A foundational activity of Zen is zazen. Zazen is coming back to the present moment. Just coming to what is rather than our idea about what is. Yet in the midst of sitting zazen we get caught. We find ourselves thinking about this or that, and then we let it go and come back to the present moment. We realize that thinking is impermanent. We realize that thinking is not necessarily a reflection of what is happening. We start to see that. Zazen happens outside the arena of the intellect. We do not "do" zazen; zazen does zazen.

From a certain perspective, we don't know what it is that we're doing. We have to have a kind of faith to engage in this practice. So, I encourage you, if you don't come to the zendo because you find zazen difficult, or you don't seem to have enough time, that you find five minutes to sit zazen. Sit for five minutes: just sit down and be quiet. If you can sit for ten minutes that's great, but if it's only five minutes, that's good too. Zazen is grounding oneself in the sincere activity of practicing the Way. Zazen is a deepening comfort and confidence with life just as it is. We don't have to judge this activity.

This is our study. This is the practice of enlightenment. Sometimes we stumble around in the dark, not knowing what to do. This, by the way, is the value of formal practice. Formal practice is a container that has been developed over hundreds and hundreds of years; it guides our body and mind. Formal practice gives us a foundation when we are confused. It is a method developed to create the conditions for awakening.

For this reason we turn to tradition for guidance. We look to someone like Dogen who teaches us that practice is realization. When we practice we are expressing Buddha. Practice is the activity of a buddha. This can seem vague, but enacting the question, "What is a buddha's activity?" helps direct us in the Buddha Way.

What does it mean to live my life as Buddha? What is the practice of a buddha? What does it mean to drive my car to the grocery store like a buddha? Does a buddha even drive a car? Maybe in our rarified notion of enlightenment and buddha-ness, a buddha doesn't drive a car. But a buddha does drive a car. A buddha goes swimming. A buddha eats cookies. Sometimes buddhas get mad. This is because you are a buddha; we're all buddhas.

❧

The practice varies initiated by faith or dharma knowledge.

Recently some of our sangha members watched the movie *Enlightenment Guaranteed,* about two brothers, Gustav and Uwe, who spent about a month at a Japanese Soto Zen monastery. Gustav seemed to be the one who would have the easiest time in the monastery because he was really gung-ho about going. Uwe, on the other hand, could not stop thinking and being angry about his wife leaving him. Yet, it turns out that Uwe was the one who had the most affinity for monastic life. Gustav struggled the most.

Although they were there for different reasons, they both threw themselves wholeheartedly into the monastic schedule. This requires faith and determination, especially when one is not sure and the practice is difficult. Neither one of them was probably thinking much about enlightenment, as the schedule and activities of a monk are all encompassing. They were fully occupied with each moment. In the midst of our mistakes and successes enlightenment takes care of itself.

While both of them followed the same schedule in the monastery, they each had different responses. There is a well-known koan about Bodhidharma (who brought Zen to China) and his disciples. Four of his disciples were in Bodhidharma's room. Bodhidharma said, *The time has come, can you express your understanding?*

One student said: *I follow the Middle Way, not too much of this not too much of that.* The second student said: *I take inspiration from seeing a Buddha's Pure Land.* The third student said: *Everything is empty, nothing is attained.* The fourth student replied by bowing three times.

These are four ways that we might express our understanding. Dogen wrote, in a chapter of *The True Dharma Eye* called "Twining Vines," that we should not assume one student's understanding was deeper than the others. We all have unique personalities. We all have different experiences. For this reason, each one of us is going to express the Dharma differently. Yet what we all express *is just this,* the awakened Dharma of this moment. For this reason, we share a basic understanding. Dharma is actualizing a wholesome, skillful interconnectedness with all beings. But how wholesomeness and interconnectedness are expressed will be predicated upon our particular life experiences and what the situation requires.

Gustav and Uwe are like Bodhidharma's four students; as are we. We are all going to have different experiences. We see this in the movie when Gustav and Uwe go to seek spiritual advice from the Abbot of the monastery. The Abbot tells Uwe he should develop empathy for his wife and see the situation from her point of view. Uwe responds that he is so angry he can't do that. The Abbot says that, if Uwe is going to hate his wife, he should really live with that hate. He should deeply experience his anger, until he realizes hating is suffering and hating will not solve his problems.

The Abbot is talking to Uwe about what Uwe needs to hear. If one of us went in and said we were angry, the Abbot might have a different teaching for us. What the Abbot tells Uwe is what Uwe needs to hear.

Gustav had another problem. Gustav was afraid of making a mistake. Gustav says to Uwe, *You know, I'm just so frightened I'm going to get it wrong.* It is easy to get caught up in anxiety about doing things right. Gustav can't pick up a teacup without spilling the tea because he's so nervous about dropping the cup. Inevitably he does spill the tea and he berates himself for making a mistake.

When Gustav tells the Abbot, the Abbot says: *I know you are afraid of dropping the teacup, but if you pay attention to how the tea smells, you might forget your fear. Ask yourself, "What is the smell of the tea? How does it taste?" If that's where you put your attention instead of being afraid of mistakes, then you won't drop the teacup.* The Abbot is connecting Gustav to the world of tea. How can you drop something that is part of yourself? This is interacting with the world. What do we do when we are afraid we are going to make a mistake?

Overcoming this kind of fear is putting our focus on the totality of the situation. To completely experience drinking tea is complete engagement—with the cup, with the smell of the tea, with the taste of the tea—thereby grounding us *in* the situation instead of our fear and anxiety *about* the situation. This is expanding our view until it includes everything, thereby letting go of and redirecting the energy of the small self, the fearful self. This is the activity of no-self and practice-realization.

Each one of us at one time or another is going to gain realization by working through our suffering. This is our practice; we can't push away our problems; we have to enter into our problems. In Uwe's situation deeply experiencing his anger was to enter into and transform his anger into compassion. When we are consumed by an emotion, or any issue, we begin by entering into and accepting the difficulty. We have to explore the nature of what it is to find ourselves in a difficult place.

Each of us has a very different way of interacting with the world. Some of us tend to be more intellectual and others are more intuitive. There is room for all of us in the Dharma. There is space for each of us to find our way. It is a very big gate.

Although there are many different ways to engage the practice, ultimately, what we understand is the interconnected, interdependent and impermanent nature of everything. Deeply engaging this truth results in wisdom, compassion and skillful response. Knowing this, the question becomes how can we express the truth of connection, compassion, and skillful means? How do we negotiate this truth? That's the basis of our practice.

⌣

If you were to gain realization without practice, how could you comprehend the Tathagata's teaching of delusion and enlightenment?

We have to negotiate our world in the midst of suffering and broken precepts. That's not going to go away. How do we do that? How do we keep our equanimity and respond skillfully? *How* we respond is practice. How we negotiate difficulties is through practice. First we stabilize our own emotions; then we respond.

If you have never been angry, how do you know what it is to be angry? If you've never been sad, how do you know how to talk with someone who is sad? If you've never had problems, how do you know how to relate to someone who is having difficulties?

Often we try to get rid of the experiences we consider outside our ideas about enlightenment. We think to ourselves "that's not the Dharma." But, that's exactly the Dharma, because how we relate to and interact with those situations is the source and enactment of our wisdom. How can we know how to respond skillfully to these difficult experiences if we cannot face them in our lives?

We are sensitized to delusion and we look for enlightenment in the wrong places. We have preconceived ideas about enlightenment. When we respond in an enlightened way, we dismiss that as everyday occurrence. Where else does enlightenment happen? Does it happen in some remote place? What is enlightenment? Is enlightenment never having problems? I think that is close to what we think it is. We think enlightenment means we will never experience suffering or make mistakes. We think this is what enlightenment looks like. We are so clouded by our notions of enlightenment that we cannot recognize when we are engaged in enlightened activity.

Despite our ideas about the unattainability of enlightenment, we do engage in enlightened activity. When we respond with equanimity to someone pulling in front of us in traffic: that is an enlightened response. When we stop and calm our minds in a difficult situation: that is an enlightened response. We actualize the enlightened mind all the time; we just don't know it is enlightenment.

🕊

You always depend upon practice to go beyond enlightenment.

We don't need to worry about enlightenment if we engage in practice. We practice by continuously coming forward with our sincere heart, doing our best, as we are. We are not trying to be somebody else. We're not trying to be some idea we have about who this enlightened person might be. It is just me. It is just you. It is just us, with all of our problems and mistakes. We continuously keep bringing ourselves back to the practice. This is the zazen of returning to each moment.

As we immerse ourselves in practice through the coming and going of our life, there is leaping beyond our individual life into the life of all beings. This leaping beyond includes our fear of spilling the tea and the world of tea itself. Nothing should be left out.

Practice-realization is something beyond delusion or enlightenment. Practice is going beyond conceptions. We say in Zen: *just this, moment-to-moment* and *things as they are*. We don't have to worry about enlightenment. We don't even have to worry about delusion as long as we are willing to completely engage in practice.

That's why the Abbot said to Uwe *hate, hate, hate, hate*. Hate until you leap beyond hate. He's not saying to Uwe, "Ok, go out and do hateful things." He didn't say go visit all that anger on other people. He said: *You just sit in the midst of your anger. Just sit in the middle of all the suffering and anger until you wear it out and realize that it won't make your life better.*

That's one aspect of sitting zazen or practice in general. When we put our bodies in a place and we say "I'm just going to sit here, even if it means I'm going to fidget, think, be judgmental, and uncomfortable. I'm just going to sit here until the bell rings." Transformation happens in the midst of your willingness to stay in your life, *as it is*. You don't know what is happening, but in the middle of your willingness to be present, something is going to happen.

If we can presence ourselves in a wholesome way, with patience, kindness and equanimity, even when we don't feel patience, kindness or equanimity, then we will find compassion for ourselves and for others. Just keep coming back and making your best effort. That's practice. You don't have to worry about enlightenment. Just keep coming back to your practice with a sincere heart and a big mind. Because it is all there.

Can we be okay with that? Can we be patient with that? Can we learn from that? Can we engage with that aspect of ourselves? Or are we going to push our life away because we don't have the right "Zen" mind?

This is not made to happen by Buddha, but accomplished by your all encompassing effort.

We make effort and that effort brings forth the realization that all beings are simultaneously making effort with our effort. The continuous effort of all beings cannot be enacted without our aspiration to make a sincere effort. Our effort is supported by faith and vow. We are encouraged by the people who inspire us. We are inspired by the life and teachings of Buddha. We are inspired by Mother Teresa, by Gandhi, and by Nelson Mandela. We are inspired by the activities of our friends. We are inspired by reading Dogen. Yet, none of these people *make* us practice. None of these people walk in our shoes. Practice does not happen for us "over there." We can only enact our practice *through* our own life.

Buddhist practice is a willingness to truly engage life as followers of the Way. There is the expression *as far as the eyes of practice can see*. As we go along the Buddha's path, we are going to see more and more and more. Our Dharma eye will be continuously awakened.

For this to happen we have to be on the path. We have to be engaged in a buddha's activity. We have to want to wake up. We have to apply the teaching to our own life. We have to directly experience what it means to open our hearts and minds and engage in the totality of the situation. We have to be willing to abide with negative emotions and ask ourselves, "What is it?" We have to be willing to question our selfishness. We have to question our clinging. We have to be willing to cultivate gratitude and appreciation. Yes, we are going to forget. But then we come back. We are going to forget gratitude, and then we come back. We are going to get caught in our anger, and then we come back. We are going to be overwhelmed by our fear, and then we come back. It's just like sitting za-zen. Come back, come back, and come back again. This is your Buddha-nature saying "Please come back. I'm right here. I've always been right here." In the midst of your life, Buddha-nature is right here; it is our treasure house.

Works Cited

Dogen, Eihei. "Guidelines for Practicing the Way." *Moon in a Dewdrop: Writings of Zen Master Dogen.* Ed. Kazuaki Tanahashi. New York: North Point Press, 1985.

Enlightenment Guaranteed. Dir. Doris Dorrie. With Uwe Ochsenknecht and Gustav-Peter Wohler. Festival Media, Buddhist Film Foundation, 2009.

Rev. Joen Snyder O'Neal *is a founder and co-guiding teacher with her husband Michael O'Neal at Compassionate Ocean Dharma Center (Jikai-ji) in Minneapolis, MN. She is a Dharma Heir of the late Dainin Katagiri Roshi from whom she received Dharma Transmission in 1989.*

Turning Words

Joen Snyder O'Neal

What we call *turning words* are expressions found in teaching stories of the ancient masters, where a few words upend usual ways of thinking and turn someone—hopefully us—toward a world that is much larger, freer, and more compassionate than we have become accustomed to.

But turning words also regularly make their appearance in our everyday lives, not just in koan collections. We just have to be able to hear them. From the time I was a little girl until now, as I enter old age, there are words that have changed my life and still echo through the years. They encourage me to keep listening.

When I was five years old and getting ready to start kindergarten, my mother took my friend Joanna Ray and me on a pre-walk to school, showing us the best, most direct way to go.

However, when school started and we were walking by ourselves, we didn't take the way she had carefully showed us. We took the way of the flowers—a way that had lots of yellow and purple and deep red, and a garage with a trellis of pale pink baby roses climbing up and over.

We were entranced by these beautiful flowers, and we would stop and smell as many as we could. Then we wanted to have one of our very own. At first we would ask the owners if we might have a flower or two, and they would kindly pick some for us. As time went on, we wouldn't bother asking; we would pick flowers willy-nilly, bunches of them. But one thing always remained the same—we would be late to school! The late children had to sit in the dark cloakroom for a while as a punishment. We would sit in the doorway, peeking out into the bright schoolroom with all the other children in a circle, singing.

One day the teacher said to the two of us, *All your friends are waiting for you.* The next day as Joanna Ray and I were walking past the garage with the pale pink roses, Joanna started to climb, drawn by the prettiest of the roses on the very top. At that moment I thought of the teacher's words. "Joanna" I said, "I don't want to be late! All our friends are waiting for us!" She kept climbing. I turned around and ran straight to school, right into the circle of all the children singing in the large bright room.

This event was the first moment I remember stepping onto the Way.

Those words of my teacher were turning words for me and have echoed down the years. Often, as I have found myself chasing after flowers, following my own stubbornness, I have thought of them. Or when I have found myself in the dark cloakroom of ignorance, cut off from others. Even now, when I don't want to get out of bed and go to zazen, I think of them.

Chasing after flowers is a wonderful metaphor for human life. We want to follow our own way, which usually means that we are caught up by our impulses, by our attractions and aversions. Hence our life becomes wobbly, and we are caught over and over by the full catastrophe.

All your friends are waiting for you. I suddenly heard my teacher's words as I stood at the bottom of the garage trellis, watching Joanna Ray go up higher and higher. My bodhisattva heart, my great being heart, was aroused by those words. I knew I wanted to be in the circle of light with all my friends. I didn't want to sit in the dark cloakroom, cut off from them. And so I turned and went in a new direction.

⩔

In 1969 I was in my late twenties and a graduate student at the University of California at Berkeley. That was an incredible time in the history of our country and in the history of the Berkeley campus. The free speech movement had rocked the campus in the mid-sixties, and now it was the height of the anti-Vietnam war protests. Governor Ronald Reagan had called out the National Guard, who surrounded the campus with drawn bayonets while helicopters flew over, spraying mace on the students below. I was studying theatre, and this was definitely high drama!

A friend of my brother came to visit and stayed with us for a few days. After doing some sightseeing, he came home one night and reported that he had stumbled on something "incredible" happening at a place called the Family Dog by the ocean in San Francisco.

I had heard of the Family Dog. It was one of the big dance halls that was popular then, hosting bands like The Grateful Dead and Big Brother and the Holding Company. I asked him if he had seen a band that night. He said no, and that he couldn't explain what it was, I'd have to see for myself.

This wasn't much to go on, but somehow I felt compelled to go. The next Monday evening I found myself pulled across the Bay Bridge, through the city of San Francisco, and down to the dance hall overlooking the ocean. I went in. There, sitting quietly on blankets on the floor, were 1500 young people—men and women dressed in all manner of clothes, hair and beards long and flowing—a large gathering of hippies! It was mind blowing. Then a conch shell was blown and everyone chanted *AUM* for several minutes. That was also mind blowing—1500 people chanting together. Then a man came up on stage and said to the hushed crowd, "I've come to tell you tonight that *samsara and nirvana are one.*"

I felt something turning inside. I wasn't sure what the words meant exactly—did he say *suffering* and nirvana are one? And what exactly was *nirvana*? But I got a sense of what he was saying—that two seemingly opposite, and central, aspects of human life were actually not separated. This was the first formal Buddhist teaching I heard in this lifetime, and it caused a revolution in me. It became a koan that pulled me completely out of a life I thought I knew, into a life of which I knew nothing.

When I was in my early thirties, I traveled to Minnesota in a converted bread van with my husband and baby. We were there to see a Zen master we had heard about, to see if we wanted to stay and study with him. We spent the first night in our van in the Zen Center's driveway. The next day I met with this Zen master, Dainin Katagiri Roshi. We talked for a little while, then sat in silence together. He gazed at me for a few minutes and then said, "Kind of deep; kind of neurotic . . . ." and then, strongly, " . . . but anyway, *you are really Buddha.*"

We had just come from living on a commune in the backwoods of Tennessee, where the spiritual practice of the community was to "speak the truth," to "straighten out" people who were on "trips." Of course, we were all on trips most of the time, so this activity was very time consuming. I remember when my father and mother came to visit, my father volunteered to help in the motor pool. He reported that they hardly got anything done because they were constantly breaking into circles to straighten the situation out. All of us were being "straightened out" by everyone we encountered, even people who had just arrived that day. The last person who straightened me out had said, "You have the vibes of a poisonous snake!" On some level, of course, there was probably truth in that.

But when I heard Katagiri Roshi say that I was really Buddha, something changed for me on a deep level. I didn't really know who or what Buddha was, but I knew that it was something very good and very different from "you have the vibes of a poisonous snake." So I stayed and studied with Katagiri Roshi for 17 years, until his death in 1990.

Now when I look at others, I remember my teacher's words, and say—sometimes silently, sometimes out loud—*You are really Buddha.*

When I was in my mid-thirties I asked Katagiri Roshi to ordain me as a priest. He said, "Next lifetime." I was very disappointed! However, I swallowed it and continued to carry on with my practice in the same way I had. Three years later Tomoe Katagiri, Katagiri Roshi's wife, came downstairs after one of Roshi's Dharma talks and took my measurements from the top of my middle finger to my elbow. I knew that this was the measurement that was taken to determine the size of the okesa, the priest's robe. Later I said to Roshi, "You said next lifetime." He said, *It is next lifetime.* I was ordained by him in my 40th year.

So many lifetimes have come and gone since then!

When I was in my early forties I decided I wanted to do monastic practice. My teacher encouraged me to go to Japan or Tassajara. But someone I had met on a retreat in Joshua Tree, California, suggested I go to Amaravati Buddhist Monastery in England. This was before the internet and I couldn't find out much about it, but I got the idea it was a Theravadin Buddhist women's monastery. For some reason I decided that that was where I wanted to go, so with my teacher's somewhat hesitant blessing I flew to England. When I got there I was surprised to see so many tall, masculine-looking nuns, but as it turned out, this was a monastery for both women and men.

There was a young Thai woman at Amaravati while I was there. She had been a postulant at the monastery, then disrobed and moved to London, where she discovered she had advanced lung cancer. She had come back to Amaravati to reordain and to die.

All of us were called upon to take care of her in shifts. I remember when I first went to her room; I was frightened because I didn't know her, and I had never been with someone who was dying. She patted the space beside her on the bed and said, "Don't be afraid, sister; I'm not."

Shortly thereafter, she became quite ill and began to go downhill at a rapid rate. I was in her room one day attending to her with one of the senior monks. She was draped over a chair struggling to breathe. Many people had been encouraging her to "let it go" since she had returned to the monastery. She had been trying her best, but at that moment she called out in despair, "I can't let it go, *bhante* [monk], I can't let it go!" He replied, *Then let it come, sister, let it come.* At that, she was able to open and be supported by the waves of life and death, coming and going; beyond life, beyond death.

A short time later she was very close to death and had announced that this was the night she would depart. The whole monastic community gathered in her room, sitting and chanting. An altar was set up at the end of her bed with a single candle burning. Then we heard a roar of motorcycles in the parking lot, followed by the sound of boots stomping in the hall. A group of young Thai men from London, friends of hers, had come down; they burst into the room and cried out, "Don't die, sister, don't die!" She sat up in bed and told the rest of us all to go, as she had decided not to die that night; she needed to take care of her friends.

She died peacefully the next evening.

So many times through the years I have heard that monk's voice saying, *Then let it come, sister, let it come.* I try my best.

A few years after this I was back in Minneapolis working at my day job. One day I was walking back to my office after lunch when I passed a "junk shop," full of used things that looked like the discards of a not-very-successful yard sale.

I felt a sudden tug, turned back and went in. I asked the woman at the counter if there was perhaps a Buddha statue anywhere in the shop. "What's that?" she said. I tried to describe what I was seeking, demonstrating the posture and holding my hands in the mudra. "Well," she said, "I don't recall ever seeing anything like that." At that moment she shifted her body slightly to the left, and I looked over her shoulder to see a two-foot-high shining golden Buddha statue sitting on the desk behind her—so beautiful! I pointed it out to her and she said, *Oh, I never noticed that before.* She sold it to me for twenty-five dollars.

One of the teachings in Buddhism is of the six realms of existence: those populated by heavenly beings, fighting spirits, humans, animals, hungry ghosts, and hell beings. The Buddha taught that these are realms—

modes of experience—that we transmigrate into moment after moment, depending on our intention, our action, and our state of consciousness. For example, if our life is centered on continually seeking to satisfy our desires, we are likely to find ourselves in the hungry ghost realm. Beings in this realm are typically depicted as having very large stomachs and tiny throats—constantly hungry, but never able to satisfy their longing.

In the visual depiction of this teaching, the Wheel of Life, a Buddha is present in each realm. For instance, in the hungry ghost realm there is a Buddha holding a container of nectar from the heavenly realm—because the only means of liberation from this realm is to substitute the desire for truth for sensual cravings. In the human realm the Buddha is holding a book, indicating our potential to study and practice and to benefit from our understanding. These Buddhas indicate that wherever we are, in whatever kind of psychological or physical state we find ourselves, there is a great opportunity to wake up!

The evening of the day I found the golden Buddha I presided over an ecumenical service commemorating Hiroshima Day at the Basilica of St. Mary in downtown Minneapolis. I was wearing my full Zen robes, and the Buddha statue was placed under the large hanging statue of Jesus on the Cross. Wow, I thought, from a junk shop to the altar of one of the largest Catholic churches in the country in just a few short hours!

There is a Buddha in every realm. There was a Buddha in the junk shop, but the saleslady had never noticed it. I'm sure a lot of people noticed it when it was enshrined on the altar at the Basilica.

I still look for the Buddha wherever I go.

Once, many years ago when I was sitting a period of zazen at the Minnesota Zen Center, I was really spaced out, traveling all over the universe in the forty-minute period. When the bell sounded at the end I was startled, and it took a few minutes for me to land. I became vaguely aware of a giant Buddha sitting upright in the middle of the universe I now found myself in. As I came to, I said to myself with amazement, "Oh, it's me!"

When I was in my late fifties a member of our sangha told a story of her fifteen-year struggle with her husband. Always before company came over she expected that he would help with the many preparations, and always he didn't, so always she was angry and disappointed. One day as she was preparing for company and at the same time preparing her anger and disappointment with her husband, she had the insight that she could do something different. At that moment she let go of any expectation of help from her husband, and with energy and vigor she stepped into the reality of the situation. She felt enormous relief and deep inner freedom.

Sometimes we like the words "letting go." Just saying them can bring a sense of relief. Lately I have been reflecting on their meaning. Some years back I was having difficulty in a relationship, and I traveled a long way to ask a certain Zen teacher for advice. After a lot of talk about the many facets of the situation, he finally said, *You need to let go of something.* He didn't say what, but it was clear that if the situation were to change, something needed to be let go of. After pondering what that could be, I awoke one morning with the clear thought that what I needed to let go of was *hope.* At that moment a joy arose, and I felt fresh air begin to circulate in my psyche. I settled in with the way things were, and this allowed me to be clearer about the opportunities available in the present moment, and the direction of the next step.

When I later thought about what had happened, I realized that I hadn't actually let go of hope, but I had let go of *clinging* to hope—of being dependent on it, being held down by it. Katagiri Roshi used to use the expression, *Keep it warm in your heart.* Looking deeply, I can see that letting go of something—for instance, hope—just means that we stop carrying around the banner of hope that flaps and waves and blocks our view when any wind blows. Rather, hope is kept warm in our heart as nourishment for the great bodhisattva aspiration to open our hearts and our arms to the suffering of the many beings.

Sometimes we *don't* like the words "letting go"; they bring up anxiety. Part of the anxiety we may experience when contemplating letting go is that we feel we will be left with nothing—that our situation will be "hopeless." In actuality, when we let go we are left with everything—the total dynamic working of the universe. It is our clinging that prevents us from feeling part of this dynamic working that seems to separate us from the freely functioning universe. We say, "I feel so alone, so cut off," but we create that delusion through our clinging.

So actually, letting go involves *letting go* of an object, but also, simultaneously, an opening of the heart that is often so defended and clenched. When we give up our clinging, the heart opens to accept whatever it is that we have been resisting. Eventually the heart becomes very wide, and "let it go" becomes "let it be." This doesn't mean passive resignation, but rather a vital engagement with the way things actually are.

In reality we can't really let go of anything—all the myriad things are already here, coming and going in the waves of the great compassionate ocean. We just let them be, stop our resistance and clinging, and enjoy swimming freely.

In the past I would often complain whenever there was something that was next on the "To Do" list of my life. "Oh," I would say, "I have to teach a class tonight." Or, "Oh, I have to visit my mother." Or, "Oh, I have to go grocery shopping." That was the way I would express myself, so of course I always felt burdened by all the things I would "have" to do.

One day my husband corrected me: "Joen, you *get* to teach a class tonight. You *get* to visit your mother. You *get* to go grocery shopping." After several years of this teaching (which I really appreciated), I began to more consistently say "I *get* to ... live my life, suffer at times, go to zazen, clean up my room." And I began to feel more gratitude for all the many things I get to do.

Of course, sometimes I backslide, but now I hear my husband's voice saying, "*Get* to," and I straighten up.

Now I am in my early seventies. Since I began working on this essay, I have become more sensitive to the many things that I hear every day that become the causes and conditions of my life as a student of the Way.

A couple weeks ago I was having my hair trimmed. My hairdresser asked what I was going to do that afternoon, and I explained to her that I was writing up some things that I have heard people say that have influenced my life. "Who knows," I said, "maybe something you say will be in the book." "Oh," she said, "nothing that *I* would say would influence your life." So I asked her what she did when her seven-year-old son was angry and acting naughty. She replied, *I hug it out of him!* After a moment of silence, I said, "Wow—as far as I'm concerned, you're in!"

Myokaku Jane Schneider *with her husband, Peter, founded and teaches at Beginner's Mind Zen Center in Northridge, California. Their practice form is Soto Zen Buddhism adapted to the needs of a lay community. After Suzuki Roshi's death, Richard Baker Roshi gave priest ordination to Jane in San Francisco Zen Center. The next year Peter and Jane went to Japan and lived there from 1973-1995. They studied Buddhism by sitting retreats in temples and studying individually with teachers of Zen and other lineages. After returning from Japan, Jane received Dharma Transmission in Suzuki Roshi's lineage from Myoan Grace Schireson at Empty Nest Zendo in North Fork, California. "The Heart Mind Library," on which this article is based, was a talk given at Beginner's Mind Zen Center on August 3, 2013 and is listed in the dharma talks on the website.*

A Guided Meditation into the Heart/Mind Library

Myokaku Jane Schneider

Come with me into the Heart/Mind Library. I call it a library because that is a place where people usually go for research, study, and information. The Mind/Heart Library is a vast space with all possibilities present. It can be called the Heart/Mind Library or the Mind/Heart Library because mind without heart is incomplete and heart and mind are one.

Within the Library there are files rather than books, and one is a file called *Self*; you have unlimited access to it because it is you yourself. Within all possibilities the *self* changes and evolves and is limited only by the choices you make. Even though you have unlimited access to this file, there are so many distractions of work, family, and friends in your daily life that you seldom look deeply into it. If efforts to understand your life have not brought you the satisfaction and peace that you would like to have, try another approach with me and look at the self that you call *I, me and mine* from the perspective of the Heart/Mind Library.

Before you enter the Library, it would help to slow down and look at what you already know. You can do that by finding a comfortable position on a cushion or chair to compose yourself since this will take a little time. If you want to lie down, that is OK, too. Everything you need is in the Mind/Heart Library, so it is not necessary to bring anything. When you are ready to begin, take a look at what you already have with you.

Memories would be a good place to start because they are an enormous accumulation of facts, fiction, and other information that have become attached to your *self*, and you have wandered through them again and again. Now that information is mixed up; remembrances and events are out of order, some are lost, and a lot of it has been changed and is still being changed today. These memories feel comfortable even when they make you feel terrible. They are very dear to you because you believe they are undeniable proof of personal, permanent existence. Although there is room for everything in the Mind/Heart Library, please put down that Memory file for now, because memories will not be needed while you acquaint yourself with the Library. You can always open that file again later when you want to.

Now you can enter the Heart/Mind Library and look around. I say *enter* so that you can imagine a beginning, but there is no door because you are already inside. You are always inside. You have unlimited access because you are always *here*. To look into the Heart/Mind Library just takes the time to stop what you are doing, to wait a few moments to clear your mind and to look around. So if you haven't already, please put your big Memory file aside and do not open it for now.

I should mention that there is another file that you are carrying, and it is exceedingly big as well. It seems to be two-in-one; the first part is about what you can do, and the second part is about what you cannot do. You can label that your Ability file. The two parts seem to be about the same size, although the "cannot do" part might be a little larger. Please put that file aside as well. There is no reason to waste your energy on something that you will not use while you explore the Heart/Mind Library.

Before you begin, you might as well check another file that you are carrying around. This one seems to be more like useless baggage, because it is full of a lot of ideas about who you are. Depending on the time, you can see yourself as kind-hearted, tough, busy, mean, irritable, happy, compassionate, slow, likeable, depressed, intelligent, lazy, hardworking, quick and so on. You should label this one Ideas-About-Yourself file. This file is endless; it is huge! Please put this one aside, also, because it too is unnecessary. In the Mind/Heart Library everything is *you*, and you are too boundless to be put in small wrappings.

You have set aside three really big files during the time you plan to look around the Heart/Mind Library and that leaves you with spaciousness and an open mind. Without something to occupy your attention, you can look at yourself from a new perspective. When you are ready, take two deep breaths and let them out slowly. After each full inhalation, slowly exhale until you have reached the end of your breath, and then push down a little further before you start your next inhalation.

When you have let out your second breath, sitting quietly with a big empty space in front of you, in back of you, and on both sides of you, quietly ask yourself, "Who is sitting here now?"

Without using the Memory, Ability or Ideas-About-Yourself files, quietly ask again, "Who is sitting here now?"

After the question wait a moment to adjust to spaciousness because this is a big library and for now, time is not important. Without consulting the usual information you normally use to understand yourself, use spaciousness to look past old ideas and ask again, "Who is sitting here now?"

When you look at your circumstances from the limited perspective of *self*, situations can only be this or that, up or down, or right or wrong. If you feel good, you see yourself with approval; if you feel bad, you see yourself unpleasantly; and if you do not care at all, you feel uninterested. But if you want to see yourself in a multitude of ways beyond the limitations of thoughts and emotions, without fear of gain and loss, you can do that in spaciousness. Speaking from the point of view of a painter, it would be like expanding your palette from a few colors to an unending supply of colors.

"Who is sitting here now?"

After the question, while you wait for a response, here is a list of don'ts to help you relate to the Library for best results. Do not expect a response immediately. Do not do what you usually do; do not pick up and open the Memory, Ability or Ideas-About-Yourself files. Leave them untouched where you left them. Do not try to answer your question in the usual way; do not supply an answer, because you will need the files you put aside to do that. Do not do anything! This time, let spaciousness be all that you need and let the question and the space after the question hang in the air with nowhere to go.

This new research method may take some practice, because the usual habit is to explain away questions as fast as they arise. Leaving questions unanswered makes us feel uneasy. Even so, however much your mind and emotions want to act, do not do what you usually do. Instead, quietly ask yourself again, "Who is sitting here now?"

Since you are sitting in spaciousness, patience is your natural ally. There is no need for action. Wait for a response from the Mind/Heart Library; it may take some moments.

Without acting on the usual impulse to produce quick solutions, ask yourself again, "Who is sitting here now?"

Remember, no matter how strongly you may feel the urge to pick up the files that you put aside, leave them where you left them. You can always go back to them later. For now be adventurous and leave your mind empty of solutions and do not do anything. To learn something new, wait quietly in spaciousness and let the question hang nowhere in the Heart/Mind Library.

When you ask the question, "Who is sitting here now?" what thought, what feeling, what sensation, what sound comes to mind? What appears is a response from the Mind/Heart Library. Perhaps it does not make any sense at all, perhaps it seems to have no connection to the question, or maybe it just makes you feel uncomfortable. But look at it; don't ignore it! What appears is a full expression of Heart/Mind reality, and if it's in your awareness, it belongs to you.

In spaciousness you have a wider perspective of yourself. For example, from the usual position of *self* you are *here* and the birdsong is *over there*. From the position of spaciousness, you are *here* and the birdsong is also *here*. So pay attention to everything, because whatever appears is a response. A thought, an emotion, a sound, or a sensation is a response that is an expression of Heart/Mind reality. Whether it makes sense or not, do not rush to label it; observe it as a momentary expression of your full being.

You probably have another rather voluminous file to be put aside. Let us call that your Judgment file. In the vast space of the Mind/Heart Library, there is no use for judgment, although you can probably pick it up again later if you need it. But in order to study your *self* as-it-is, put the Judgment file aside and once again ask the question, "Who is sitting here now?"

Remember, do not touch any file; let the question sit here with nothing to do. And as you wait, I would like to bring up another important point about spaciousness. Previously you put your large files aside, and now it is important to put the responses from the Mind/Heart Library aside as well. Let them be present for a moment as-they-are, look at them carefully, and then let them go.

Once again quietly ask yourself, "Who is sitting here now?"

When thoughts or emotions arise, let them hang there untouched, no memories to justify them, no abilities to make them reasonable, no ideas to explain away the emotions they arouse, no judgments to give a sense of control. Whatever need you feel to put a personal touch on them, do not do it. Usually you would put them into the files that you carry around and then forget them until another time. But you decided not to do what you usually do. So you let the responses of the Heart/Mind Library sit there in space because there is nothing to be achieved, nothing to be solved, and nothing to be explained. Your awareness, the responses, and spaciousness will bring about a new perspective of you, yourself. This time, just being with responses as-they-are is enough.

Do not confuse your immediate experience by adding thoughts or by trying to reconcile your experience with emotions. When you allow thoughts, emotions, and sensations to exist just as-they-are, the connection between reality and you is such an intimate relationship that it should not be exchanged for a watered-down, thought-out version of it. Stay with each response to the question no matter what it is, let it go, and give full attention to the next moment.

Since *self* relates to experiences in an exclusive way, using opposites such as *this or that,* and *here or there,* maintaining a secure position is important. But in spaciousness, such opposites are irrelevant and there is no position to maintain because spaciousness is inclusive. Without the need for a position from which to act, you can embrace change as adventure and learning. In spaciousness, *I, me and mine* becomes one with *you, they and their.* In spaciousness, empathy and compassion open and bloom.

So for now, while you are learning in the Mind/Heart Library, do not explain away anything. All that is necessary is to be fully aware of the presence of each experience, moment after moment.

In the Mind/Heart Library, there is no room even to hold on to questions or to take the time to create more files, since you are going to let everything go anyway. If you hold on to your discoveries, whether you think them important or not, the vast space with all possibilities will be forgotten. Instead, you will wander around in a limited space. But since there are infinite learning possibilities in the Heart/Mind Library, why confine yourself to such a small area?

For now, release the thoughts, emotions, and sensations as quickly as they come and look again to see what is there now. If you want to understand *self-existence* better, then pay attention to your activities, because *self* is the emotions we feel at the moment; *self* is the thoughts and sensations we feel at the moment; *self* is the sounds we hear, the things we touch and feel, the world we see at the moment. A fluid and flexible mind experiences the world directly as-it-is. Holding on to a thought or feeling creates an obstruction, like damming up a stream with trash.

It may feel like denying yourself to let go of thoughts and emotions as fast as they come, because without something to dwell on, it is difficult to reaffirm your *self-existence.* It is true that in the Mind/Heart Library dwelling on limited *self* is not important, but it is time to meet your fluid, changing, unfathomable *being. Self* changes from moment to moment, but unfathomable *being* is the inquiring mind that experiences each moment fully, immediately releases it, and looks with awareness again and again, uncluttered with even one moment's past experience. When ungraspable *being* is forgotten, you become only the limited *self* you believe you are. But even if you forget ungraspable *being,* in the

Mind/Heart Library limited *self* and indescribable *being* are not separate. Whether you understand your full potential or not, even in daily affairs limited *self* can act freely, unfathomable *being* acts freely, and when acting together with awareness, all things are possible.

You can practice this anywhere. The Heart/Mind Library is always here and you have unlimited access to it. Whatever happens, if you stop for a moment to remember the vast world with no files to clutter up your mind, spaciousness returns and the Heart/Mind Library will be present.

Remember, even in the midst of activities, take a few moments to stop, breathe, ask, "Who is here now?" and don't supply answers or hang on to anything. Pay attention to the next moment and, especially, entrust yourself to spacious, ungraspable *being*.

In the Mind/Heart Library, every moment is an untouched page, but because you are limited *self* as well as ungraspable *being*, you have to deal with the weighty files and cluttered pages as well as each new, untouched page. Whatever affairs you are engaged in, clinging to thoughts, memories, and sensations can confuse your perception of events. So the first thing to do is to drop the heavy files you depend on and, for a few moments, allow spaciousness to function in place of activity. Then look with a clear mind at your circumstances. It may take some practice to convince yourself of the need to remember indescribable *being*, but if it gets too challenging, remember that the big files you put down are still there if you really want to carry them again.

Myoan Grace Schireson, Ph.D., *is a Zen Abbess, president of Shogaku Zen Institute (a Zen teachers' training seminary), and holds a doctorate in Clinical Psychology from the Wright Institute in Berkeley, California. She received Dharma Transmission from Sojun Mel Weitsman Roshi in the Shunryu Suzuki Roshi Zen lineage. The late Fukushima Keido Roshi of Tofukuji Monastery, Kyoto asked her to teach the koan she studied with him during her practice there. Abbess Myoan Grace leads two practice centers and a retreat center, Empty Nest Zendo, under the Central Valley Zen Foundation.*

Abbess Myoan Grace is the author of Zen Women: Beyond Tea Ladies, Iron Maidens and Macho Masters (Wisdom, 2009), *and has published articles in* Shambhala Sun, Buddhadharma *and* Tricycle *magazines. She has also been anthologized in* The Book of Mu, Receiving the Marrow, *and* The Hidden Lamp *as well as in a book on spiritual training:* The Arts of Contemplative Care. *She has been married for 45 years and lives with her husband part-time on Stanford campus and at her Zen retreat center, Empty Nest Zendo in North Fork, California. She has two grown sons and four grandchildren.*

Awareness: From the Zen Cushion to Everyday Life

Myoan Grace Schireson

Here we are, all together in sesshin turning inward, turning toward Fall. I want to talk to you about how to practice in retreat and beyond. All sesshin activity aims to "turn on" awareness. Through active and purposeful turning towards, you may discover your relationship to intrinsic awareness, and during sesshin, together we cultivate that awareness. For those of you who are new to the art of sesshin, the techniques and behavior used for this cultivation could seem a little weird.

For example, you don't engage in the casual conversation that is customary in your everyday social setting. And yet, you begin to feel rapport and bonding without words. What happens to you is the opposite of weird; you become more deeply connected to the details of life. What does it feel like to breathe in this moment, or to walk outside to an infinite space? Luminous awareness arises and strengthens, shining on every ordinary moment.

The essence of sesshin practice develops a process for deepening your awareness resulting in the freedom to use awareness creatively in your daily life. There are four steps in this process of deepening awareness and making it useful.

The first step is finding awareness. Awareness is the self-reflective quality of the mind that can grow in brightness, focus, depth, and quality. Awareness is what observes your mind thinking; sometimes it is called the observing self or the essence of mind. The second step is amplifying awareness. This stage develops and strengthens awareness by focusing and concentrating. In this step you use meditative technique— whether it be breath or koan—to strengthen your concentrative "mind muscle" and settle more deeply into awareness. The third step is circulating awareness through the body/mind equipment. Sometimes we purposely direct awareness to a felt mental or physical blockage. Sometimes awareness bubbles out on its own, illuminating and fulfilling sesshin activities like *oryoki* and chanting. Occasionally, an insight spontaneously arises, connecting a painful stuck place with the specific way to let it go. The fourth step in developing awareness, is cultivating your ability to use it freely. You have the confidence at this stage to trust your life to your awareness. You choose to allow awareness to guide you instead of relying on ingrained habitual reactions.

Finding the Light of Awareness

The first step in my process of finding awareness has been described in traditional Zen. In Case 86 of the *Blue Cliff Record*, Yunmen said: *Everyone has their own light. If you look for it you can't find it* (Cleary, 2005). In other words, the light can illuminate your mind, but with an idea in your mind that you will "get" this light, it does not appear. When you are after something, you create a mindset of gaining activity, or more mental commotion—a separated self, looking for something. One part of your mind has separated and is chasing after a prized goal. This is like a dog chasing his own tail; lots of activity, but the goal is not accomplished. No way this will work; to find your awareness, you need to practice without a gaining idea. So how do you do this?

Actually, the light appears on its own when you become unified; this is why Yunmen cautioned against seeking it. When you settle into your own being, your own breath, your own body, when you unite body, breath, and mind, you connect with your Self. Naturally, your mind reflects the light of awareness. This light is what allows you to watch your own thoughts as they arise. Through finding the light or luminosity in your mind, you can observe the subtle movements of the mind without being pulled around by them. You enjoy a sense of grounded connection while just watching what arises in your mind—not grasping and not averting. You are developing an unfiltered intimacy with what is.

Experiencing the light that permeates your body and mind may occur reliably in meditation practice, and sesshin activities facilitate this experience. You don't need to engage in extreme physical activities or go to the end of the earth to develop familiarity with the brightening, self-reflective, and boundless qualities of mind. Just as important, please realize that the light of awareness is not limited to the experience of meditation, but can be experienced spontaneously in nature, athletic activity, relationship, art, and potentially in every spiritual or religious training. Zen does not own the process of intimacy with awareness, but it does specialize in it.

There is a risk that you will miss finding the light of awareness if you just imitate what you have been taught by a Zen teacher, if you seek some special state of mind, if you rely on memorizing what you think you are supposed to do, or if you just go through the motions. Suzuki Roshi described the hazards of imitating and going through the motions with the expression "Looks like good." You want to look good to avoid the rejection you anticipate, or you attempt to lessen hardship. You attach to the forms of practice rather than connecting with the essence of practice. "Looks like good" means that from the outside, the Zen student appears to be sincerely involved in practice, but inside the student is faking it and is more interested in avoiding imagined wounds than being present. It is the teacher's job to uncover the pretense and encourage the student to get real.

Zen invites intimacy with the light, but there is a mistake in practicing zazen as strict observance of a medieval ritual or as a means to avoid unpleasant states of mind. Zen is an experiential practice; you need to be there as yourself to connect to your awareness. It is experienced personally; it can't be found through imitating someone else in some other time and place. *You* need to actually do this despite your fear of what you may experience.

Koun Ejo, one of Dogen's disciples, said in his essay "Komyozo Zammai":

> I have some earnest advice for those who sincerely aspire to practice. Do not be pulled by a particular state of mind or by an object. Do not rely upon intellect or wisdom. Do not carry in your hands what you have learned on the seat in the sangha hall. Cast your body and mind into the Great Komyozo (the Treasury of Radiant Light) and never look back. (Okumura, 1987)

Koun Ejo admonishes us not to memorize or imitate. Instead, you must make the effort to experience unity with the radiant light of awareness. No matter how smart you are, you won't be able to do this through an intellectual approach. This is something you do, not something you study. Koun Ejo further describes opening to the light of awareness. *Then, when the light appears, throw yourself into it completely.* Discovery of the light, followed by purposeful immersion in it, leads to the next step—amplification of the light.

Amplifying the Light of Awareness

Many of you will notice that you can feel something about other people in the meditation hall without making eye contact or exchanging words. In fact, with the attention turned on, and with verbal input and output reduced, your sensory awareness is stronger, more vivid. When people are angry you can feel it, and when people are joyous you can feel that. When people are concentrating, you feel it. When we meditate, we generate a different kind of energy, and you can feel that too. When you are meditating with other people, your own ability to be present and concentrate will be amplified by their energy. It's like dolphins swimming together; they lift each other up. Meditating with others who are sincerely present and concentrating will lift you up; it will light up your mind and will amplify your awareness. This is a unique opportunity of sesshin and a benefit of practicing with others. When we do our practice together, it benefits all of us.

How do we use practice effort to amplify awareness without seeking an outcome? We throw ourselves into the process of meditation without a gaining idea. Hongzhi, Dogen's Dharma uncle, described the necessary conditions for amplifying the light in his essay "Roam and Play in Samadhi":

> *Empty and desireless, cold and thin, simple and genuine, this is the way to strike down and fold up the habits of many lifetimes. When the stains from old habits are exhausted, the original light appears, blazing through your skull, not admitting any other matters.* (Leighton, 2002)

In this passage, Hongzhi describes the light *appearing and blazing* only after the discipline has been applied to old habits of mind. We can translate his advice to very rigorous practice conditions—conditions appropriate to our age and culture—that we hope to create during sesshin. Note that he says *empty and desireless, cold and thin, simple and genuine.* He does not say "satiated and still craving, fat and sassy, complicated and duplicitous." Hongzhi places an emphasis on the letting go, the facing of hardships nakedly without props, and the complete responsibility for our own awareness. In sesshin, we try to exchange our usual tendencies, cravings, need to be right, and special requirements for simply following the practice. We do not do what we want to do or what we feel like doing. We do not engage in the complex "He said-she said," intending to put a stop to the non-cooperating factors in our life. Please allow yourself to be forlorn and hungry, tired and irritable, solely motivated to follow the schedule without your usual litany of selfish insistence on getting your way. This is part of the process of loosening the grip of our selfish demands to allow more intimate contact with a larger Self—the Self that is universally aware.

When your personal ideas and needs arise during zazen, try not to push them away; try to invest more energy into your meditative focus. Redouble your attention to your breath and mind, creating a luminous space in which to allow the thoughts and feelings to arise. Focus. Concentrate. Expand the space of awareness.

I am very sorry to report that we have had few verified accounts of enlightenment experiences resulting from sitting in a hot tub, gazing at the moon while sipping wine. In most everyday life you are often a "comfort-seeking-missile," driven forward through a mindless pursuit of relief of suffering or just relief of biological states of discomfort. Hence, Hongzhi's admonition to be *empty and desireless, cold and thin, simple and genuine*—just get down to basics so you can heighten single-mindedness. Try not to scratch that itch; try not to self soothe. Instead, take meditation itself as your energetic and intentional focus. The feeling is one of letting go of desire for comfort in exchange for pursuing the truth of this moment. This amplifies the light of awareness. This awareness may grow so strong and bright that Hongzhi describes it as *blazing through your skull*. Hongzhi has previewed for you the transformative qualities of awareness; we change not only the quantity of awareness, but also the quality. Awareness may become a transformative cauldron. At the time we merge with this light, small concerns can no longer be found, because awareness has dissolved them. As most of us know, nothing is permanent, but a strong experience of the transformative qualities of the light gives you faith in practice and encouragement to continue.

In this stage you may benefit from understanding the expressions "essence of mind" versus "content of mind." Awareness itself—the light of awareness—perceives and illuminates the contents of the mind, the formed thoughts and impulses. Awareness itself is intimate with the essence and the content of mind. As we strengthen or amplify the awareness and consider what is arising in our mind, we note a difference between the essence of mind and the contents of mind. We are strengthening our relationship to that essence within which the contents arise. Intimacy with the essence of mind, through the application of awareness to it, becomes like warm water in which the contents of mind—thoughts, feelings, and sensations—float like ice cubes. Awareness consists of two elements: essence of mind and the contents of mind. Everyday life relies on processing the contents of mind; Zen meditation deepens intimacy with the essence of mind.

If you amplify the energy with which you connect with essence, the contents of mind dissolve back into the essence. The essence now has more energy, having absorbed the energy of the dissolving contents. The essence becomes brighter, more energized, and is capable of continuing to see and dissolve more formed content—thoughts, emotions and attachments. There is fluidity to the awareness, and as you become more intimate with the essence of mind, awareness is freed from your attachment to the outcome of the compelling circumstances of content. You begin to sense your potential freedom.

Perhaps you have noticed that life seems to lurch towards disorder. We keep trying to manage and survive in a changing environment. I remember Suzuki Roshi's words about how you put everything in a boat, get into the boat, and go out to sea, fully aware that the boat will sink. It's always falling apart; that's what's true of life. To compensate for this unsatisfactoriness, we're constantly shifting and redoing and straightening ourselves out. This is another way to describe impermanence. In fact, that's really what we're working on in our practice of zazen; we're returning to shore. Practice-enlightenment is not something we get—it's a verb. The boat that is sinking is our concept of self, and we have invested everything we have in it. You cannot find peace within that sinking without confidence in your practice.

Zazen is the means through which we gain confidence in practice. I saw a sign on a local church that read: "Calm seas do not good sailors make." In zazen the sea may be wild, but we find a deeper balance. We keep returning, returning to presence and newly arising circumstances and conditions. We're shining back the radiance (Buswell, 1991). We're bringing our concentration and our awareness back to itself. This is the process that I call amplification of awareness. There is a steady return of our awareness, it grows and we participate in that growth. It is wonderful to know that there is something that grows more vital even as we age and life falls apart. Uchiyama Roshi called it *settling the Self on the self* (Wright, 1983).

Circulating the Awareness

When you have strengthened or amplified the awareness to be self aware and intimate with essence of mind, then you need to let it circulate through your body. Of course, with or without our conscious efforts, awareness is circulating. But it is good to participate. We have various sesshin activities to help you circulate the awareness. If you just sit there and contemplate your navel and your breathing, there is a tendency to become stuck. You may feel fragile; you may feel that doing meditation is the only place you are safe. You may feel baffled and disappointed when you re-enter your life. And you may be tempted to say: "Wait a minute here, you people are not following my schedule or even basic politeness."

From the beginning of Zen training, we learn to circulate awareness by connecting it with the body. We teach everyone from their first experiences of meditation to circulate energy by including their posture and their body in the meditation. Connecting with the body is an integral part of meditation instruction and practice. When aligning your posture, you scan the whole body, becoming aware of all the parts of your body and their relative comfort, discomfort or stress. The body is consciously brought into contact with vital awareness. Awareness connects with and expresses itself through aware bodily movement. This is the first way that you may begin to circulate awareness throughout the body.

There can be negative effects from isolation and self-study in a Zen retreat even when you are circulating awareness in the body. If you are meditating for several days, there is a danger that your behavior may become too self-conscious; your affect or emotions may become deadened. Most of your attention is focused on your own body, breath, and mind, and while your awareness may become activated and strengthened through this persistent effort, you may become self-absorbed and feel more isolated. Watching your arising thoughts with exquisite attentiveness is a necessary first stage, but if you continue to gaze *only* at yourself, you are in danger of becoming increasingly self-centered. It is important to not become so self-absorbed that you become isolated and lose your connection to other people and reality. While your inner life can be infinitely fascinating, you have to stay connected to your Bodhisattva vow to practice for the benefit of others.

Even though you circulate awareness and energy in your own body through the postural body scan you do during zazen, you need to learn to use your awareness in relating to other people. To avoid withdrawal from people, sesshin activities include group walking meditation, chanting, doing *oryoki*, working together, wearing robes, and listening to talks. All these sesshin activities help you circulate and integrate practice energy into your life. My experience is that when I leave my mind spacious and aware, there is room for other people to enter. Hakuin Zenji taught that meditation in action is one thousand times better than meditation in stillness. He exemplified this practice by helping the town people and using his Zen know-how and calligraphy to write on signboards for local merchants. Hakuin demonstrated that mature awareness was a dish widely served in many settings, not something meant to be enjoyed only within the monastery walls.

Hongzhi described the process of developing deeper intimacy with the absolute through being empty and desireless. These instructions were most likely meant for formal practice. You may question whether you are also required to be empty and desireless when off the cushion. Clearly no matter how much you practice, desire and suffering will arise in certain situations. What then?

There is an essential koan by the Zen philosopher Hisamatsu, *What will you do when nothing will do? What then?* When there are no practice guidelines, no sesshin rules, no schedule, and your mind has met its match—what then? Please understand that this is how your life is. More than ninety-nine percent of Western Buddhists do not live in monasteries. What do you do when you are fired, when your spouse leaves, when your child is in trouble? What then? Actually, this is not a new question; "What then?" was the question posed to the Buddha on his deathbed. Of course, the worst had come to pass; Buddha was leaving his disciples. What then?

The question of "What then?" arose in the "Mahaparinibbana Sutta" (Walshe, 1995) when the Buddha instructed his monks from his deathbed. Using women as a metaphor for (the monk's) desire in this conversation, Ananda pressed the Buddha with "What then?" Ananda persisted in questioning the Buddha about meeting with desire, even as the Buddha was dying. Ananda wanted clarification from the Buddha about how the monks should act toward women. The Buddha first responded with his policy of avoiding women and repressing the whole experience of meeting the feminine. Stay away from trouble: *Don't see them, Ananda.* Ananda continued to probe: *But if we see them, how should we behave, Lord?* Or in other words, "What then?" Avoidance didn't work, what then?

The Buddha advises further avoidance. OK, Ananda, you saw a woman even though you didn't want to see a woman—what then? *Do not speak to them, Ananda.* But Ananda perceived that not speaking to women wouldn't work. What if women still tried to talk to you? What if they were there for the Dharma? What then? Finally Ananda asked the Buddha what to do if all previous efforts have failed to avoid contact with women: *But if they speak to us, how should we behave, Lord?* Only after this third inquiry does the Buddha offer realistic practice. If all else fails, what then? Call up awareness: *Practice mindfulness, Ananda.* That's what!

You too will need to meet your desires with awareness. Trying to avoid desire, suffering, or loss won't work; it will still arise. Circulation of awareness means that you can call on awareness when you are out and about. With slings and arrows, with arising desire, you can dial into awareness. Through engaging and connecting awareness with activity in sesshin, you have learned to apply and circulate awareness. Even when you have stressed out your body-mind equipment, and even during emotionally demanding experiences, learn to call on the awareness you have been developing. It's down to this: will you trust your old patterns, or will you call up awareness?

While I have heard that there are Buddhist practitioners who have transcended all emotions, I have not yet met any such beings. I hold open the possibility that they exist. For most of us, though, there is no question that we will continue to struggle with emotion. After all, that is one reason that you came to practice. Sadly, people at some Zen centers always seem to look and act serious and dour, as if to say, "I don't have any feelings, I'm a Zen person." Actually, I think there is a danger of becoming a Zen Zombie—someone who has lost ability to enjoy this human life. I find it distressing that Zen can be harmful to your emotional life. Joko Beck taught that if you don't find a way to use Zen off the cushion and in your daily life you are better off not practicing at all. Which brings me to the fourth stage of awareness practice—using it freely in your life.

Using Awareness Freely

Awareness must move from the absolute state of awareness itself into the relative world of thoughts, feelings, impulses, and activities. This is the teaching of the *Mahapranjaparamita Sutra, The Heart Sutra: Form is no other than emptiness, emptiness no other than form.* In other words, awareness itself needs to embrace and guide your particular life. Just as awareness was amplified when the contents of awareness were dissolved into the essence of awareness, so the essence returns to the relative by cooking up creativity specific to the moment. Like pouring nectar between two cups, the absolute is poured into the relative, and the relative is poured into the absolute. You are the intermediary, receiving the awareness and using it freely and flexibly.

Alive and aware, zazen is not a relic or holy activity and it is not static—it moves. When a student asked Joshu, "What is meditation?" He answered "Non-meditation." The student was puzzled and asked Joshu what he meant. He shouted: "It's alive!" (Green, 2001). Meditation that becomes fixated in Zen teachings or dependent on sitting on the cushion is not conducive to liberation.

Fukushima Roshi taught that the Zen word for freedom, *jiyu*, means *depending on the Self*. He emphasized that the unselfish self is the one that you can depend on. He clarified that the meaning of freedom in the traditional Zen lexicon differs from the Western use of the word. *Jiyu* means "freedom to" in Zen language. Westerners think of freedom as "freedom from." "Freedom to" means freedom to engage flexibly and creatively, without obstruction. "Freedom from" means freedom from oppression or freedom from suffering in the Westerner's mind. Fukushima Roshi taught that while Zen training is strict and disciplined, the Zen path only reaches fruition when it enables creativity and flexibility in your life.

Suzuki Roshi enjoyed lecturing on the two ninth-century Chinese Zen companions, Seppo and Ganto, to highlight relationship and Zen freedom. After these two monks received Dharma transmission from Tokusan, they went on pilgrimage. Even after realization, they were integrating and refining their awareness. Rather than entering secular life, they visited many temples to engage in practice and discussion to refine their awareness and understanding. While traveling they were caught in a heavy snowstorm and took refuge in a cave. Seppo was sitting all night long. Ganto was sleeping, and he was at ease. But every time Ganto woke up, he saw Seppo sitting in meditation. Ganto said to Seppo: *This village is like a fortified town, why don't you sleep?* In other words, you are rigidly guarding yourself and your practice, what's up? Seppo, rubbing his chest said: *I do not feel easy in my heart.* Ganto answered: *Please tell me one by one what you have acquired.* Seppo recounted all the Zen principles he had learned from Master Tozan and Tokusan.

Ganto cared about his friend and listened patiently while Seppo recounted all that he had memorized in the Dharma hall. When his friend had finished, Ganto spoke to him emphatically, speaking from his own experience and from his own heart. Ganto said, *Don't you know that which enters through the front gate is not the family treasure. Let it flow from your heart!* Seppo had his first awakening experience then and there (Foster and Shoemaker, 1997).

In this traditional Zen story friendship and caring provide the cauldron for Seppo's realization. There was trust and honesty between the two friends; they were connected emotionally. The friendship must have helped Seppo finally integrate what he had studied and practiced over so many years. Seppo exposed his sense of deficiency, and Ganto, his friend, met him with a stream of loving heartfelt awareness, a connected wisdom that included an original and creative command. *Let it flow from your heart.*

As you begin to connect with your own awareness in sesshin, remember that you are in it for the long haul. You may use your sesshin time to learn discipline to amplify the light, and you may learn to connect the practice to your activities with others. Finally, you need to enjoy the fruit of this practice with friends, loved ones, at work or with family. Let it flow from your heart!

Works Cited

Buswell, Jr., Robert E. *Tracing Back the Radiance: Chinul's Korean Way of Zen.* Honolulu: University of Hawaii Press, 1991.

Dogen, Eihei and Kosho Uchiyama, commentary. *From the Zen Kitchen to Enlightenment: Refining Your Life.* Trans. Thomas Wright. New York: Weatherhill, 1983.

Ejo, Koun. "Komyozo Zammai." *Shikantaza: An Introduction to Zazen.* Trans. Shokaku Okumura. 3rd ed. Tokyo: Sotoshu Shumucho, 1996.

Hsien, Hsueh Tou Ch'ung and Yuan Wu. *The Blue Cliff Record.* Trans. Thomas Cleary and J. C. Cleary. Boston: Shambhala, 2005.

"Mahaparinibbana Sutta." *The Long Discourses of the Buddha: A Translation of the Digha Nikaya.* Trans. Maurice Walshe. Boston: Wisdom Publications, 1995.

The Recorded Sayings of Zen Master Joshu. Trans. James Green. Boston: Shambhala, 2001.

The Roaring Stream: A Zen Reader. Ed. Nelson Foster and Jack Shoemaker. New York: Harper Perennial, 1997.

Zhengjue, Hongzhi. "Roam and Play in Samadhi." *Cultivating the Empty Field: The Silent Illumination of Zen Master Hongzhi.* Trans. Taigen Dan Leighton with Yi Wu. Boston: Tuttle Publishing, 2000.

Misha Shungen Merrill, *the head teacher of Zen Heart Sangha in Menlo Park and Woodside, California, has practiced Zen since 1984. She was ordained as a Zen priest in 1988 and received Dharma Transmission in 1998 from her teacher, Keido Les Kaye Roshi, the abbot of Kannon Do Zen Center and Dharma Heir in the lineage of Shunryu Suzuki Roshi, the founder of San Francisco Zen Center. As an adjunct to her Zen training, she practiced Japanese Tea Ceremony in the Musha-no-koji-senke school for the past twenty-six years. Misha also teaches elementary and middle school children at Peninsula School in Menlo Park where she is the librarian. She resides in Woodside with her husband and four-footed friends.*

Stewardship: The Bodhisattva Way

Misha Shungen Merrill

When I began meditation practice, my first Zen center had the normal work positions of *ino, tenzo,* and *doan*—all Japanese titles that came from our founder, Shunryu Suzuki Roshi. There were many other work positions, however, that came under the English heading of *steward* including dharma school, community outreach, sewing, and lecture recording. I never questioned the term and when it came time to start my own group, I set up our work practice in a similar way. Over the years, I have realized that this was a very particular word choice made by my teacher and I began to think about that word and why it seemed so appropriate.

What is a steward? Webster's Dictionary tells us that a steward is *one entrusted with the management of the household or estate of another* and that *to entrust is to trust or invest with a trust or duty, to assign the care of something.* So stewardship is *entrustment:* being trusted to take care of something for others. The word *stewardship* is often used today by environmental groups or governments when a small group of people are entrusted (or take on the responsibility themselves) to take care of something for the country as a whole. But what would a steward be in terms of practice?

My teacher, Keido Les Kaye, used to talk a lot of *taking care practice,* something I think he learned from Suzuki Roshi. Many of my early memories of practice with him were about working on some project—a stone wall, a garden path, painting walls—with patience and care. I remember that the stone wall took years, and I watched as new members would kneel in the dirt with him as they carefully chose the next rock and fit it into place. There was no sense of urgency or efficiency, no need to get it done. He was showing by example how to take care of even the smallest thing (like a rock) and appreciate your relationship to it.

Stewardship is at the core of Mahayana Buddhism, exemplified by the beings called bodhisattvas. These are the buddhas who vow to help others attain enlightenment before enjoying their own. One of the most famous is the Bodhisattva of Compassion, Avalokitesvara (Kannon).

She is often depicted with one thousand hands, each containing an eye, with which she takes care of the world—surely marking her as the ultimate steward!

The practice of stewardship begins with Avalokitesvara, but there are many teaching stories that embrace this practice throughout the history of Zen. The founder of Soto Zen, Eihei Dogen Zenji, wrote of one such experience upon meeting an old tenzo during his sojourn in China:

> *During my stay at Mt. Tiantong, a priest named Yong from Qingyuan Prefecture held the position of tenzo. One day after the noon meal when I was walking along the eastern covered walkway to a sub-temple called Chaoran Hut, he was in front of the Buddha Hall drying some mushrooms in the sun. He had a bamboo stick in his hand and no hat on his head. The sun was very hot, scorching the pavement. It looked very painful; his backbone was bent like a bow and his eyebrows were as white as a crane.*
>
> *I went up to the tenzo and asked, "How long have you been a monk?"*
>
> *"Sixty-eight years," he replied.*
>
> *"Why don't you let a helper do it?"*
>
> *"Others are not myself."*
>
> *"Reverend Sir, you follow regulations exactly, but as the sun is so hot why do you work so hard as this?"*
>
> *"Until when should I wait?"*
>
> *So I stopped talking. As I was walking further along the covered walkway, I thought about how important the tenzo's position is.* (Tanahashi, 1985)

This story presents the essence of stewardship: others are not myself. The life of a steward—of a person of practice—is absolute; no one can live it for us, no one can feel it for us because others are not me. Intellectual understanding can take us only so far; until we have an actual experience of this absolute nature, we will keep trying to manipulate our life, wanting everything to be just a little bit different, a little bit more comfortable. The steward is the one who owns the pain, the joy, the responsibility of life and, therefore, experiences true freedom: the end of dualistic thinking that is always constructing a second-hand reality.

In true stewardship, comparisons are useless; the old tenzo's admonition that *others are not myself* is reminding us not to worry about what others are doing, but what we know we should be doing. During my first practice period as a newly ordained monk, I was part of the *doan ryo*, the group responsible for all the activities within the zendo. This included taking care of all zendo forms (instruments, chanting, services), as well as being assigned a particular area of work which in my case was to be the *chiden*. This is the person who takes care of all of the altars and I spent long hours trimming candles and cleaning incensers, eager to show my skill and dedication to the teacher and the community.

There was another member of the *doan ryo*, however, who seemed to do as little as possible, often retreating to his cabin during work period to avoid his daily assignment. Eventually this began to annoy me as I thought he was not pulling his weight as part of the *doan* team. I finally went to speak to the head teacher about this, thinking that he should be aware that this person was shirking his responsibility. Instead of rolling his eyes or sharply reprimanding me (which was what I really deserved!), the teacher was very kind in his response. Rather than focusing on what the other student was not doing, he turned me completely upside down by saying, "What I see in front of me is a competent Zen student doing her job." I was chagrined to realize that I had been caught in *comparing mind*, concerned about what someone else was doing rather than focusing on what I should be doing—my stewardship as *chiden*—the best I could do.

After studying in China, Dogen returned to Japan and wrote once more about the tenzo's position:

> *After I came back to Japan I stayed for a few years at Kennin Monastery, where they had the tenzo's position but did not understand its meaning ... the monk who held the tenzo's position ... did not personally manage all of the preparations for the morning and noon meals. He used an ignorant, insensitive servant, and he had him do everything—both the important and the unimportant tasks. He never checked whether the servant's work was done correctly or not, as though it would be shameful or inappropriate to do so ... He stayed in his own room, where he would lie down, chat, read sutras, or chant. For days and months he did not come close to a pan, buy cooking equipment, or think about menus. How could he have known that these are Buddha activities?*
> (Tanahashi, 1985)

The *tenzo* made a common mistake, one that we are all guilty of at some time or another: believing that certain activities (like chanting or reading sutras) are somehow more important than so-called mundane activities like cooking or cleaning. Dogen's understanding—and hopefully ours—is that all activities are Buddha's activities and therefore worthy of our care and attention. When we understand this, true stewardship occurs.

I had a marvelous teaching about our tendency to judge certain activities to be worthy or not of our *taking care practice* when I visited Plum Village in France many years ago. This is the main Western practice center of Zen Master Thich Nhat Hanh, and practitioners come from all over the world during the summer months to receive his teachings and participate in the community's practice. Because there are so many people, all visitors are assigned to a smaller practice group led by one of the monks or nuns as a way to keep the practice personal and to organize work practice in a manageable way.

My friend and I arrived too late on the first day to be assigned to a group, so we attended a couple of lectures and meditation sessions until the next morning when we were then assigned. As long-term Zen students we were well trained in work practice, and so when it was announced that there would be a work period after lunch we were both ready and willing to do our part for the benefit of the community. The nun who led our group had a list of jobs that needed doing and one by one people raised their hands to volunteer. However, when it came to cleaning the bathrooms—something my own teacher felt to be one of the most important jobs anyone could do—we were very surprised when our two hands were the only ones in the air, despite the fact that several people still had no assignment.

The nun needed one more person and finally another woman grudgingly agreed to do it. The three of us went off to the bathrooms (which were really glorified Port-a-Potties and fairly stinky!) and proceeded to do our job. While my friend and I were being very thorough and cleaning every surface, I watched as this other person raced through the job doing as little as possible. As she left us, she remarked that she wanted to get done quickly so that she could get a good place in the meditation hall for the afternoon lecture.

At the time I was surprised that she had made such a distinction between cleaning the bathrooms and hearing the teacher's lecture, but after years of teaching others I realize that this is a common mistake reinforced by years in our so-called *normal* life. When we are really paying attention, we begin to notice that we are always making these kinds of distinctions, creating a whole hierarchy of dualistic judgments—good, bad, important, unimportant, like, dislike, sacred, or mundane—and that everyone else is, too. Like many, this woman had missed the most important point: whatever the teacher would be lecturing on were just words pointing to the importance of taking-care practice—steward-ship—not the actual practice itself which in her case was cleaning the bathroom.

I remember him talking that afternoon about the care of a rose that he held in his hand. It was beginning to droop and as he talked about taking care of each thing that is in front of us, he carefully snipped off the end of the stem and placed it back in fresh water. In minutes, that rose had begun to look alive again and I thought, "That's it—it's just the same with a stinky toilet! A little bit of extra care, of real attention, and it is alive and useful again." Everything is like this and only we can do it—others are not myself and no one can clean that toilet for you, nor cut the stem of a wilting flower that is in your hand. We must each be a steward for every moment that arises in front of us. It is important to understand that the phrase *others are not myself* also means that others *are* myself because of the truth of emptiness. Not understanding this, we will fall into dualistic thinking of right, wrong, self, or other, and then fall into the trap of pride in our position or performance because we believe it to be "mine."

When I was in Japan years ago doing a summer practice period in a small temple, the abbot whose temple this was came for a visit. Naturally, our teacher wanted the temple to be absolutely perfect for his teacher's arrival, so we started cleaning with a vengeance! I was asked to wash windows and after replying "Hai!" (Yes!), I went off to find clean-ing equipment. After fifteen minutes the best I could come up with was a rather soiled rag from the bathroom area, a bucket with hot water, and my own bar of soap. I could not understand why there were no clean-ing chemicals or even simple soap, but my job was to wash windows and I had to find a way to do it. However, once I had started washing in this manner, the head monk came up and very politely said, "Shungen-san, no ... please, this way." And then he pulled out a piece of newspa-per, folding it in half over and over again until it was no bigger than a sponge. He dipped it in water and then pressed it against the window until the surface was wet. Then he unfolded it enough to find a dryer part, refolded it to the same size, and used it to dry the window which now shone perfectly clean!

Apparently, the ink of the newspaper served as a chemical cleaner and had the advantage of not leaving any material from a cleaning cloth on the surface! He handed me the newspaper and I proceeded to clean dozens of windows in this fashion. Later I reflected on the kindness of his instruction—he never once admonished me for doing it "wrong," nor did he ever say that his way was "right." He merely asked me to do it the way that everyone else was doing it. That was my first real understanding of emptiness: there is no me or you, only us. And when that happens, dualistic thinking falls away and real freedom occurs.

In the first story of the old *tenzo* and Dogen Zenji, Dogen asks the *tenzo* why he is working so hard in the hot sun and the *tenzo* replies: *Until when should I wait?* The *tenzo* has accepted responsibility for his job; he knows that he is the steward entrusted with this work and once this is fully accepted, the next question is: when is the best time? Right now! If we really wish to be free from self-concern and foolish dualistic distinctions, now is the only time that actually exists. The true steward realizes: only I can take care of the self from morning to night, only I can receive life in this moment. Stewardship means that we cannot wait for others to do what must be done or until someone tells us to do it; we must take responsibility for things even if they are not directly our responsibility but we see that it needs to be done. As the poet Rumi wrote:

> *There is one thing in this world which you must never forget to do. If you forget everything else and not this, there is nothing to worry about, but if you remember everything else and forget this, then you will have done nothing in your life. It is as if a king has sent you to some country to do a task, and you perform a hundred other services, but not the one he sent you to do. So human beings come to this world to do particular work. That work is the purpose, and each is specific to the person. If you don't do it, it's as though a knife of the finest tempering were nailed into a wall to hang things on. For a penny an iron nail could be bought to serve for that.*
> (Barks, 1997)

When we penetrate the truth of no-self, taking care of what is in front of us means taking care of all beings. That is the vow of a bodhisattva; that is the work of a steward of the world. Stewards are entrusted with a duty to take care of things for others; in Zen, stewards are the bodhisattvas who make it possible for all beings to practice together in harmony. We come to do particular work starting with the self, but we do not end there: as bodhisattvas, we do this work for all beings until everyone wakes up together.

Works Cited

Dogen, Eihei. "Tenzo Kyokun." *Moon in a Dewdrop: Writings of Zen Master Dogen.* Ed. Kazuaki Tanahashi. San Francisco: North Point Press, 1985.

Rumi, Jalal Al-Din. *The Illuminated Rumi.* Trans. Coleman Barks, illus. Michael Green. New York: Broadway Books, 1997.

Eido Frances Carney *received Dharma Transmission from Niho Tetsumei Roshi in 1997 at Entsuji Temple, Japan, in lineage with the hermit priest Ryokan. She is the founder and teacher of Olympia Zen Center in Washington, and abbess of Fukujuji Temple in Kurashiki, Japan. She is the editor of* Receiving the Marrow, Teachings on Dogen by Soto Zen Women Priests *and the author of* Kakurenbo Or the Whereabouts of Zen Priest Ryokan.

Rattling Teeth

Eido Frances Carney

... never rattle your teeth until you are fully awake and aware. —Ryokan

What shall we do then about our need to talk? When Ryokan uses the words "awake" and "aware," is he writing about stumbling out of bed in the morning and waiting until we are somewhat conscious before speaking? Or does he mean "Awake" and "Aware" as to speak only from a realized practice? We might answer: of course he means speaking from the mind of awareness, that which is essential to right speech. Yet even if someone has had awakening experiences, these are momentary events and the relative world must still be negotiated where most of us are not "fully Awake and Aware." We live in a relative world with an array of levels of consciousness and many of us are oblivious to the consequences of our actions much of the time. No matter how deep an Awakening, we still discover the rattling of teeth at one time or another with some degree of unconscious activity. Thus we have the Buddha seal of speaking from Awakening as a Noble Truth and the precept of Right Speech for speaking from the action of human fairness and peace.

These days we have a sense of incivility in our public discourse. Perhaps the political arena and our popular culture instigate this behavior, but the cause of the blaming, hurtful, bullying, misdirected speech is less important than understanding the effects of such poisonous dialogue. Of all the difficulties we have in our relationships, thoughtless, flippant, imprudent speech gives rise to the greatest ills. Which of us doesn't want to call back a hastily spoken meanness that seeds separation? Who hasn't been the recipient of a verbal wounding that festers hurt? Who has not seen the path to war paved by heated threats that summon armies? Has anyone not played out an angry speech in the mind to settle a feud? We're all in it, one way or another, and the business of sharing language is not easy. Yet we speak. We speak even when speech is nonverbal. We say something even in silence and stillness. And we must involve ourselves and interact, eat and play together, have fun, pray, make music, laugh, joke, grieve, weep, say loving words, encourage our children, and somehow master the emotional field in the language of making sense and meaning together.

Right speech is one branch of the Eightfold Path found in the Buddha's Four Noble Truths; this practice helps us to reside in the deep heart of happiness and come to terms with suffering. Right speech at once ennobles everyone together in practice, because it expresses Buddha Nature as a generative imperative in our human interactions. The ten prohibitory precepts that we vow as Soto Zen practitioners also have everything to do with active right speech. The Buddha was well aware that in this area of communication and relationship we need the most help. Clear and right speech is essential to the harmony of our Sanghas, marriages, children, and friendships. Clear and right speech has also to do with what we sit with, how we hear the language of the world around us, and what we allow ourselves to dwell on in our own minds. Other precepts such as "Not dwelling in anger," or "Not praising oneself at the expense of others," address keeping internal speech in right balance so that we do not resort to problematic language for selfish or shortsighted reasons.

If one is not ashamed to tell a lie then there is no other evil that he would not do, said the Buddha. We all know that once we exaggerate the size of the fish we caught, we ourselves begin to believe that the fish was twice as large as it actually was. Social researchers have investigated the nature of lying and found that once a person tells one lie, it becomes easier and easier to tell more, and lying can become habitual. A lie is simply set up to make ourselves look good, or to hide something we've done wrong. We don't want to get into trouble, so we fudge and cover over the actuality, injuring our own integrity in the process.

The practice of awareness is to know what is operative in us when we speak and to commit ourselves to choose to speak with integrity rather than deception. A response in a difficult situation might have consequences in either direction. If we speak the truth, we might have to pay a penalty for some kind of infraction. If we lie, we have a worse consequence, which is a poisonous outcome. For instance, Ray Bradbury in *Zen in the Art of Writing* says that if we plagiarize, if we do not stand in our own field of creative honesty, it will take us at least three years just to recover from one single act of piracy, one act of using someone else's words as if they were our own. Our honor and character are vastly diminished by deceit and we will know within that we misrepresented ourselves. We were not what we said we were. Years of dogged character restoration are a high price to pay to make ourselves look good. But the true way of right speech is not rooted in personal concern; it is an act of clarity and openness with others because of the truth of Buddha Nature, the groundwork of our essential being and connectedness. This is true even if, at this moment, we have not realized it.

Involvement in right speech requires recognizing that all species have their forms of communication. Listening is at the deep core of attention to right speech. Listening to nonverbal speech and the dimensions of how and what the world is saying to all sentience is right engagement with a Buddhist practice life. Various species are calling for help, and while some people are listening and responding, many are ignorant of the pleas, because they don't recognize or hear a different language. In this moment, we are being informed directly by the distressed voices of trees, plant life, mountains, rivers, oceans, land and sea mammals, sea species, insects, reptiles. To ignore the world around us is to listen with only one ear since every form of life is communicating its existence. As conscious Buddhists, it is our calling to try to respond to the suffering species unable to stand against predatory human pressure. At root level, we can listen and hold these voices in our Zazen, opening ourselves to the global collective of breathing life. We can be the ears of Avalokiteshvara, hearing the cries of suffering and responding with compassion to the needs around us. In doing so, we immediately support all efforts to face the problem of climate change and to call upon our whole society to realize what we must do to bring civilization through the trials of climate revision. This activity is called Right Speech. *The whole universe in all ten directions is a monk's everyday speech,* says Dogen Zenji. Nothing is excluded.

Listening begins in the womb, and throughout our lives we are living in a field of vibrations active all around us with some vibrations pulsing at decibels from a slight whisper to sounds that can rupture a human eardrum. Other high pitched or low toned sounds vibrate beyond our ability to hear, although animals and insects can register some of these frequencies. Absolute silence is artificial and is created to test what happens to the human mind when we are beyond any sonic information. I want to say that there is still some form of speech, even if we are in a totally darkened room with no sound. There is continuous speech in the work of the brain and there is continuous speech in the absence of speech. Perhaps I want to say that consciousness itself is a field of communication of one kind or another that creates a field of continuous interactions. There is only the flow of activity in each moment, and this is what I'll call "speech being."

Dogen Zenji believed that speech was a means to bring about Awakening. He used language to teach and we have his written words that bring his teachings alive right now, speaking to us directly.

> *Even though it may be merely for a moment, when someone, whilst sitting upright in meditation, puts the mark of the Buddha seal upon his three types of volitional actions— namely, those of body, speech and thought—the whole physical universe and everything in it becomes and is the Buddha seal; all of space, throughout, becomes and is enlightenment. You should do your utmost to thoroughly explore through your training the arising of body, speech, and mind, along with your inner experiences and the outer conditions that affect you.* (Nearman, 2007)

Dogen Zenji expresses that the development of our awareness of speech, lifted out of the purely relative and functional and into the state of the pure practice of right speech, transforms us and manifests the totality of our being in the ten directions. Thus, right speech is not merely a prohibitory exercise, but a means to fully realize and express enlightenment.

For Ryokan, right speech was an extremely important practice. He voices his teaching in practical ways, saying that kind and compassionate words keep us on a correct path that honors the teachers and the teachings.

> *When you encounter those who are wicked, unrighteous, foolish, dim-witted, deformed, vicious, chronically ill, lonely, unfortunate or handicapped you should think: "How can I save them?" And even if there is nothing you can do, at least you must not indulge in feelings of arrogance, superiority, derision, scorn, or abhorrence, but should immediately manifest sympathy and compassion. If you fail to do so, you should feel ashamed and deeply reproach yourself saying: "How far I have strayed from the Way! How can I betray the old sages? I take their words as an admonition to myself."*
> (Abe and Haskel, 1996)

Here, Ryokan is considering the internal dialogue and thinking patterns that can steer us away from our vows. He reminds us to manifest sympathy and compassion, to keep clear communication as we walk down the street in our towns or cities, in our supermarkets, or wherever we go in daily life. We are not better than anyone else, even someone fallen down in the gutter. He urges us to guard our tongues and keep in mind the internal chatter and never engage in hurtful conversation as much as possible. Our own interior conversation is a primary area of concern, so that we do not develop a misshapen space within ourselves that does not live up to our true spiritual potential. We can have a wrong view of ourselves as well as others. Condemnation directed at our own self is just as harmful as condemnation directed toward another. Ryokan says: *Always keep control of your mind. The mind is fearsome as a poisonous snake, a wild animal, or a murderous brigand. It is hard to restrain as a mad elephant without a chain or an ape free to leap among the treetops. It must be promptly subdued and not allowed to run wild* (Abe and Haskel, 1996).

The dedication in our morning ceremony calls for: *Lasting peace of the Sangha; tranquility of daily practice; dissolution of all misfortune; fulfillment of all relations.* To this end, Ryokan's counsel on right speech for the health of a Sangha is lengthy, but useful to put into practice. He recommends that we: not gossip, not triangulate by speaking behind the back of another or carrying stories to one another, not argue, not talk back rudely, not ignore others, not speak when angry, not bad-mouth others. His list is long and these are but a few, yet important, recommendations for maintaining harmony and working out our differences, which are bound to arise in this human soup. These prohibitions are simple manners—not only for Sangha, but also for families, work groups, or any assembly of people intent on living in a healthy and virtuous way. Each one involves applying and using wisdom in our practice. If we have a difficult time with someone, we can use personal restraint to take the time to ask whether what we want to say is beneficial to this person. While something beneficial may be very difficult to say, we can bring our own selves to a quiet, settled mind and be at ease. Then we can ask ourselves if it is possible to say what needs to be said so that our response can be received and clearly heard without injury to the person. *Wise speech is a gate to what the Dharma illumines for by means of it we will recognize that all names, voicings, and words are simply like vibrations,* says Dogen Zenji (Nearman, 2007).

If we have caused injury to someone or to ourselves, we can face the matter in Zazen, working our way toward the central issue of love. Ultimately we've been given language to express love. Zazen is the ground where we hear the speech of the lotus flower emerging from the mud of our existence and restoring our acquaintance with a pure heart. Zazen is where we equalize and feel the grasp of arrogant speech turn into a phantom with no hold on us. Zazen is where the true speech of posture becomes the Samadhi of speechless speech. Zazen tempers the heated mind and transforms the gnarling of chattering despondency. In Zazen we restore intimacy in our interactions and in our right relations.

We can each be happier and manifest a thriving environment if we speak with clarity instead of with the mind of delusion. Instead of anger, we speak with kindness; instead of greed, we speak with generosity. We can borrow the words of Ryokan and say to ourselves each morning: *How can I betray the old sages? I take their words as an admonition to myself!* Then we can stand in the strength of Buddha Dharma, realize our essential equality, celebrate our interconnectedness, and manifest the true Sangha, allowing the rattle of teeth to turn into a song of praise.

Works Cited

Bradbury, Ray. *Zen in the Art of Writing.* Santa Barbara: Joshua Odell Editions, 1994.

Dogen, Eihei. *Shobogenzo.* Trans. Hubert Nearman. Mt. Shasta, CA: Shasta Abbey Press, 2007.

Ryokan, Daigu. *Great Fool, Zen Master Ryokan.* Trans. Ryuichi Abe and Peter Haskel. Honolulu: Univ. of Hawaii Press, 1996.

---. *The Zen Poems of Ryokan.* Trans. Nobuyuki Yuasa. Princeton, NJ: Princeton University Press, 1981.

Rev. Teijo Munnich, *abbess of Great Tree Zen Women's Temple, is a Soto Zen priest and Dharma Heir of Dainin Katagiri Roshi. She received formal training at Hokyoji in Minnesota, Tassajara Zen Mountain Center in California, and Hosshinji Sodo in Japan. Great Tree Zen Women's Temple is a residential practice center for women and a retreat and practice center for men and children, near Asheville, North Carolina. She also serves as teacher for the Zen Center of Asheville and Charlotte Zen Meditation Society.*

The Middle Path: A Little Bit of Nothin'

Teijo Munnich

When I first started practicing Buddhism, I was looking for balance in my life. In the first few lines of the Buddha's first discourse, he emphasizes just that, discussing the importance of the Middle Way. This is what the Buddha said:

> Bhikkhus, these two extremes ought not to be practiced by one who has gone forth from the household life. What are the two? There is devotion to the indulgence of sense-pleasures . . . and there is devotion to self-mortification. . . . Avoiding both these extremes, the Tathagata has realized the Middle Path: it gives vision, it gives knowledge, and it leads to calm, to insight, to enlightenment, to Nibbana. And what is that Middle Path . . . ? It is simply the Noble Eightfold Path, namely, right view, right thought, right speech, right action, right livelihood, right effort, right mindfulness, right concentration. This is the Middle Path realized by the Tathagata, which gives vision, which gives knowledge, and which leads to calm, to insight, to enlightenment, to Nibbana. (Rahula, 1975)

After making this statement, the Buddha goes on to talk about the Four Noble Truths, the fourth of which is the Eightfold Path. So when I was first introduced to The Four Noble Truths by my teacher, Dainin Katagiri Roshi, I thought it was a worthwhile endeavor to study them one by one. But right off the bat, I struggled to understand the first truth, which was presented to me as: *Human life is suffering.* I simply disagreed. If anyone looked at my life they could see that it was mostly not suffering. To say that human life is suffering just didn't make sense to me. I realized that I should probably look more deeply, since those far wiser than I believed that this was true.

When I tried to look further into the First Noble Truth, however, I still had some difficulty. Even if one dismisses the word *suffering* and concentrates on alternate meanings of *dukkha*, the word the Buddha used, there is still the problem of how to understand what *dukkha* is. I tried, but quickly moved on to the Second Noble Truth: the cause, which is desire. But because I didn't understand what *dukkha* was, looking into the cause didn't help much. The Third Noble Truth is cessation, that we can be free from *dukkha.* But hey! What is *dukkha?* Then I remembered that the Buddha started his discourse by talking about the Fourth Noble Truth as the path to awaken to the Middle Way, so I decided that's where I should start.

Practicing the Eightfold Path

My first pursuit was the meaning of *right* in this context. Most sources I read explained that it was not right as opposed to wrong, but they didn't mention how to understand it. I got some insight into this with something Katagiri Roshi told us: that the Sanskrit word for right is *samma,* which comes from a term that means "to unite" (Katagiri, 1998). So, rather than seeing the Eightfold Path as a list of specific ways to be or behave, *samma* suggests that we consider behavior that harmonizes with all of life. This points us to the relatedness of all of life, and directs us to consider the bigger picture of life rather than getting stuck in our personal needs and wishes. *Samma* encourages us to consider how our understanding, our thinking, our speech, our actions, our livelihood, our effort, our mindfulness, and our meditation can benefit all beings and can help us experience unity.

Right View

The first aspect of the Eightfold Path is usually translated as right view. Right view is commonly seen as understanding the Four Noble Truths. In other words, in order to know what right view is, we have to understand the first three truths—what is *dukkha,* what is its cause, and what does cessation mean? There's no way around it, this is where we have to start.

The First Truth, *dukkha,* is the feeling of discontent. It feels a little like a deep itch that we can't scratch, yet we believe that, if we dig deep enough, we will eventually be able to get to it. We feel that when we find the right access, we'll be able to eradicate the itching forever. But though we try and try again, we continue to find that we are unable to relieve the itching. Sometimes we may hit it just right, but the itching returns. This causes us to either experience a sense of failure or to run around looking for a new method.

Moments of satisfaction that we feel about ourselves and life in general are short-lived. Both the fact that things are constantly changing in life and the perceptions we have of how life could or should be cause us to be constantly chasing after something different from how things are. Even when we get what we want, it doesn't last, and when we don't get what we want, we feel as if we've failed. Every transition in life is a moment of letting go and experiencing the reality of this moment. If we can't recognize this, we suffer: from fear of change we don't understand, or from the experience of loss when what we thought we had for good dissolves.

It is usually said that the Second Noble Truth, the cause of *dukkha*, is desire, clinging, grasping. The desire is to get something we think will give us lasting happiness: we want to be smarter, wiser, more attractive, thinner, sexier, more flexible. The clinging is to try to hold on to something that has brought us pleasure; the grasping is not being able to let go when things change. Desire is based on what we often call "control issues."

The Third Truth is cessation of the suffering of *dukkha*. Cessation doesn't mean that we are totally free from yearning, it simply means that we recognize the feeling of yearning and aren't gripped by its influence, so it is no longer a source of suffering. Seeing the yearning and understanding its cause gives us the clarity we need to see the possibilities of each moment and know how to proceed, going forward in spite of difficulties or letting go and changing direction when necessary.

My experience of the fourth truth, the Eightfold Path, is that it is a reminder to be clear in every aspect of our lives and live in ways that bring about balance. Practicing the path helps us to keep in touch with what is happening in each moment and to respond with wisdom. When we try to practice it, we find the best way to respond to each situation.

Right view means simply to see things as they really are without grabbing or denying. We humans are so easily distracted by promises of happiness or wishes to escape what we don't like. And, because things are constantly changing and interdependent, the belief that there is a lasting happiness to be found or that we can get away from what we don't like will create the suffering of *dukkha*. Right view is to be free from the delusion of permanence and independence.

I began to get a glimpse of right view during an early session in Alexander Technique, a method of observation through which we can find ease in our bodies by noticing body habits and releasing them. In order to notice, we have to tune in to what we are feeling and where we are feeling it.

When a woman named Helene came to the monastery where I was practicing in Japan, we immediately became friends. Early in our conversations I learned that she was a teacher of Alexander Technique, something I'd been interested in for a long time, but had not taken the time to pursue. She was eager to show me some things and began to do hands-on work with me very quickly. But I felt resistance to what she was trying to show me. I felt physically uncomfortable with her suggestions, especially about zazen posture. I had asked Katagiri Roshi to help me with my posture at one time and I was holding myself exactly as he had shown me. It never occurred to me that what he showed me might not be right for my body. At the time I thought because he was Japanese he knew everything about Zen.

As much as I liked Helene, I lost my enthusiasm for working with her in this way and tried to change the subject when she brought it up. But she persisted. I felt awkward saying no, so I went along with her, though in my head I was still resisting. Then I suddenly noticed what my mind was doing, and I wondered, "Why am I resisting? What am I afraid of? What is the worst possible thing that could happen even if what she's telling me doesn't work?" I realized there was no good answer, and I gave in and decided to try what she was suggesting. It was a turning point for me. In addition to learning a great deal about my body habits, I became very aware of how much my perceptions affect my ability to see life directly. The moment I recognized my resistance, my mind let loose of my fixed ideas about my body and opened up space for new ways of seeing it. My fixed ideas about how to use my body prevented me from recognizing the obstacle I was creating for myself.

Right view is not a matter of seeing things in a particular way. At a young age we create a structure of thought that helps us make sense of all the things we encounter in life. Whenever we encounter a new idea, we try to find where it fits into the understanding we've created so far. If it doesn't fit into what we understand, we discard it. We continue to build on this thought structure throughout our lives, turning it into a definition of reality. Although adhering to this structure as reality helps us to function in society, it is nothing more than a single view of reality, and it makes it difficult for us to think outside the box. We forget that we're the ones who created our belief system—the box—and we become one-sided in our thinking. Right view means to find the Middle Way.

To do this we have to see life anew in each moment. Dogen Zenji says that there are 6,400,099,150 moments in a day. That means things are moving swiftly; impermanence and our interconnection with other beings means that everything, including us, is changing at a very fast speed. In that context, trying to maintain control is delusional.

Katagiri Roshi once told us that silence is right view. Silence is not something we create or impose on ourselves; it is something we can access at any time. The silence is already there. When we pause, breathe, watch, and wait, when we let go of our idea of who we are and what life is, we develop flexibility of body and mind. Silence is the quality of integration, which allows us to have right view in any one of those 6,400,099,150 moments.

Right Thinking

We all have habitual ways of thinking that we cling to, and they become beliefs. These beliefs affect the way we behave. We also have beliefs about our bodies. To notice and let go of our beliefs, even for a moment, brings us broader insights and shows us life in ways we hadn't considered.

One way to see how our thinking affects us is to observe our bodies, or ask someone else to observe. F.M. Alexander, the Shakespearean orator and originator of the Alexander Technique (AT), discovered this method of observation when he almost lost his voice. He spent a long time searching for the cause and a cure. Medical doctors couldn't find anything wrong. Finally he set up some mirrors and began observing himself. It was then that he started to notice things about how he held his body when he spoke and how certain orations triggered certain habitual movements. He noticed that before he even opened his mouth to speak, certain thoughts caused him to tense up in particular ways. He noticed that whenever he started to perform, he threw his head back in such a way that it caused pressure in the back of his neck. Because of these observations, he began to look for a way to change his body habits. He found that he could release the pressure by simply moving his head slightly away from his body, and he noticed that when he did this, his entire body moved with it. He began to pause before speaking, which allowed him to choose not to engage in the habits that caused him to tense in that way.

After returning to the United States from Japan in 1988, I began studying Alexander Technique with one of F.M. Alexander's students, Marjorie Barstow. Marj was ninety-two years old when I met her, but she was very sharp and continued to embody awareness of her body.

As a result she was a very good teacher. Like Zen practice, AT teaches that there is no fixed way to be; that life is a constant process of awareness through pausing and observing. Marj could tell you a lot about what you were doing. She was a very short woman reaching about to my shoulders when she was standing. One day when she was doing hands-on work with me she was looking up at my face and gently touching my neck with her hands. "Why are you curling your toes?" she asked. I was, in fact, curling my toes, something I wasn't aware of until she mentioned it. She hadn't been looking at my feet, but she knew more about what I was doing than I did.

We do unconscious things with our bodies all the time. If someone is irritating us, we may lean away from him or her with our head or shoulders. Later we wonder why we have a stiff neck or our shoulder is tight. Once I had so much stiffness in my shoulder that my entire arm became numb. I'd been trying to figure out what was wrong for some time. One day, an AT teacher was trying to demonstrate to a small group of us how much our thoughts influence our bodies. He suggested that we drop our heads to our chest and, without moving anything, just think about lifting our head. As I thought about it I felt myself tighten my neck, and as I lifted my head it spread to my shoulder. Just noticing this tightening allowed me to make a change. For some reason I had an idea that I needed to do that tightening in order to lift my head.

Letting go is not simply to ignore what we don't understand and move on. When we try to ignore something, we are actually attaching to it. We put up a screen so we can't see it, but by not looking at the problem, we are unconsciously being dragged around by it. To completely let go in any moment we have to make an effort beyond what we think we can do, embody it fully, become sick of it, take a deep breath, let go, return. It's a process. Marj used to talk about the release we experienced as *a little bit of nothin'*. We often think that to get to the Middle Way from what we consider an extreme takes a giant step, a lot of effort. Before discovering the Middle Way, the Buddha did this exact thing. He went from a life of wealth and complete comfort to the severe life of an ascetic. Finally, he found that neither extreme was beneficial, and he chose the way of balance. This became his primary teaching.

My yoga friends tell me that in yogic study, *dukkha* is often described as "obstructed space." We create obstructions by not being attentive to how we are thinking and how our thinking influences everything we do, including how we use our bodies. Shifting our thinking just slightly can clear our minds and help us notice how our thinking creates obstructions that don't allow us to move freely. Right thinking is the practice of stepping back and noticing or considering what others notice about imbalances and obstructions. Very naturally there will be a slight shift toward the middle.

Right Speech

We need to choose our words carefully. Our words are a reflection of our thinking. Every year I co-lead a retreat at Southern Dharma Retreat Center with Alexander Technique teacher Meredith McIntosh. We call this retreat "Beginner's Mind: The Undoing of Doing." Meredith practiced Soto Zen at Bukkokuji Temple in Obama, Japan, a stone's throw away from Hosshinji, where I practiced. We both see the strong connection between AT, which I call "body Zen," and the beginner's mind practice often talked about in Soto Zen. Both practices require that we inhibit the inclination to "do" something, the not-doing of which allows us to recognize what is happening in the moment.

"I'm always listening to the words that people use in their lessons," Meredith says, "because the way they talk about what they're noticing clues me in about their understanding and attitude about body awareness. If they use *doing* words rather that *allowing* words, or stagnant words such as *position*, or passive phrases such as *the way you adjusted me*, it helps me to understand how I can guide them further." Noticing the words we choose can tell us a lot about the way we think about ourselves and the people we are with. Choosing words that elicit what we really want to communicate is a form of Right Speech.

Another way of looking at Right Speech is to investigate what is behind our speaking or not speaking. Sometimes we can speak too much and sometimes silence is not Right Speech. The balance lies in this awareness.

Harada Sekkei Roshi, abbot of Hosshinji Monastery, always encouraged us to come to *dokusan* (interview with a teacher). One time he told me I should come more often, and I responded that I sometimes didn't have anything to say. Come anyway, he told me. So I did. Time and time again I went to *dokusan* with nothing to say. Sometimes I understood something without exchanging words with him. At other times, conversations happened spontaneously that were very relevant and showed me something that I wasn't noticing. One time I went to *dokusan* and he asked me, "Do you have anything to say?" I said, "No." He paused for a moment, then said, "Sometimes you have to say something." I realized at that moment that I had fallen into a stupor.

Talking excessively can create confusion about what we really want to say. Talking thoughtlessly can cause others to stop listening—or run away. Talking pointlessly can get us into trouble. Not talking when something should be said can support what might be a harmful situation.

I had a friend who talked a lot. I was away from him for a year and when I returned, people told me that, in an effort to stop talking excessively, he had vowed to not talk for three months. They said it was terrible—he created just as much unnecessary distraction and "silent noise" when he was trying to communicate without words. They were very grateful when the time was up.

Pause, breathe, observe. The practice of choosing words carefully and of being aware of when to speak and when to be silent creates harmony in life. Harmony means to find the balance when we speak: to be neither excessive in our speech nor to hold back when something needs to be said; choosing words which are helpful, not deceptive or confusing; and speaking in ways that help us to understand each other. This is the Middle Way.

Right Action

This usually refers to the practice of the precepts, which help us bring about harmonious, unifying actions. To not kill, lie, or steal, and so on is not just a philosophical idea. Without recognizing the bigger picture, it's easy to simply categorize these things and not be aware of how our actions actually affect others and ourselves.

From the perspective of our bodies, inattentiveness can be a way of breaking the precepts. People often die young, for example, because they have not been attentive to their bodies. We push ourselves to achieve, ignoring pain that is an indication of imbalance. Marj Barstow, in discussing one of the discoveries Alexander made, says, "He began to see how often we just push ourselves up and stick our chests out and pull our shoulders back. That's a fixture. Now, you don't hold that very long, because if you're going into activity you really want flexibility." And she adds, "When I find myself pushing, I have not taken the time to see where I am before I start to move."

When we pause and notice before we respond, we can be aware of the best way to move. Maybe it means we need to stop and rest. Maybe we discover that we need to take a walk. How we take care of ourselves also affects how we treat others.

I had been practicing Soto Zen for fifteen years when Katagiri Roshi died. It had been a lot of pushing: fifteen years of practice, both at Minnesota Zen Meditation Center and monasteries in the United States and Japan, then dealing with his illness and death for over a year. I made a list of objectives for the next five years, and among them was to be a hermit. I needed some space. A friend offered to let me use her small cabin in the mountains, with wood heat and no running water. It sounded perfect. For the first three months I slept a lot. I had no schedule except to take care of my basic needs. One morning I woke up and felt rested, but something inside of me told me I still had more to learn from this experience, so I stayed. One day I was listening to a tape of Thich Nhat Hanh in which he suggested taking a walk without a destination. He explained that at first you have to resist the tendency to have a destination. It sounded nice, so I tried it. Although I didn't have any time or schedule restrictions, I quickly noticed how geared I usually was to those restrictions. I wanted to have some kind of destination: "I'll walk for 30 minutes," or "I'll take this loop." When my mind finally settled down and I stopped trying to create a goal for my walks, I started seeing beautiful things along the way, things I had walked by many times and not noticed.

My next practice was to try to learn how to do nothing. I told myself I would sit on the porch every day for fifteen minutes without doing anything. I would sit down but soon find myself jumping up to do something, then remember my intention and sit back down again. Sometimes I felt guilty, like I was wasting my life. I had to keep reminding myself about what I was doing for a long time before I settled into an appreciation of doing nothing. Someone said of my lifestyle at that time that I was being irresponsible. My response was that this was the most responsible thing I had ever done.

The time I spent at the cabin caused me to become aware of how exhausted I had become. My body was running on adrenaline, and it was a false energy. My teacher had done that for many years, and the first cancer doctors found in him was in his adrenal gland; the tumor was the size of a grapefruit and ninety-percent cancerous.

I'm not suggesting that inaction is better than action, just that if we have awareness, we can make choices. We can learn to find the balance before we are caught in extremes. Marj once said, "I know when I want to have more freedom, I know what I can do and what I must do, then I make the choice of whether or not to do it."

I often say that patience means simply to let life unfold. This means to pause, breathe, watch, and wait before we act. Sometimes we don't have time to wait, but pausing and breathing will help us to know that. To simply let life unfold, rather than imposing our ideas of how it should be, is right action. Therein lies balance.

Right Livelihood

What does it mean to support ourselves? We are more than our various titles; we are all the things that we do. How are we sitting when we work? How do we walk? We may be very familiar with the activity that is the source of our livelihood, but we don't know what each moment will bring. It's not just what we do; it's how we do it. Whatever we do can be helpful or harmful depending on our awareness and our response.

We had a statue in our Buddha hall at Minnesota Zen Center made by a friend of Katagiri Roshi's. I didn't like the statue; I felt it was ugly and wondered why it was on the altar. One day Katagiri Roshi told us about the person who had carved it. He was a friend of Roshi's who was forced to go into battle during World War II. He was a pacifist, so he always shot his gun into the air. Afterwards I came to like that statue, because every time I looked at it I thought about him shooting his gun in the air so he didn't have to kill. Even though I don't believe in war, a soldier I've never met inspired me by his spirit of right livelihood. Though he was forced to work at a job he didn't believe in, the way in which he did it was so inspiring that seventy years later someone who didn't even know him was affected by his story.

It's easy to get caught up in the belief that to make money is the goal of our work, or that being busy is the way to be productive. It's worthwhile to consider whether our idea of what is productive is actually helping to create harmony in our lives and in our culture. Whatever we do, we need to consider the bigger picture of life, not just whether it makes us feel good or helps us live a comfortable lifestyle. The choice of our livelihood is important, but equally important is how we live out each moment of our life, how we take care of our bodies and minds, how we consider those with whom we are relating. The Middle Way is to find within our livelihood, within all our relationships, the best way to respond to each situation.

Right Effort

I often say that right effort is just getting yourself to the meditation cushion. When we sit quietly we see where the imbalances are in our lives, and we can discern what kind of effort is necessary to restore balance. After learning the process of stepping back and observing, it becomes more natural to find the right amount of effort needed in everyday life.

When I first started practicing at Minnesota Zen Meditation Center (MZMC), I felt that I needed to jump-start my life. I thought meditation would help me become more productive. But I found just the opposite. I began to see that I was doing too much, and always had the sense that nothing was done well. Little by little, I dropped some things and entered more wholeheartedly into others.

Someone else who started at MZMC at about the same time had the opposite experience. He found that he needed to engage more, do more, delegate less, which is a great example of the self-correcting nature of zazen. When we sit, we find what right effort is for us.

There is a story about an AT teacher who had a robbery at her home. When the police came they checked for fingerprints and were amazed to find that the fingerprints on her teacup were perfect. They said it was an unusual thing to find because fingerprints are usually smudged. She understood how to apply just the right amount of effort needed for picking up a teacup. The kind of effort we use in picking up a teacup is different from the effort we use to pick up a load of rocks. When we pause and breathe, whatever we do we can do with just the right amount of effort.

Marj Barstow used to tell us that to slouch is an inefficient use of the body. When we use our bodies efficiently, she pointed out, we feel better. I could add that when we use our bodies efficiently, we don't harm our bodies. The Middle Way is not too much effort and not too little. For someone like me, less is more. For others, more is more. For some others, more may be less. And then that changes, too, because everything in life is changing constantly, including us. Awareness needs to be present in each moment. It is important to know ourselves as well as our circumstances.

Right Mindfulness

Mindfulness is the opposite of trying to accomplish something. It means to pause and see where you are as you move from one thing to another, and even before you transition. It is taking a breath and returning to deep silence again and again.

When I was practicing at Tassajara, Thich Nhat Hanh came and taught us about mindfulness. Prior to that I hadn't thought much about it, but he inspired me to try being more mindful in my activities. I started with my job of cleaning the meditation hall, which included clean-ing all the globes for the kerosene lamps. I had done this many times before and it was something I enjoyed doing. But the day I tried hard to perform this task mindfully, I broke one globe after another. That was the day I learned what mindfulness is not—true mindfulness requires a balance of effort and ease.

We can also see this dynamic in our relationship to time. I attended a retreat led by Thich Nhat Hanh in the late '80s. I didn't have a watch, so I was always worried about being late. I would ask people in my room what time it was and managed to get myself to the meditation hall on time, often to find that the event had been delayed. At first I became upset when this happened—why weren't things happening on time? But at a certain point I stopped watching the time and started just showing up without worry. I was amazed to find that I consistently arrived just a few minutes before things started.

People rarely noticed when Katagiri Roshi made a mistake. I used to watch him very closely, so I'd notice. What he did was just to continue, to take a breath and not miss a beat. He let his mistake inform him, but he didn't linger there or beat himself up. He simply returned to the mo-ment. This is mindfulness too. The title of his first book, *Returning to Silence,* is a reminder to us that we can always return to the present mo-ment, the place of mindfulness. Sometimes we think that, by focusing our mind on something, we are being mindful. What I've learned about being mindful is that it requires that we let go at the same time that we are being attentive. It's not being hyper-awake, but not asleep either.

Being mindful is an ongoing process too. It is a practice of noticing how we are feeling, thinking, acting, and reacting. Our response to each situation is very natural when we are truly mindful.

Right Samadhi

Meditation is *samadhi.* In Dogen's teaching, every time we sit down in zazen we experience awakening. What is it that we awaken to? The reality of life, which is impermanence and interdependence.

It's hard at first to recognize the awakening Dogen refers to, because most of us think of awakening as some lofty state that always feels calm and peaceful. But true peacefulness is the result of coming to terms with life as it is whether it's quiet or stormy, hot or cold, comfortable or un-comfortable. What we awaken to is what is happening in this moment. When we sit quietly and face a wall, we look at our life squarely and realize there is really nowhere to escape to; we see that we're right in the middle of life, we're part of life. Seeing things in this way is freedom. If we can't escape our beliefs and fears, then why not take a good look at them? When we do, we see they have no substance.

Samadhi is often translated as "concentration." If we think of *samadhi* as concentration, though, we should recognize that it is the kind of concentration that has no particular goal, no expectation of some result, because within the rapid movement of life, adhering to an outcome only leads to frustration. This concentration is simply to be present with what is. Returning to the silence within is the awareness of the true self. Sometimes *samadhi* is referred to as "one-pointedness." This too means to return to the deep silence where we experience the Truth of life that is found in each moment

Finding the Balance

There is always movement, even within stillness, just as there is stillness within movement. The first time I sat on my cushion in front of Marj, she began by asking me questions about meditation: What do you think about when you're sitting there? How long do you sit there? Do you sit perfectly still? Finally she said, "Just remember that even when you're sitting still, there's always movement."

Something awakened in me when she said that. I knew what she said was right; I felt the movement in my body whenever I sat. When people asked me if I still danced, I often told them that sitting quietly is a kind of dance, but I could never explain what I meant.

Even beyond the movement that is constantly going on inside our bodies, within stillness we experience the movement of life, which is impermanence. That can be an unnerving experience; because things are changing very rapidly, we have to acknowledge a lack of control over our life. But although it may feel uncomfortable, this is the real point of balance. Seeing life as it really is means we can be aware of the *little bit of nothin'* that helps us find the Middle Way in each moment.

I used to describe the Middle Way as what we glimpse in the middle as we swing from one extreme to the other. Over the years I've learned that balance is actually not so far away from what we perceive as the extremes. Meredith McIntosh describes the Middle Way like this: "You're interacting with your environment, but you're in neither fight nor flight mode. Meeting the circumstance, we can respond appropriately with flexibility. Alexander's idea is that there's not a right place, but there's a right direction."

The Middle Way is seeing what is happening in any moment and responding appropriately. This is very subtle at first, but through the practice of the Eightfold Path we can learn to see differently, to observe life and engage with it rather than adhere to a certain set of beliefs.

To live fully is to find the balance between using our beliefs as a framework for action and acting as a natural response to what is happening in the moment. It's like dancing with life. As it changes, we step back and observe, take in the reality of each situation and all beings, then improvise our way into the next moment. As my revered old AT "Zen Master" Marjorie Barstow taught me long ago, it's just *a little bit of nothin'*.

Works Cited

Rahula, Walpola. *What the Buddha Taught.* New York: Grove Press, Inc. 1975.

Katagiri, Dainin. *You Have to Say Something: Manifesting Zen Insight.* Ed. Steve Hagen. Boston: Shambhala, 1998.

Daijaku Kinst, *ordained in 1988, received formal authorization as independent Zen teacher in 2005 from Sojun Weitsman, Roshi, Abbot of the Berkeley Zen Center. She has taught and led retreats in a variety of settings, including Gampo Abbey with the Venerable Pema Chodron. She received a Ph.D. in Buddhism and Psychology from the California Institute of Integral Studies and is currently a core faculty member and director of the Buddhist Chaplaincy Program at the Institute of Buddhist Studies, an affiliated graduate school of the Graduate Theological Union, Berkeley, CA. Along with her partner, Shinshu Roberts, Daijaku is cofounder and teacher at Ocean Gate Zen Center in Capitola, California.*

The Path by Moonlight:
Dogen's Guidelines for Following the Way
Daijaku Kinst

Zen practice requires us to bring every aspect of our being into relationship with the teachings. Living the Way means living it in all dimensions—nothing is excluded. This requires great courage, great humility, great trust, and a good guide. Dogen's fascicle, "Gakudo Yojin-shu" (Tanahashi, 1985), is one such guide. It is quite possible to read and reflect on this fascicle from many perspectives and to learn new things with each reading.

Dogen starts off with the admonition: *You should arouse the thought of enlightenment.*

This is central—a pivot point and touchstone in our practice. *Bodhicitta,* the thought of enlightenment, is completely present, in this very moment, and it is expressed in the intention to realize awakening. The awakened mind seeks the realization of awakening. The term *bodhicitta* is also a way to describe the point in our practice when we face our lives and say with conviction: "I want to wake up. I actually want to wake up. I'm not sure what that means, but I know that I do not want to perpetuate delusion and suffering in this life. I want to embody the teachings in all aspects of my life and I trust that by doing this I will bring greater sanity to this world and my life in it." This has a visceral feel to it, a sense of coming into alignment with true north. It does not exclude learning or thoughtful consideration of our lives, but, in essence, it is not based on intellectual understanding or coming to know anything. It is deeper than knowing or not knowing.

Aligning with the teachings, in zazen and in the everyday moments of our lives, is an act of awakening. We do not need to have an idea of what enlightenment is to do this. Ideas about enlightenment are just that—ideas. They are fine, if they keep us close to the teachings; they are obstacles, if we are distracted by them. And we are inevitably distracted by them. So we return again and again, and that returning is the activity of awakening.

❦

Dogen says: *The practice of the Buddha's way is always done by receiving the essential instructions of a master, not by following your own ideas. In fact, the Buddha way cannot be attained by having ideas or not having ideas.*

Dogen is asking us to give up our habitual delusions and stubbornness and to assume a posture of dignified receptivity. We need to study what supports this receptivity in our lives. We need to listen to the essential instructions of a master. This means we seek out teachers and teachings that guide us on the Way. But, it also means we must cultivate the voice of the true master within ourselves and listen for it in all aspects of our life. We must ask ourselves, in zazen, at work, in our relationships, in each moment: What is the instruction of the true master, here, now? How do I listen and respond? When we stay close to this question it becomes, not an intellectual exercise, but a way of living and moving in the world. Beyond our ideas, what is alive in this moment, this relationship, this heartache, this need, this joy, or act of generosity?

Practicing in this way, we are alert to life and to the ways in which we fool ourselves. This is inevitably uncomfortable, inconvenient, and disruptive, as well as joyful and enriching, and it requires great courage intelligently applied.

❦

Dogen says: *Courageous people who study the way, should first know the correct and incorrect practice throughout the way.*

What is correct and incorrect practice? We should investigate this from many perspectives. First we should ask: What supports the growth of wisdom and kind action in my life? What encourages me and nourishes awakening? These are important questions and they are particular, concrete, and specific. Answering them provides us with guidance as we live our ordinary life—*our* life, the life we have, not another one, or the one we think we need in order to wake up. To consider one's life as anything other than a Buddha field in which awakening is completely possible is to step away from our deepest responsibility to ourselves and to this world. So we think, we consider, we make choices, and we enact them day-by-day. We take our lives seriously, recall over and over what is most important. We plant our deepest values in the center of our lives and, when we stray from them, we return.

But this is not the whole picture. Dogen's teachings also require that we move daily into a realm in which we allow ourselves to be transformed from the inside out and to trust something other than our own ideas. This is risky and deeply challenging, and it is the realm in which a great, quiet courage is most needed. To allow ourselves to be transformed in this way, we must come to know, in our bones, that letting go of the self as we habitually experience it does not result in our destruction, but in our liberation. This requires deep trust in the dharma and in our true nature. According with this trust becomes our way of life.

Dogen is asking us to practice in two dimensions at once. First, we are asked to observe, to think, to listen, to use our discriminating minds and make judgments about what works and what doesn't. Second, we are asked to trust the practice completely, to let go of our ideas and allow ourselves and our lives to be transformed.

Many of us have heard: *Do not mistake the finger pointing at the moon for the moon itself.* The moon, in Zen teachings, is often used as a metaphor for enlightenment, and the finger, those aspects of our life that point us toward it. This phrase tells us something about the relationship between thoughtful effort and awakening. We should attend to the finger and the direction in which it points. We should come to know concretely how we support a life of practice. If we focus exclusively on the finger, however, we will never see the moon. Instead we will convince ourselves that, by studying the finger, we are living practice. We will not move into the unknown, into a place beyond our habitual definitions and assumptions. But this is exactly what we must do, because remaining in the comfort of the world we know only reinforces it.

We must be willing to enter into the darkness of not-knowing, for it is in the dark that we allow something new. It is also in darkness that we come to know, without a doubt, that it is the light of the moon that allows us to see the finger pointing the way and the moon itself. It is our awakened nature that allows us to see.

Over time we also come to know that, even when we cannot see the moon, even when darkness seems complete, the moon is there. There is a stage in the development of children when, if a thing is not visible to them, they think it does not exist. We can be like children in that way— we think if we cannot see the moon, cannot see what we think of as awakening, it does not exist. We do not trust that no matter what, the moon is there, our awakened nature is there. We do not trust that who we are is not simply a person studying a finger or looking at the moon, but a moment that includes all things seen and unseen. How often do we take our limited viewpoint as defining the nature of reality? This is delusion. We are the intersection of finger, moonlight, path, body, breath, wandering mind, distracting emotions, inconvenient relationships and responsibilities, birth, death—the whole of it.

Dogen, referring to the great sage Nagarjuna, says: *The mind that fully sees into the uncertain world of birth and death is called the thought of enlightenment.*

Our world has depth, beauty, and meaning and is not graspable with our ordinary minds. We construct theories about this reality, and what it is like to see clearly and fully into the uncertain world of birth and death. These theories can guide and can also obscure. Perhaps we think that if we have the aspiration for awakening and see clearly, we will not experience distress and pain. But this is not the way of things. To see fully is to live in this world as a human being.

The great poet Issa had many losses in his life. After the death of his beloved daughter he wrote:

> *The world of dew*
> *Is the world of dew*
> *And yet, and yet . . .* (Stryk, 1991)

We are not saved from "and yet . . . ," nor would we want to be. This too is the mind of awakening. This is the way in which our lives are a response to and with each moment—this encounter, this heartache, this need, this joy, this act of generosity, this breath. If we do not live in this human realm, but try to transcend it, we will keep ourselves from risking an encounter with the moon.

How difficult it can be to unseat the self-centered self, the one who knows and will not let go of that knowing. This habit is rooted in fear and its antidote is trust, great trust.

Dogen says: *Those who practice the Buddha way should first of all trust in the Buddha way. Those who trust in the Buddha way should trust that they are in essence within the Buddha way . . . . To arouse such trust and illuminate the way in this manner and to practice accordingly are fundamental to studying the way.*

Notice that Dogen is asking us to arouse trust in the Buddha Way in the same way he has asked us to arouse the thought of enlightenment. We do not manufacture trust or the thought of enlightenment; we arouse it. Like a sleeping lion. This is fundamental. Such trust illuminates the way just as the moon illuminates a path in the dark.

To trust in this way, we must study trust; we must take opportunities to become intimate with trust. Recently, I returned to a temple in Kyoto in which it is possible to descend into the womb of the *tathagatha*, into the earth, into pitch blackness, guided only by keeping one's hand on a very large mala that forms a railing for guidance. Twisting and turning in complete darkness, one eventually comes upon a rock with the Sanskrit character *hrih*, the seed syllable associated with compassion, lit only by sunlight coming from a hole in the earth above. I am struck, each time I visit, by how clearly this descent expresses our practice. We cannot see ahead, we cannot see behind, yet we know there is a path, and if we stay close to the teachings, we will be guided. Each time I have been there, I have also felt the silent presence of the people before and behind me, even though I could not see them—each of us in darkness being guided in the same way, taking each step trusting in the mala for guidance.

We do not need to see the totality of the Way. Like driving in thick fog, we cannot see far, but we do not need to. If we stay on the road, we will get where we are going. And, at the same time, this moment in the fog is our complete life. What is "going" other than our life in this moment? What is "where" other than right here? And yet we are going, we have aspirations and goals—and we should. We want to live our lives for the benefit of all beings; that is an aspiration and a goal. In our daily lives, we want to get along with our boss and coworkers, be more patient with the lonely fellow down the street that likes to tell the same story over and over, handle the stress of this busy world well, and make thoughtful choices. Awakening takes place in the life we have, not the one we think we should have. And the small choices we make have a tremendous impact. Did you sit this morning or not? Did you allow anger to hijack your mind and heart or not? And when it did, did you apologize and return to your intention or not? By allowing our actions to be guided by the teachings, like a mala in the dark as we descend into the womb of the *tathagata*, we live out our deepest intentions and stay close to the path of awakening. This is an active process based in intelligent reflection.

At the same time, we maintain a posture of not knowing, of humility and receptivity. We know that what we know is a version of reality, not reality itself. We align ourselves with the way and allow ourselves to be guided and transformed by it.

Cultivating and expressing great courage, great humility, and great trust is an everyday affair. It occurs in each choice we make and is also beyond our knowing or not knowing. Living at the intersection of knowing and not knowing, we arouse the thought of enlightenment and the trust that illuminates our way. We risk an encounter with the moon and seeing fully into this world of birth and death. In other words, we risk waking up.

Works Cited

Dogen, Eihei. "Gakudo Yojin-shu (Guidelines for Studying the Way)." *Moon in a Dew Drop: Writings of Zen Master Dogen.* Ed. Kazuaki Tanahashi. San Francisco: North Point Press, 1985.

Kobyashi, Issa. *The Dumpling Field: Haiku of Issa.* Trans. Lucian Stryk. Athens, OH: Swallow Press, 1991.

Hoko Karnegis *serves as communications director at Hokyoji Zen Practice Community in southern Minnesota, having previously headed the Milwaukee Zen Center. She received Dharma Transmission from Shohaku Okumura in 2011 after completing her training at Toshoji Senmon Sodo in Okayama, Japan, and completed zuise that same year. An adjunct college instructor in Eastern Religious Traditions, she also writes occasional articles for national Buddhist magazines and websites.*

The One Left Behind

Hoko Karnegis

The impermanence of this floating world
I feel over and over.
It is hardest to be the one left behind.

—*Rengetsu* (Stevens, 2005)

How wonderful it would be if, once we got things the way we wanted them, nothing ever changed. The best elements of our lives, the people we love, the activities and experiences we enjoy most, would go on and on forever. Our suffering would come to an end.

And yet, we know from our own life experience that it isn't possible. All around us, things are arising and fading. Sometimes it seems like it's all going by too fast, like everything is changing and we can't keep up. We can feel like we're being left behind.

The Japanese recognized this feeling a very long time ago, and called it *hakanashi*. *Haka* can indicate the time period for planting and cutting rice, so it refers to a measurement of time. Adding *nashi* creates a meaning like *past the limits*. Planting or harvesting rice at the wrong time—outside the usual window—could result in a devastating crop loss, so naturally people would be disturbed if the proper times of year came and went, but they were unable to complete their tasks. *Hakanashi* is about the gap we experience when the outside world is moving too quickly, and we feel like we can't match its speed. It seems like time is flying away beyond our control, and we have a sense of deep regret.

In fact, of course, we're not standing by while the world whizzes past us. We, ourselves, aren't the same people we were even a moment ago; we've breathed in and out a few more times, had a few more thoughts and insights, gotten a bit older. This impermanence is universal and doesn't leave anyone out. Even when everything seems perfect, and we have everything we want, in the next moment something changes. There's nothing we can really hold onto.

Otagaki Rengetsu (1791-1875) was born into a samurai family and became a nun in the Zen Buddhist tradition following the death of her husband. She was an expert in painting, calligraphy, poetry, and pottery. As both an artist and a nun, she would have had a highly developed sense of *mono no aware*, the deep beauty inherent in the unavoidably transitory nature of existence. In her poem above, she enters directly into the feelings of loss and longing that come with watching the things we love, enjoy, or admire come and go, arise and fade away. We repeat the pattern of welcoming something into our lives, coming to value its presence, and suffering when it moves on. This cycle is not a distraction or disorder in our lives. It *is* our lives.

When Zen Buddhism arrived in Japan, it had a profound influence on the country's art and culture. The Japanese already had a deep appreciation for the fleeting nature of beauty and felt some affinity with teachings about the three marks of existence: unsatisfactoriness (*ku*), the lack of an abiding self-nature (*muga*), and impermanence (*mujo*, literally, *without constancy*). Under this Zen influence, rather than seeking beauty in the ultimate perfection of an external object, the Japanese sought it in the totality of their experience of the object. Seeing and appreciating a lovely blossom in this moment includes remembering the nondescript bud on the branch and the withered petals that will fall to the ground. The experience of this moment may be quite intense and powerful, yet it remains fragile because, in a flash, it is gone.

Indeed, some of the most powerful symbols of the beauty of impermanence are flowers. In Japan, April is the time for *hanami* (flower viewing). Usually the flowers are fragile cherry blossoms, whose life on the branch of a tree is especially brief. The weather bureau makes a forecast about the best week or two for viewing, and tracks the "cherry blossom front" as it moves across the country. The Japanese hold picnics and parties under the trees, enjoying the once-a-year color and fragrance and each others' company.

Here in Minnesota, the equivalent is the much-awaited fall color, one of the most celebrated happenings in our "theater of seasons." People make plans to visit the spots that have the most beautiful and colorful fall leaves, and the most popular accommodations fill up weeks in advance. The wave of color begins in northern Minnesota, where the colder temperatures arrive first, and moves steadily south, tracked by TV weather folk and newspaper travel writers. We look forward to being in the middle of the short-lived riot of orange maple, yellow birch and red oak leaves over our heads and under our feet.

Once the leaves have fallen, of course, the next moment arrives, bringing its own fresh changes. Each day when I wake up in my little room at Hokyoji and look out the window, there's something new to see in the meadow or the woods, and as communications director, it's my pleasure to share something of Hokyoji's daily life with our many friends around the world. One October morning, I was supposed to meet someone to do some work on one of the buildings. "Please go on ahead," I told him. "I'll be right there. See how the sun is burning the overnight frost from the roof of the toolshed? I have to get my camera. I hope I'm not too late!" I could see that the clouds of moisture billowing from the shingled roof would not last long as the sun grew stronger. Now is all we have! And now! And now!

Singing together, supporting each other

When I was training at Toshoji in Okayama, Japan, we performed a lot of funeral and memorial ceremonies. Sometimes I had the chance to sing *baika* at these services. *Baikaryu eisanka* is a type of Japanese Buddhist hymn created by the Soto Zen school in 1952 in honor of the 700th anniversary of Dogen Zenji's death. It pairs both very old and more contemporary melodies with the teachings of the Buddha, Dogen Zenji, or Keizan Zenji. *Baika* is part of a broader category of Buddhist songs of praise called *goeika*.

The literal translation of *baikaryu eisanka* is *plum blossom style recitation praise song*. In the "Shisho" and "Baika" fascicles of the *Shobogenzo*, Dogen Zenji writes about the plum blossom as a symbol of the true transmission and flowering of the dharma from person to person and generation to generation. *Baikako*, or groups of people who meet at the temple to sing together, form an important social network. Most often, *baikako* consist of laywomen, few of whom have any formal training in music or singing. Yet, somehow all the voices, bells and movements are accepted and come together (including even those of an ordained foreigner!). As members, we not only hear, discuss and sing the teachings together, we provide friendship and moral support to each other. Singing at services and celebrations, we share the words and encouragement of our ancestors with many listeners. It's obvious from the Baikaryu Vows that we recite before each practice session that we do not sing for ourselves alone.

> *We will live according to proper teachings through baikaryu eisanka.*
>
> *We will live in harmony with others through baikaryu eisanka.*
>
> *We will create a cheerful world around us through baikaryu eisanka.*

There are *baika* songs marking various events in the Soto Zen liturgical year (Buddha's birth and death days, anniversary days for Bodhidharma, Dogen and Keizan, etc.) as well as songs dedicated to bodhisattvas Jizo and Kannon, songs that summarize key points of Soto teaching, and songs for events like precepts ceremonies, weddings and memorials. In happy times, the *baikako* gathers joyfully to practice and perform together. However, it can be hard to practice memorial songs when one has recently lost a family member or friend. The *baikako* offers understanding and empathy whenever one of its members feels a rush of memories and emotions that makes it difficult to sing.

Hoji (memorial services) are an important part of Zen practice. The singing and chanting that are part of the service are opportunities to come in contact with Buddha's teachings at a time when we may be the most vulnerable. With our defenses down and our sense of certainty shaken, this might be exactly the moment when we're best able to throw ourselves into the refuges of Buddha, dharma and sangha. None of us can avoid this kind of loss at some time in our lives. We wish it wasn't so, but we will all have the opportunity to do this kind of practice.

A good sendoff nourishes everyone

One of the songs I sang most commonly at funerals and memorials was the *Tsuizen Kuyo Gowasan*. (*Tsuizen kuyo* is another term for a memorial service; *wasan* is a kind of song, and *go* is a polite prefix.) A memorial service can bring up all kinds of difficult or painful feelings, but actually it's our opportunity to say a proper farewell to our loved one. *Tsui* means to send off, and *zen* is good, right or excellent. *Ku* is to offer and *yo* is nourishment. We do our best to provide some respectful and meaningful closure to this stage of our relationship with our loved one, bidding him or her farewell with blessings and good wishes.

The words to this song are as follows:

> *Among the drops of dew, strung like gems, that have settled on the lotus leaf, a single drop is our life—so short, though we want it to be long. The physical form that existed yesterday, today appears as a reflection in a dream, and what is real is that we put our hands together in gassho despite the shadows in our hearts. When we quietly speak the name of the deceased, our feelings grow even stronger, and although our tears naturally arise, we know there are profound karmic*

reasons. Amid the many lovely flowers that have been offered, the candles that are bright with our true feelings, and the enveloping incense, may your spirit be at ease in eternity.
(Traditional)

What a lovely picture it makes to imagine each of us as a shining drop of dew settled on the lotus leaf! Our lives are supported by the unfolding awakening that is the lotus, and we are living each day together in upright stability, reflecting each other and everything around us right in the midst of that unfolding. It's a pretty good place to be, that lovely lotus leaf. And yet, dew is transient. All too soon, it evaporates and returns to the atmosphere, losing its form as a dewdrop, yet not really disappearing. The constant change that characterizes form is simply a natural manifestation of emptiness. With no abiding self-nature, it's impossible for anything to remain in a fixed state. That includes all the intangible elements that go with our physical existence—thoughts, emotions, intentions, sensations, memories, plans, dreams—and the tangible form of the body as well.

That changing form is one of the reasons we may feel that we've been left behind when someone dies. Even when we deeply understand impermanence, this human form feels solid. We may have vivid memories of physical contact with our loved one: dancing, hugging, playing sports, or just being together. Suddenly we're confronted with empty sweaters and shoes, favorite tools that lie unused, a phone that doesn't ring. We might realize how reliable and enjoyable the physical forms of our relationship have been. While we take some comfort in our memories, they don't have the same solidity.

In our quieter moments, we have the opportunity to consider what that means. Memories don't have solidity because they are our own creation based on our interpretation of past events. If we ourselves are changing moment by moment, of course our memories are changing too. We may remember a conversation one way today and another way next week. Maybe the day comes when we can't recall our loved one's face as clearly as we used to. The person we thought we knew is slipping away, even though we took it for granted that our impressions and understanding of him were reliable, unchanging reality. We still have a relationship with him, but what is the true character of that relationship? Taking comfort in our memories isn't at all a bad thing. We just need to fully understand the nature of our memories.

We can't go back and relive or change those times with our loved one. If the relationship was difficult, we may harbor some guilt or regret that we didn't patch things up before she died. Maybe we're still angry that we didn't get the love, respect, care, guidance or support we wanted, and now she has moved beyond our reach and left us and our unresolved feelings behind. As Lily Tomlin says: *Forgiveness is giving up all hope for a better past.* We have only this moment in which to act—the only moment that is real. What will we do now?

What is real is that we put our hands together in gassho despite the shadows in our hearts. In this moment, even in the midst of our pain and confusion, we practice as well as we can and do our best to free all beings. Unable to change the past or control the future, we simply take care of our lives right now, even if small things are all we can manage. It can be hard to break our preoccupation with our pain and sorrow and even to think about the rest of the activity of our lives, but the reality is that it is no less possible to live out our vows during this difficult time than in any other. By doing our best to manifest our Buddha-nature even now, we clarify our relationships with all beings, including those whose physical forms are no longer a part of our daily experience.

This is not so easy. This kind of loss is never what we want. Sometimes our memories are comforting, but sometimes they remind us of what we've lost. Nonetheless, if we hold onto our intention to live in Buddha's way in honor of our loved one, the despair becomes a dharma gate. *Although our tears naturally arise, we know there are profound karmic reasons.* Often, as I sang at a funeral, I could hear the family members weeping quietly behind me. I imagined that the words of the song expressed their feelings of bereavement, but I also hoped that it helped them put their loss into perspective. Somehow, for a time our lives intersected with those of our loved ones. Somehow, those great lives came to an end. Since everything that happens is an unfolding of beginningless and endless karma, this isn't a random, isolated occurrence. It isn't the act of a hurtful universe, aimed at us personally and designed to cause us devastation. Naturally, we grieve at the death of someone close to us, but he or she is part of a larger picture than the one we can see. Each of us is creating our own karma, but we're also involved with the playing out of the karma of others. That being the case, there's no getting away from interdependence. We are intimately connected with each other, always have been, and always will be, affecting each others' trajectories in ways we don't even realize. What would your life have been like had this person not been a part of it? What would her life have been like without you?

Tsuizen Kuyo ends by mentioning the offerings of flowers, candlelight and incense to the deceased. In America, it might feel strange to make such offerings, but they play an important part in the *hoji*. For instance, the smoke from the incense not only acts to purify everyone at the service, but it is said to carry our thoughts, prayers and intentions to the deceased. One person is the designated *seshu* for the service, perhaps the eldest son or daughter of the deceased person. We often translate *seshu* as *chief mourner*, but the actual meaning of the kanji would be closer to *chief benefactor* or *chief donor*. The job of the *seshu* is to create merit by making offerings to the Buddha or chanting sutras and then to transfer that merit to the deceased and to the ancestors, sincerely praying that all beings realize the Buddha Way. In the midst of the snows of December and January in Japan, the plum tree is already blooming, expressing the complete functioning of its life even though spring has not yet arrived. In the midst of the sorrow of loss, already the dharma is flowering and the *seshu* is reaffirming our vow. There's no waiting until things settle down, or our hearts have healed a little, or we've gotten used to the idea that our loved one is gone. This body and this moment are the ground of our practice—exactly these tearful eyes and just this instant when we just want everything to be the way it was.

Practice in the midst of pain

When my dharma great-grandfather Kodo Sawaki Roshi died at Antaiji in 1965, the normal course of events would have been the staging of an elaborate series of funerals and memorials. Instead, his disciple Kosho Uchiyama Roshi decided to hold a memorial sesshin. Tradition says that there is a 49-day transition period after death, during which the deceased has the chance to review with Jizo Bodhisattva the unfolding of his or her karma before taking up a new form. Thus, for 49 days, Antaiji practitioners silently engaged in what came to be known as *sesshin without toys*. There were no dharma talks, no sutra readings, and no work periods—just hour after hour of zazen. In the midst of the loss of their great teacher, these practitioners chose precisely that moment to intensify their commitment, put aside all other activities, and just sit in honor of his dharma life.

The Buddha's own *parinirvana* caused great despair among his disciples, despite his declaration that he had actually been around for a very long time and wasn't really disappearing, but was, in fact, appearing to die in order to encourage their commitment to diligent practice.

When Dogen talked about this with his own monks, he quoted the *Lotus Sutra* (Leighton/Okumura, 2010) and said: *Again and again I declare that I am entering into nirvana [as a skillful means]. All beings are sad with longing, and their tears overflow. Although we trust his words that he always resides on Vulture Peak, how can we not be sorry about the coldness of the twin sala trees?*

What a challenge it presents us to deeply enter into the truth of the three marks of existence and realize non-attachment, and at the same time deeply enter into our human suffering and grief at the death of a loved one. Both of these things are the nature of reality, and neither can be ignored. Dogen was all too aware of this, and wrote in his *Genjokoan: Since the Buddha Way by nature goes beyond [the dichotomy of] abundance and deficiency, there is arising and perishing, delusion and realization, living beings and buddhas. Therefore flowers fall even though we love them; weeds grow even though we dislike them* (Okumura, 2010). Beauty and sadness cannot be separated, just as life and death cannot be separated. This moment of life is one hundred percent this moment of life, but it depends on death for its existence. The next moment of death is one hundred percent the next moment of death, but it depends on life for its existence. Life and death are completely integrated. Even so, as grieving humans we lose sight of the truth of this and see only our immediate loss and pain. This is OK. It's the way things are.

Kobayashi Issa (1763-1827), a lay priest in the Jodo Shinshu sect of Buddhism and one of Japan's great haiku poets, was intimate with loss. His early life included multiple difficulties and tragedies, and his first-born child, a son, died shortly after he was born. When his little daughter also died two and a half years later, he wrote this verse:

While the dewdrop world

Is the dewdrop world,

Yet— yet—   (Aitken, 1979)

Our lives and those of our loved ones are single drops of dew in this dewdrop world: so short, though we want them to be long. We recognize that things are fleeting—including the things we love most—and sometimes we can even accept this. And yet, we can't deny our sadness and longing when the life of someone close to us comes to an end. We do our best to go on living and practicing, and maybe somehow, we begin to see there is beauty in that longing—not because we are indulging in some idea about who we are as the ones left behind, but because our sadness is the truth of the reality of this moment. Can we completely jump into it, with no separation? If so, we can find the beauty of this moment, and by extension, all other moments. There is gentle sadness for now in the loss of a loved one, and there is an ongoing sadness about the transient nature of all things. Beauty is not separate from sadness.

If we're sensitive to the true nature of things, we can begin to feel both the joy of being together with loved ones and the gentle melancholy that comes with our certain knowledge that things will change. We can wholeheartedly enter into both of these emotions at once, recognizing and appreciating each of them without identifying with them or using them to write stories about ourselves. This kind of combined feeling, and the beauty that goes with it, is subtle. It does not lead to either exultation or anguish. It is simply what's there in this moment, quite apart from whatever we think about it. We could choose to ignore it and only acknowledge the sensations that we think will make us happy, but to do so is to choose to remain asleep.

Fleeting loveliness everywhere

In old Japan, many everyday things were considered gateways to this kind of sad beauty. The lonely cries of wild birds, the sound of a far-off temple bell in the evening, the cracked teacup—all were invitations to fully enter into the beauty of transience. After all, to endlessly search for and cling to only the happiest and most comfortable of moments is to miss the beauty of all the rest of the moments that make up our lives. In his famous 1332 work *Tsurezuregusa (Essays in Idleness)*, Yoshida Kenko asks:

> *Are we to look at cherry blossoms only in full bloom, at the moon only when it is cloudless? ... To long for the moon while looking on the rain, to lower the blinds and be unaware of the passing of the spring—these are even more deeply moving. Branches about to blossom or gardens strewn with faded flowers are worthier of our admiration.* (Keene, 1967)

Somehow, in spite of our direct experience, change comes as a surprise. Kenko notes: *It does not matter how young or strong you may be, the hour of death comes sooner than you expect. It is an extraordinary miracle that you should have escaped to this day; do you suppose you have even the briefest respite in which to relax?* We must care for and appreciate our relationships with others in this and every moment—even when those relationships are strained—because no one knows what the next moment will bring. We enjoy them even in the shadow of their future absence.

When a loved one dies, it can feel as though he or she has moved on, moved away, left us behind. It seems that while he or she has changed in a very deep way, we are still here, still the same, going on with the day-to-day routine. Yet when we look closely at the reality, we see that both we and our loved one are changing together—not in the same way, but not alone. Since impermanence doesn't leave anyone out, we continue this dance of change together. We can't be left behind.

That means that our relationship with our loved ones also continues to grow and change. We have the opportunity to value his or her presence in our lives in new ways as we continue to develop and mature. New insights can emerge about the ways we connected and communicated, what we learned from each other, and the aspects of our loved ones that we've internalized and now embody, continuing to make them available in the world. We can appreciate the beauty of our time together—beautiful because it is fleeting.

Works Cited

Aitken, Robert. *A Zen Wave: Basho's Haiku and Zen.* New York: Weatherhill, Inc., 1979.

Dogen, Eihei. *Dogen's Extensive Record: A Translation of the Eihei Koroku.* Trans. Taigen Dan Leighton and Shohaku Okumura. Boston: Wisdom Publications, 2010.

Kenko, Yoshida. *Essays in Idleness: The Tsurezuregusa of Kenko.* Trans. Donald Keene. New York: Columbia University Press, 1967.

Okumura, Shohaku. *Realizing Genjokoan: The Key to Dogen's Shobogenzo.* Boston: Wisdom Publications, 2010.

Rengetsu, Otagaki. *Lotus Moon: The Poetry of Rengetsu.* Trans. John Stevens. Buffalo: White Pine Press, 2005.

Setsuan Gaelyn Godwin, *Abbot of Houston Zen Center (HZC), practiced at San Francisco Zen Center for eighteen years, twelve of those years at Tassajara Zen Mountain Center, and in Japan at Hosshinji. She received Dharma Transmission in 2003 from Tenshin Reb Anderson in the Shunryu Suzuki lineage, and has resided at HZC since 2003.*

A Storm in the Zen Center Garden: Three Levels of Mindfulness

Setsuan Gaelyn Godwin

Zen practice isn't always performed during work. Work is certainly not always Zen practice. Nevertheless, Zen and work are intimately associated with each other. Our work and our Zen practice illuminate each other, co-evolving together. It's the nature of the human mind to be interested in how things function, and how we participate in the process. As Zen practice develops, we become more free and flexible in jumping into the process of work, play, and activity. We jump in with less hesitation. Then we learn how to jump out—we learn the value of rest.

Shakyamuni Buddha performed by teaching, for the most part, a noble form of work, as all teachers know. Learning how to teach, learning how to learn is excellent work.

In the Buddha's time, monks weren't particularly involved in labor. They didn't till the fields or build temples as they would in China and Japan. A monastery in India would be a gathering place for monks to take refuge from the rains, to study, hear teachings, discuss and debate. There would be begging practice and basic self-care, but spiritual development was the primary focus for monks.

As Buddhist practice evolved in China, monastic life looked quite different owing to the different cultural understanding of work: work is a natural activity, and monks were not considered to be outside the fabric of mutual care, of growing food and caring for the land. The way monks work came to be a visual representation of spiritual understanding.

In Chinese and Japanese monasteries, the monks and lay residents gardened, cooked, built and maintained structures, and sewed clothes as well as studying, listening to the teachings, meditating. Until this very day, Zen is characterized by this approach. In a Zen place, it is assumed that practitioners will learn and participate in many things, including full participation in all work activities.

A story of the great teacher Baizhang illustrates this. It is said that he was preparing to work in the fields with the rest of the monks but couldn't find his tools—the monks had hidden them so the old master would have no choice but to rest. He duly returned to his quarters. Later, when the call came for the midday meal, he declined to eat, saying: *A day without work is a day without food.* This is now a standard Zen saying. In fact, it is brushed on a scroll hanging in the Abbot's quarters at Houston Zen Center, with a painting of a monk industriously repairing his robes.

A day of no work is a day of no food is an expression of the centrality of physical effort, the interweaving of work with all the basic human activities including eating, meditating, sleeping, and studying. It is an expression of egalitarianism as well. Every human works in an appropriate way: the master of a Zen monastery works in a natural way in the fields. The younger monks may work more energetically, but the master weeds and works the ground appropriately alongside the monks.

This ethic of work in Zen monasteries is commonplace now, fully accepted. Monasteries are places of meditation, study, work, chanting, celebration, and ceremonies. Meditation practice animates work activity; work activity grounds meditation and understanding. Our ability to be present livens activity, including all forms of work —laundry, caring for our library books, cleaning the temple floors—everything.

When Myogen Steve Stucky, the Central Abbot of San Francisco Zen Center, visited Houston Zen Center, he offered a story from the record of Suzuki Roshi. The head cook brought a concern to Suzuki Roshi. He was agitated and upset that his kitchen crew wasn't doing a very good job. Suzuki Roshi advised him: *When you're cutting the carrot, just cut the carrot.* This provided some relief, but not for long. The head cook came back a few more times and received advice. Finally, Suzuki Roshi sat in silence. He then said: *It takes a calm mind to see virtue in others.*

How does a cook in turmoil get from the mind in turmoil to the calm mind? The cook in turmoil had placed his awareness on the cutting of the carrot, resulting in a period of calm. Is that all there is? What is this awareness, what is mindfulness?

I am grateful for the work of Gil Fronsdal who described three types of awareness, or mindfulness: clear, open, and lucid. We will use these to investigate an incident of stormy turmoil during a work project in the garden. Gardening and cooking provide so many good examples of Zen practice!

Mindfulness, like concentration or compassion, develops along with your practice. It has different flavors, if you will; it functions differently. Three of the flavors are: Clear awareness, open awareness, and lucid awareness. Or we could say, clear mindfulness, open mindfulness, and lucid mindfulness. How do they differ?

Gardening is one of our very important activities at this Zen Center and, as is usual, a few of us got together to mow the lawn, trim the hedges, and spruce up the temple grounds. The vegetable beds, trees, and other plantings are cared for on different days. The Friday team concentrates on the street view—the plantings people see upon arrival. Robert dedicated himself to edging the lawn with exemplary concentration. I finished one task and turned my attention to pruning back a vigorous vine called Asiatic Jasmine that was surrounding a little newly planted native tree, a Texas Wild Olive tree.

I had noticed that the Asiatic Jasmine was getting too close to the tree trunk. I wanted to give the Wild Olive a little breathing space, room to grow. The earth was quite moist near the tree, quite workable. It appeared to be a straightforward project; my goal was simple—clear a space of about three feet encircling the tree and mulch that three-foot diameter circle. From across the yard this seemed reasonable. But the vine was more than a match for me. I soon found that it was tangled, wiry and strong. Also it is gooey and slippery when cut. The jasmine was growing right next to the tree trunk, beginning to grow up the little tree itself. As I started pulling it back and cutting it with hand clippers, I felt pulled deeper into the border, losing my balance. After quite a while, I had a large pile of jasmine behind me, but the circle around the tree was not three feet in diameter—it was about 10 inches in diameter!

Clear Awareness

Gardening itself requires clear observation of the plants, the conditions, the tools. It can be serene. Here, though, clear observation of the activity included awareness of feelings arising, emotional states, judgments arising. I noticed thoughts: this task is much more difficult than I prepared for. I observed "reluctance to continue" arising. Then questions arose: why am I doing this alone? Where is the whole community and why aren't they helping with this? A psychic storm was brewing.

Kneeling in the jasmine, my head just inches above it, my hands working with the clippers, by feel instead of by sight, I was immersed in the tangle. Naturally, because I am a Zen practitioner, I reminded myself that this was an impermanent situation; it will end and my mind will probably reflect that it was easy after all. I strategized in that way.

However, the difference between what I had wanted to accomplish—the three-foot circle around the tree—and the progress I was making was challenging to equanimity. It was Very Unpleasant. I observed the psychic storm of impatience with elements of sadness slowing developing in the situation. I cast my mind about for explanations and the thought came: it is very bad that this tree is not better cared for. It is indicative of the decline of True Zen Practice. The observation was Clear: clearly observing the arising of the elements. The thought arose that if Zen Center couldn't care for this tree appropriately, well, it was a very Bad Sign.

I hope you can see the humor in this. At the time, the humor was not obvious to me! I saw only the problem, six inches from my nose: a neglected tree, unruly tangled vines of jasmine, miniscule progress in the face of the situation. And me, alone, determined to solve the problem.

Later in the day I would reflect on this and be rewarded with some new insights. The situation of being faced by an insurmountable obstacle, all alone and yet responsible, feels like my eleven-year-old self's world. But the difference, in the garden, was that I was clearly observing what was coming up in my mind.

Returning to the garden, in the midst of the tangle, clear observation seemed sufficient. It seemed that it would be sufficient to survive this calamity and then move on to the next thing. Perhaps this was similar to the relief the head cook felt when Suzuki Roshi advised him: *When you are cutting the carrot, just cut the carrot.*

Open Awareness

When Robert completed edging the lawn and walked over to help me for awhile, I stood up, stepped back, ambled over to the other side of the property, played with the dogs, looked around, at the trees, the clouds. I gave up on the jasmine. My attention opened to a broad array. I rested a bit before beginning to tinker with a different task.

When I eventually remembered the jasmine from across the expanse of the lawn, with the trees, clouds, dogs, and air included in my view, from the Open perspective, the little area I had been concentrating on looked just that: little. In fact it looked fine, just as it was.

It was just a little corner of Zen Center with a new little tree. As soon as I had some perspective on it, the elements of my concern changed their relation to one another. My thought, during the pruning, that the jasmine indicated neglect of the Zen Center, became just a thought, and not a very potent one at that.

A series of thoughts took their proper place as just thoughts. This series: people will think that we neglect our grounds; our Zen Center will fail because we haven't been able to cut Asiatic Jasmine; if we're not the kind of place that can take care of Asiatic Jasmine, we should just shut the doors.

With Open Mindfulness, the fruits of practice flowed in, along with the broader landscape in which I was working—clouds, trees, dogs, the friends who were helping. Appreciation of the efforts of the sangha flowed in; the fruits of the practice of other people flowed in. A sense of humor appeared. The vigorous jasmine did not evaporate, but the problem appeared in its proper proportion, and other methods to meet it arose.

Lucid Awareness

An awareness that is *lucid* is *infused with light*. From across the expanse of the lawn, I realized that the little area around the tree had looked pleasant all along. It could use a little attention, but that is what Zen Centers are for—to attend to little corners. Our minds perceive the world directly and mediate it into meanings, into categories. My mind recognized the beautiful Zen Center, noticed the various growing things, and categorized them into things that should be trimmed or not trimmed. My mind's categories included areas of Zen Center and Not Zen Center. The meaning of an untrimmed area of garden changes with states of awareness.

The psychic storm, the anguish and frustration I experienced in the garden that morning, encouraged me to pay attention to mindfulness itself, not just to the Texas Wild Olive tree and the Asiatic Jasmine. Clear awareness, clear mindfulness is direct contact, looking very closely, as precisely as you can. The spaciousness of open mindfulness comes about as we practice with our limitations, as we get to know ourselves and our habits. From the open perspective, we can open to the insight and help that is available—and there is always help available.

Lucid mindfulness, lucid awareness, would be the perspective of a Buddha, an enlightened being. One could ask about the Asiatic Jasmine situation: How would a Bodhisattva see this? How would the situation look if it were suffused with light, if light were flowing through the lattice? It wouldn't necessarily be a simple answer. For example, a Buddha, an awakened one, understands that suffering, such as the suffering I was enduring in my escapade with the Asiatic Jasmine, can be useful. As a result of suffering, I met the eleven-year-old me who often felt that she was given tasks that were too big; but she, only she, was responsible for them, and only she could accomplish them correctly. I think she believed she lived inside a Brothers Grimm fairy tale, and, if she could only complete the task, all would be well. Meeting her, and learning how to allow her to play, was a reward and a delight.

We need, and can use, all forms of mindfulness, of awareness. Lucid awareness is just one of the three tools. We wouldn't sidestep clear awareness or open awareness in order to abide in lucid awareness. Work practice, competent gardening, skilled cooking—all require clarity, clear awareness. From lucid awareness, there is no challenge in accepting that, for example, a gardener can make mistakes. One of the gardeners energetically pulled out all the new lettuce sprouts—they looked like weeds! Lucid awareness sees the beauty in non-differentiation between lettuce and weeds. But lunch needs to be made and lettuce salad is on the menu. We take a moment to instruct the new gardeners in clear identification of what we call weeds and what we call lettuce.

Roshi Joan Halifax, Ph.D., *is a Buddhist teacher, Zen priest, anthropologist, and pioneer in the field of end-of-life care. She is Founder, Abbot, and Head Teacher of Upaya Institute and Zen Center in Santa Fe, New Mexico. She received her Ph.D. in medical anthropology in 1973 and has lectured on the subject of death and dying at many academic institutions and medical centers around the world.*

She studied for a decade with Zen Teacher Seung Sahn and was a teacher in the Kwan Um Zen School. She received the Lamp Transmission from Thich Nhat Hanh, and was given Inka by Roshi Bernie Glassman. Roshi Joan is founder and director of several organizations focused on applied Buddhism in diverse environments. Her books include: The Human Encounter with Death *(with Stanislav Grof);* The Fruitful Darkness; Simplicity in the Complex: A Buddhist Life in America; Being with Dying: Cultivating Compassion and Wisdom in the Presence of Death; Being with Dying: Compassionate End-of-Life Care *(Professional Training Guide); and* Seeing Inside.

The Circle of the Way

Joan Halifax

On the great road of buddha ancestors there is always unsurpassable practice, continuous and sustained. It forms the circle of the way and is never cut off. Between aspiration, practice, enlightenment and nirvana, there is not a moment's gap. Continuous practice is the circle of the way. This being so, continuous practice is unstained, not forced by you or others. The power of continuous practice confirms you as well as others. It means your practice affects the entire earth and the entire sky in the ten directions. Although not noticed by others or by yourself, it is so.

—*Zen Master Eihei Dogen* (Tanahashi)

When we were building Upaya's temple, we named her Dokanji, Circle of the Way Temple. The name originated with Japanese Zen Master Dogen. I think it was Kaz Tanahashi who thought of using this name, or was it me, or was it all of us? Of course it was dependent co-arising. At the time, the name felt so clear to all of us because of the practice style and ethos here at Upaya.

Our temple's name, Dokanji, Circle of the Way, applies to how we endeavor to live our lives here at the Zen center. However, it's important to note that this is our aspiration, not a description of how we already are. We aspire to realize continuous practice in an integrated, inclusive, non-compartmentalized way. Reality always prevails, however, so we struggle to actualize our ideal and we often flounder.

We need to expect these struggles, because we live in Western culture where compartmentalized, non-integrated behaviors are the norm. It's common, for example, for people to cherish Saturday or Sunday as their days, freed from work, days for play or rest. There are Friday night behaviors, Saturday night behaviors, Sunday night behaviors, then Monday morning behaviors. We compartmentalize our behaviors into these different timeframes. It's how the Western world is structured.

This segmented approach to time is a clear challenge that we experience at Upaya. We're committed to taking these vertical behaviors that differentiate time and function and create something like a musical staff, where the lines and the spaces between the lines are one whole, continuous movement, where our daily lives of service to others and our practice are not separate from each other.

Yet getting rid of compartmentalized behaviors is not easy, even here. We've acknowledged that all of us need "days off." We renamed these days "personal practice days," feeling it would be more congruent with our ethos to not think of them as an "off-day." However, what has happened is that people usually do laundry, answer emails, and cook on these days, that they still treat them as "days off." It wasn't enough to rename them; people slipped back into compartmentalization and differentiation. "These are my days, my time," and the rest is "monastery time."

But can we understand that "monastery time" is every minute we live? The vision of the circle of the way is that everything we do is practice. Underlying everything, there is a deep continuity in all our thoughts and actions and beneath our thoughts and actions. Western people find it very difficult to comprehend the continuous way. We like to separate things into pieces and take them apart. It is how science is practiced, how business is done, and how we see the world. It's the genius of Zen Master Dogen to bring us into seeing how we don't have to structure our lives into cells, that instead we can experience "being" in flow, and shift our perspective on time into time-being.

The Buddha says: *To practice the dharma is swimming upstream.* For Westerners, it's not just swimming upstream—it's swimming against a tsunami.

We have to change the view from it's my life to this is our life. As one man dying of prostate cancer said to me: *We belong to each other.* We belong to the earth; we belong to the sky. We inter-are. Wisdom, compassion, body, mind are not separate. The same applies to our very moment-to-moment experience, to our experience of time, which is not separate from being. Each moment is causally intertwined with all other moments. We are intertwined with each other in a causal flow of multiplicities and multiple processes that Dogen calls time-being.

Dogen teaches: *Continuous practice is the circle of the way.* All the musical notes are there, making a chord moment by moment that shifts and progresses through time, creating an unrepeatable melody. This is simply the nature of life, whether we see it or not, this flow and weave of non-repeatable events that co-arise.

This being so, Dogen continues, *continuous practice is unstained*. It is unstained by any contrivances, by thinking, by naming, categorizing, or wishing. He then says that this is, *not forced by you or others*. The music of life unfolds with its complex non-repeating harmonies and progressions that also includes silence and also, humorously or tragically, our delusions and disharmonies.

Yes, our blindness keeps us from seeing that we inter-are in time-being. Yet sometimes we see remarkably well. I remember one day being in Joshua Tree National Monument. An artist turned to me and said: *Everything is in the right place.* Maybe as an artist she had some kind of impulse to change things "artistically." But instead, she had let go into the perfection of just that moment as it was. She let go into the music of the natural world and, in her surrender, experienced that she too was part of it; that she too was in the right place.

We cannot be forced into this deep experience of letting go into the music so that we are the music. We cannot be forced into this experience by being admonished that *washing the dishes is enlightenment*. We only arrive there by relaxing into what Dogen calls *the miracle of the moment*. Then you might find yourself in the vast field of collective realization, not forced by you or others. So washing the dishes is just washing the dishes, *unstained* according to Dogen, by thinking, naming or categorizing. Unstained—spontaneous and miraculous.

The same might be said of the practice of *shikantaza*, just sitting—panoramic nonjudgmental inclusive receptive awareness. You can't force *shikantaza*. You can't sit down and say, "O.K., I'm going to do *shikantaza*." Dr. James Austin, in the Zen Mind, Selfless Insight retreat, pointed out that receptive attention, or *shikantaza*, is an involuntary process. It happens. *Shikantaza* happens. Not because you want it to. You can't sit down and willfully make *shikantaza* happen. The brain doesn't work that way. *Shikantaza* is involuntary. Trying to "just sit" is not "just sitting." Trying interferes with "just sitting." When you "try to just sit," you are practicing "trying." You are not "just sitting."

The circle of the way also is involuntary. The structure can point to it but to realize it means you realize it. A strange way to say this is that "it makes you real." You become real. You become authentic through this involuntary letting go. You can't make it real by will. You make it real by letting go—it arises from this deep experience of selfless letting go, or the self letting go, what Dogen calls *the dropping off of body and mind*.

Some people are resistant to "zen" structure. One of my good friends in dokusan said about sesshin: "This is a lot like being in the Army." Well, maybe yes, maybe no. There are some differences and there are some similarities. One of the most important differences, but also one of the most important similarities, is the continuity of all functions. The functions of our life inter-are. You can't come into the dokusan room and say, "I'm a bodhisattva. I want to be ordained," and then grab an object and say, "This is mine."

What we ask for here at Upaya is congruency: to notice the split in our behaviors, and then not to split from the split. When you notice that your behaviors are not congruent with your ethics or ethos, for example, you don't hold yourself up in judgment and abuse yourself. Instead, you bear witness to how many times you leave life by objectifying and compartmentalizing. When you discover you are alienated, that you have objectified "the other," then you might be so broken-hearted that there is nothing else to do but to let go into the "study of the way." In the best (or maybe, the worst) of circumstances, this is involuntary. It's not even an imperative. It's deeper than an imperative. It can't not be when it arises. There is simply nothing else but being let go into the dharma as one gets renounced by one's alienation.

I have a small sense of this in my own life; small, and yet enough to recognize when I encounter someone who has been actualized by this to some degree in their life. I always experience an incredible sense of relief at discovering: Oh, here's one who's not living in a compartmentalized way. Here's a person who is not objectifying other beings. Here's a person who confirms or is mindful of each being and each thing.

Dogen goes on: *The power of continuous practice confirms you as well as others.* To confirm each other and ourselves reminds me of the Zen Ancestor's words: *Not knowing is most intimate.* This experience of being confirmed is to be penetrated by each being and thing, including ourselves, in an unmediated and intimate way, beyond ideas of who and what. This experience of confirmation arises from the base of receptive attention, being in an open attentional field. Our experience of connectedness with and through the world is easily visible in fishes as they swim in a school, in tango dancers, or in a mother holding her baby. Whenever we experience being released from the tight fist of fear, when the music and the dance become one thing, we know mutuality, interbeing, dependent co-arising. The mother and child are not separate from each other; dancers flow around each other; fishes move as one body.

We meet, really meet, in a field beyond all thoughts and conceptions. Thus, *the power of continuous practice confirms you as well as others.*

The structure of the sesshin is a powerful example of interbeing and co-confirming. Sometimes four or five days into the sesshin, when everything is flowing, we discover that we are in harmony, not like a machine, but like birds flocking. We are one body, confirmed and confirming each other.

One time in Mexico I was invited to go to a sugar cane field where the swallows gather in great numbers every afternoon. I went and sat on the hillside with some friends to witness this beautiful event. Just before dusk, a few swallows flew in without giving any indication that something special was about to happen. Then suddenly, thousands upon thousands of swallows were there, and whoosh, they made a giant swallow that stretched across the sky. This miraculous formation of beings interdepending dipped and dived, swooped and danced, without anyone directing the dance. It was just this vibrating mass of beauty in the sky dancing as one body. And then, just as suddenly, right before the sun dropped below the horizon, thousands of black swallows flowed out of the sky like a dark river at dusk; they flowed downward and disappeared into the sugar cane. All the Mexicans applauded and I did too.

Next morning, I ran down the hill to the sugar cane field. Platoon after platoon of swallows flew up; each group did a little macro-swallow dance, then disappeared in different directions as they went to search for food. At the end of the day, they would find each other again and give themselves over to the dance of interbeing.

The swallows are a visual experience of the reality that truly we're all connected to each other; that this life, this existence, is all connected, causal, unrepeatable and continuous.

This is what we hope to cultivate during sesshin, and during our daily lives, yet we can't make it happen. But before we are let go of, there is preparatory work to do. First, we learn the craft of the practice. And then, as we practice, like an artist, our self-consciousness slips away without us even realizing it. Then, the behaviors in the zendo become like a dance, a dance characterized by beauty and gravity, concentration and subtlety. The dance goes from the sub-atomic to the molecular to the individual, then to the collective and out into the cosmos. Then it circles back again into the very pulsing of our blood. It is a dance of selflessness, and it happens only as all of us release into the field of time-being.

It won't work if we feel oppressed or directed by ourselves or any particular person. It doesn't happen because we have been ordered to do it; we can't be afraid that we are going to disappoint the abbot. At a certain point, we have to recognize that the structure, craft, and discipline are here to support us; they are present to provide deep nourishment for a collective and inter-independent experience of flow, of interbeing, of awakening.

To repeat Dogen: *The power of continuous practice confirms you as well as others.* The more we simply cooperate with the whole process of sesshin, the more mutually confirming it is. The more we stay in the structure and don't break it by emailing or talking, the more deeply confirming it is. What's confirmed is not only our own experience. Although our own *samadhi* has the chance to deepen, we experience that the *samadhi* of others is deepening also as we do this together with and for each other.

We can also experience this with the precepts. Even though some people do not like the idea of the precepts, most of us at Upaya have discovered that practicing precepts is a saner and more practical way to live. If you live at Upaya with all this wonderful cultural diversity, you have the opportunity to realize what it means to live in a way that does not disturb you and others. It doesn't mean being selfish or self-centered; it means being generous, kind, and considerate, having mental stability, not being caught in the reactive conditioned mind. It also means having the heart to deeply cooperate with one another to support the deepening of practice. One day, we might discover that the precepts are how a Buddha would live. This might seem simplistic. Yet we are all buddhas, suffering buddhas and happy buddhas, moon-faced buddhas and sun-faced buddhas. So why not realize it right now? We're playing hide-and-seek with our own goodness; we're hiding from our own basic nature. We're seeking something that is already here. It is already everywhere.

The precepts themselves are practices of liberation, not to be used to blame ourselves or others, not done judgmentally or with a kind of piety (which is just insecure self-importance). We do these practices simply because we love. We love. Without an object. Simply because we love. Our practice acknowledges and confirms interbeing, causality, dependent co-arising. We inter-are.

Dogen completely understands this. He says: *Your practice affects the entire earth.* Every time you turn off a light, you're reaching right into the heart of Iraq, right up into the Arctic, right into the sky. Dogen says we reach right into the entire sky in the ten directions. This is a time when the demand for oil is radically degrading our very atmosphere. A friend in Nanking said, "We never see the sky here." China is polluted, Vietnam is polluted. Vietnam is the fastest growing economy in Southeast Asia, poisoned with our dioxins from the war, now booming economically by making more and more irrelevant things for us consuming Americans. They are being poisoned directly and indirectly by our consumerism. We inter-are.

We need to ask ourselves, how much do we really need? We're creating a phenomenal economic boom in Southeast Asia and in China as a result of our rampant consumerism, and we are inspiring consumerism throughout the world. But do we need so much? Can we take exactly what we need in our bowls and not yearn for more? Can we see how our hunger for things is polluting not only our mind and lives but this very earth and sky? And especially can we notice how consumerism keeps us away from our true essence?

What do we really need to actualize the best in our hearts? When I went to Tibet in 1987, I was there for four months, hitchhiking. I bought the Chinese army's version of power bars from some woebegone soldiers in a remote outpost in Western Tibet. I was grateful to be eating these thick rectangles of lard, salt, sugar and refined flour. I'd take a big bite and chew it slowly, recognizing that from one point of view they should be on the "no eat" list for the whole world. But I'd eat this thing and think, the fat will give me warmth, the carbohydrates will give me energy, the salt will help me out, and it will kill my appetite; and then I'd smile inside and confide to myself, well, it might kill not only my appetite but might kill me. But no matter—these kinds of judgments were not interfering with my enjoyment. I was just happy; I was grateful. I wasn't calling up my local nutritionist for counsel and consolation.

I ran out of these power bars when I ended up on the northern shore of Lake Manasorovar, where there seemed to be nobody about and nothing growing but nettles. So I did as Milarapa did: I gathered wild nettles and made a simple soup. Drinking the pale green broth, I thought it was the best soup I'd ever eaten. Then one day, walking, I discovered a lama in a cave near a broken-down gompa. I begged food from him because I had nothing to eat. He gave me the last of his very funky rice and some white flour with weevils in it. He was so kind, so utterly humble. He could have given me a big stir-fry and I wouldn't have been happier. I wept from sheer gratitude.

So what is it we need? Do we need gold or jewels or do we need to awaken our sense of the incredible enrichment of just this moment as it is? When Roshi Bernie Glassman and his wife Jishu and others were up in Upaya House working on the precepts, Bernie came up with, "Do not cultivate a mind of poverty in yourself or others." Thich Nhat Hanh often describes the time he was walking in Plum Village, and he came upon a Western woman with a tight and unhappy face. He saw her as a hungry ghost. She had that look in her eyes, that there's nothing that's enough.

The deeper our consumerism penetrates us, the farther away we get not only from our own liberation but the liberation of all beings. The hungrier we are for things, the more we objectify the world around us and the easier it is to plunder and destroy the very ground of life. It means that your practice, as Dogen says, affects the entire earth in the ten directions.

Dogen also says: *Although not noticed by others or by yourself, it is so.* There's no prize or award for living honestly and with kindness and compassion. One does not self-praise: "I'm a good bodhisattva." You don't win the lottery by being good. *It's not noticed by you,* says Dogen, and *it's not noticed by others.* The natural, uncontrived state of mind and heart is sufficient, and leaves no trace.

The heart-mind involuntarily arises in the experience of the body and mind studying-realizing the way. Awakening is involuntary. "Continuously" doesn't mean only practicing on Saturday or Sunday. Dogen means continuous practice. Be Buddha continuously, all the days and nights of the week. Awaken continuously, allow continuous awakening to be the natural thread of your life.

Dogen, by the time he was 23, had already lost a lot—his parents, his two most precious teachers, and he'd traveled to China on a harrowing boat trip. He writes:

In May of 1223 I was staying aboard the ship at Qingyuan. Once I was speaking with the captain when a monk about sixty years of age came aboard to buy mushrooms from the ship's Japanese merchants. I asked him to have tea with me and asked where he was from. He was the tenzo from Ayuwang shan.

He said, "I come from Xishu but it is now forty years since I've left there and I am now sixty-one. I have practiced in sev-

eral monasteries. When the Venerable Daoquan became abbot at Guyun temple of Ayuwang, I went there but just idled
the time away, not knowing what I was doing. Fortunately,
I was appointed tenzo last year when the summer Training
Period ended. Tomorrow is May 5th but I don't have any special offerings for the monks, so I thought I'd make a nice noo-
dle soup for them. We didn't have any mushrooms, so I came
here to give the monks something from the ten directions."

"When did you leave Ayuwangshan?" I asked.

"After the noon meal."

"How far is it from here?"

"Around twelve miles."

"When are you going back to the monastery?"

"As soon as I've bought the mushrooms."

I said, "As we have had the unexpected opportunity to
meet and talk like this today, I would like you to stay a while
longer and allow me to offer Zen Master tenzo a meal."

"Oh, I'm sorry, but I just can't. If I am not there to prepare
tomorrow's meal it won't go well."

"But surely someone else in the monastery knows how to
cook? If you're not there it can't make that much difference to
everyone."

"I have been given this responsibility in my old age and
it is this old man's practice. How can I leave to others what I
should do myself? As well, when I left I didn't ask for permis-
sion to be gone overnight."

"Venerable sir, why put yourself to the difficulty of working as a cook in your old age? Why not just do zazen and
study the koans of the ancient masters?"

The tenzo laughed for a long time and then he said, "My
foreign friend, it seems you don't really understand practice
or the words of the ancients."

Hearing this elder monk's words, I felt ashamed and surprised. I asked, "What is practice? What are words?"

The tenzo said, "Keep asking and penetrate this question
and then you will be someone who understands."

But I didn't know what he was talking about and so the
tenzo said, "If you don't understand then come and see me
at Ayuwang shan some time. We'll talk about the meaning of

words." Having said this, he stood up and said, "It'll be getting dark soon. I'd best hurry." And he left.

In July of the same year I was staying at Tiantongshan when the tenzo of Ayuwang shan came to see me and said, "After the summer Training Period is over I'm going to retire as tenzo and go back to my native region. I heard from a fellow monk that you were here and so I came to see how you were making out."

I was overjoyed. I served him tea as we sat down to talk. When I brought up our discussion on the ship about words and practice, the tenzo said, "If you want to understand words you must look into what words are. If you want to practice, you must understand what practice is."

I asked, "What are words?"

The tenzo said, "One, two, three, four, five."

I asked again, "What is practice?"

"Everywhere, nothing is hidden."

We talked about many other things but I won't go into that now. Suffice it to say that without this tenzo's kind help, I would not have had any understanding of words or of practice. When I told my late teacher Myozen about this, he was very pleased. (Tanahashi)

When the tenzo said: *One, two, three, four, five*, he meant this includes everything. To realize the circle of the way is to realize nothing is hidden, that everything is included. To understand that our very aspiration is awakening, no different than the practice of the precepts, no different than cooking in the kitchen, no different than the production of phenomena in the mind, that everything is a vehicle of liberation.

On the great road of Buddha ancestors there is always unsurpassable practice continuous and sustainable. The great road of the Buddha ancestors is everywhere. It's the road between Santa Fe and Sedona. It's the path between here and the kitchen. It's the kitchen itself, the utensils, the ladles, the chopsticks. It's cleaning the temple; it's using the toilet. It's right here, between us, connecting us. It threads through our very blood and nerves, bones and marrow. It is our skin, our heart, our life. It is the realization that all beings and things inter-are. The path and the temple are the way. That is the very heart of continuous practice. *It forms the circle of the way and is never cut off.* It is never compartmentalized. It is never special. It is never different than what is right here in this moment. It is not fabricated through narrative. And it is unrepeatable. We cannot travel this path again. It is always new, and always fresh.

Between aspiration, practice, enlightenment and nirvana there's not a moment's gap. Continuous practice is the circle of the way. This being so, continuous practice is unstained, not forced by you or others. It arises involuntarily, not because you have willed it or another has forced it. It is completely within the experience of letting go. *The power of continuous practice confirms you as well as others. It means that your practice affects the entire earth, the entire sky in ten directions. Although not noticed by others or by yourself, it is so.*

When we named our temple Circle of the Way, when we named this center Upaya (skillful means), we aspired to live these names. By naming ourselves thus, we set a standard for ourselves. There is something important to understand about the relationship between organizations and their names—whatever you call a thing will also present you with the shadow of that name. This is a clue about Upaya—the issue of skillful means is present for us all the time. We are accountable to that name and we must also expect that unskillful means are happening in the shadow, outside of our awareness. We need to recognize this and be vigilant, to constantly ask, "What are we not seeing? What do we need to see?" And the same is true of this temple, The Circle of the Way. In its shadow, we'll find behaviors that compartmentalize, that separate, that deny that we inter-are.

A key aspect of our practice, then, is to bear witness to and reflect the obstacles we see in our institution, each other, and ourselves because we have publicly and bravely committed to these names and are willing to look in their shadow. Our names are clues and thus can be lights that illuminate our shadow selves with and through each other. As we endeavor to be the circle of the way, to develop skillful means, we will discover that this Upaya, which is our life and our refuge is, of course, vulnerable to the illusion of separateness.

In our daily lives, we often struggle to embody these courageous names. We also are swimming against the stream of Western culture and our conditioning. The willingness to live within the truth of all of who we are is a precious, rare and often difficult thing. These struggles in our sangha and ourselves make us more open, more humble and more disciplined. It is the heartbreaking failures through which we pass as individual practitioners and as a community that are the very means for our compassion, clear mind, and resiliency to develop.

In the end, it is the depth and strength of our compassion and humility that develop us as human beings, humans who have the aspiration to awaken from the behaviors that produce suffering. Can we do this? Can we look honestly and fearlessly into the face of suffering—in ourselves, in our community and in our world? We can and we must. How else will we discover:

> "What is practice?"
> "Everywhere, nothing is hidden."

Works Cited

Dogen, Eihei. *Treasury of the True Dharma Eye: Zen Master Dogen's Shobo Genzo.* Ed. Kazuaki Tanahashi. Boston: Shambhala, 2010.

Directory of Teachers

This directory does not constitute the entirety of all Soto Zen teachers in the Americas, only those whose teachings appear in this book. Please visit the Soto Zen Buddhist Association website, SZBA.org or, global.sotozen-net.or.jp, to see a larger listing of Soto Zen teachers and temples and further information about Soto Zen practice opportunities in regions throughout North America.

Austin, Shosan Victoria
Dharma Teacher
San Francisco Zen Center
San Francisco, California
sfzc.org
Iyengar yoga with Shosan:
iyisf.org or manouso.com

Bays, Jan Chosen
Teacher and Co-Abbot
Zen Community of Oregon and
Great Vow Monastery
Portland and Clatskanie, Oregon
zendust.org

Boissevain, Enji
Teacher
Floating Zendo
San Jose, California
aboiss5@comcast.net

Burk, Domyo
Teacher and Director
Bright Way Zen Center
Portland, Oregon
brightwayzen.org

Carney, Eido Frances
Founder and Abbess
Olympia Zen Center
Olympia, Washington
olympiazencenter.org

Coghlan, Myoen Jisen
Teacher
City Dharma
Pittsburgh, Pennsylvania
citydharma.wordpress.com

Cutts, Eijun Linda Ruth
Central Abbess
San Francisco Zen Center
San Francisco, California
sfzc.org

Elbert, Meian
Abbess
Shasta Abbey
Mt. Shasta, California
shastaabbey.org

Godwin, Setsuan Gaelyn
Abbot
Houston Zen Center
Houston, Texas
houstonzencenter.org

Habermas-Scher, Myo-O Marilyn
Teacher
Dharma Dance Sangha
Minneapolis, Minnesota
facebook.com/DharmaDanceSangha

Halifax, Joan, Ph.D.
Abbot and Head Teacher
Upaya Institute and Zen Center
Santa Fe, New Mexico
upaya.org

Karnegis, Hoko
    Communications Director
    Hokyoji Zen Practice Community
    Eitzen, Minnesota
    facebook.com/hoko.karnegis

Kinst, Daijaku
    Co-founder and Teacher
    Ocean Gate Zen Center
    Capitola, California
    oceangatezen.org

Krahl, Etsudo Patty
    Founding Teacher
    Ashland Zen Center
    Ashland, Oregon
    teachers@ashlandzencenter.org

McCandless, Myoshin Kate
    Resident Teacher
    Mountain Rain Zen Community
    Vancouver, British Columbia,
    Canada
    mountainrainzen.org

Merrill, Misha Shungen
    Head Teacher
    Zen Heart Sangha
    Menlo Park and Woodside,
    California
    zenheartsangha.org

Munnich, Teijo
    Abbess
    Great Tree Zen Women's Temple
    Asheville, North Carolina
    info@greattreetemple.org

Nakao, Wendy Egyoku
    Abbot and Head Teacher
    Zen Center of Los Angeles
    Los Angeles, California
    zencenter.org

O'Hara, Pat Enkyo, Ph.D.
    Abbot
    The Village Zendo
    New York, New York
    roshi@villagezendo.org

O'Neal, Joen Snyder
    Co-Founder and Guiding Teacher
    Compassionate Ocean Dharma Center
    Minneapolis, MN
    joen@oceandharma.org

Phelan, Josho Pat
    Abbess and Teacher
    Chapel Hill Zen Center
    Chapel Hill, North Carolina
    chzc.org

Postal, Jion Susan
    Founder and former Teacher
    Empty Hand Zen Center
    New Rochelle, New York
    emptyhandzen.org

Ragir, Byakuren Judith
    Guiding Teacher
    Clouds in Water Zen Center
    St. Paul, Minnesota
    cloudsinwater.org, judithragir.org

Roberts, Shinshu
    Co-founder and Teacher
    Ocean Gate Zen Center
    Capitola, California
    oceangatezen.org

Schireson, Myoan Grace, Ph.D.
    Abbess
    Empty Nest Zendo and Modesto Zen
    Group
    North Fork and Modesto, California
    emptynestzendo.org

Directory of Teachers

Schneider, Myokaku Jane
 Founder and Teacher
 Beginner's Mind Zen Center
 Northridge, California
 beginnersmindzencenter.org

Szymanski, Meiren Val
 Dharma Teacher
 Bamboo in the Wind Zen Center
 Sunnyvale, California
 val@bamboointhewind.org

Wolfer, Jikyo Cheryl
 Founder and Teacher
 Joyous Refuge
 Port Angeles, Washington
 joyousrefuge.org

Jikyo Cheryl Wolfer *received Dharma Transmission from Eido Frances Carney in the Order of Ryokan at Olympia Zen Center's Ryokan Memorial Hermitage, Gogo-an, in 2010. She trained in residence at Olympia Zen Center for eight years and received monastic training with the monks of Shasta Abbey in Mt. Shasta, California. She founded the Port Angeles Zen Community, now known as Joyous Refuge, in Port Angeles, Washington in 2009.*

Jikyo earned her B.A. in Language Arts and holds a Masters in Counseling Psychology from St. Martin's University in Olympia. Jikyo trained as a mediator and hospice grief group facilitator, and has worked as a journalist, proofreader, typesetter, legal assistant, and public library administrator.

Made in the USA
Charleston, SC
10 October 2014